This book is a gift of
THE FRIENDS
OF THE
MORAGA LIBRARY
Moraga Branch, Contra Costa County Library

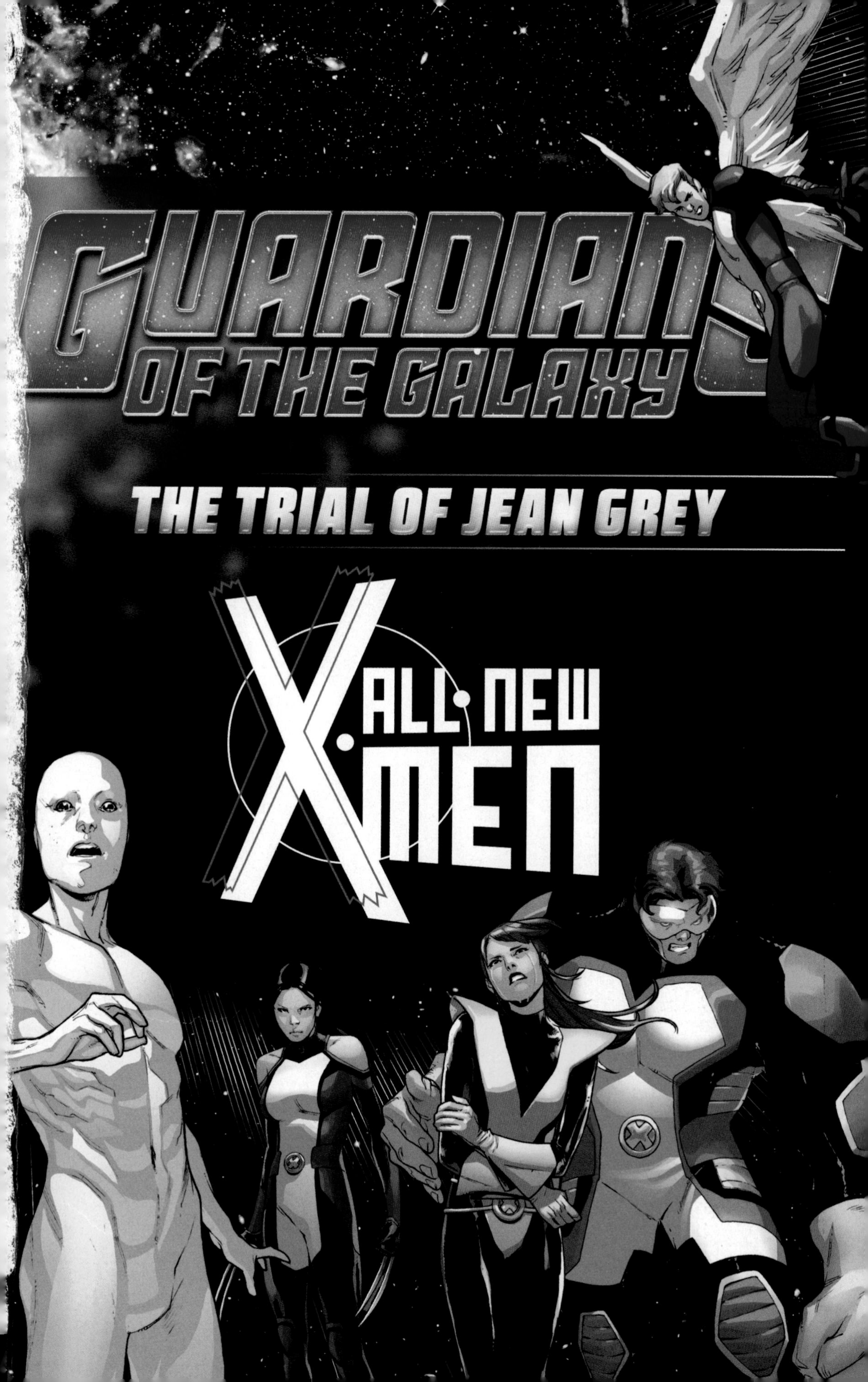
GUARDIANS OF THE GALAXY
THE TRIAL OF JEAN GREY
ALL-NEW X-MEN

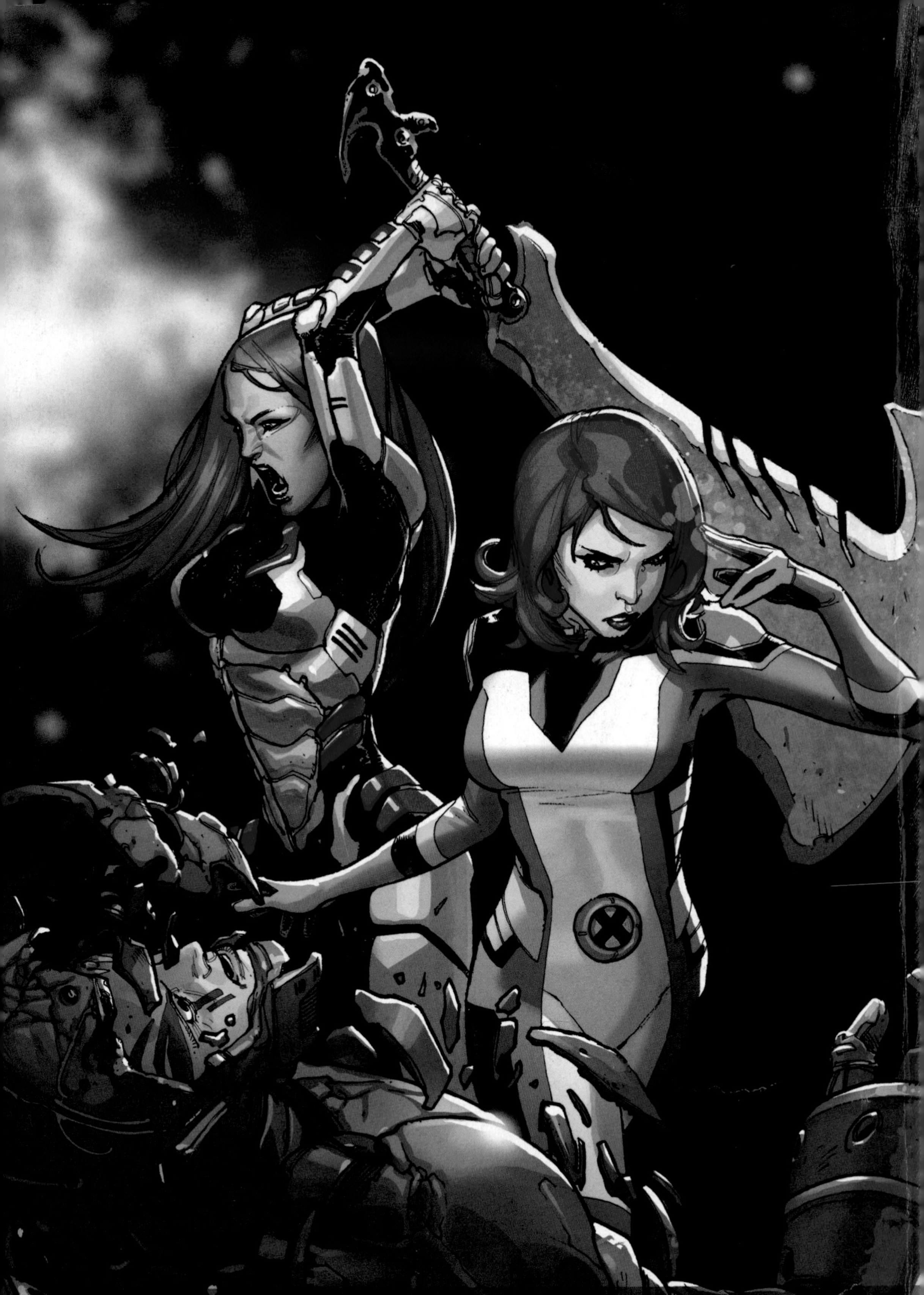

GUARDIANS OF THE GALAXY/ALL-NEW X-MEN: THE TRIAL OF JEAN GREY. Contains material originally published in magazine form as GUARDIANS OF THE GALAXY #11-13 and ALL-NEW X-MEN #22-24. First printing 2014. ISBN# 978-0-7851-6830-0. Published by MARVEL WORLDWIDE, INC., a subsidiary of MARVEL ENTERTAINMENT, LLC. OFFICE OF PUBLICATION: 135 West 50th Street, New York, NY 10020. **Printed in the U.S.A.** ALAN FINE, EVP - Office of the President, Marvel Worldwide, Inc. and EVP & CMO Marvel Characters B.V.; DAN BUCKLEY, Publisher & President - Print, Animation & Digital Divisions; JOE QUESADA, Chief Creative Officer; TOM BREVOORT, SVP of Publishing; DAVID BOGART, SVP of Operations & Procurement, Publishing; C.B. CEBULSKI, SVP of Creator & Content Development; DAVID GABRIEL, SVP Print, Sales & Marketing; JIM O'KEEFE, VP of Operations & Logistics; DAN CARR, Executive Director of Publishing Technology; SUSAN CRESPI, Editorial Operations Manager; ALEX MORALES, Publishing Operations Manager; STAN LEE, Chairman Emeritus. For information regarding advertising in Marvel Comics or on Marvel.com, please contact Niza Disla, Director of Marvel Partnerships, at ndisla@marvel.com. For Marvel subscription inquiries, please call 800-217-9158. **Manufactured between 3/28/2014 and 5/12/2014 by R.R. DONNELLEY, INC., SALEM, VA, USA.**

10 9 8 7 6 5 4 3 2 1

STAR-LORD GAMORA ROCKET RACCOON GROOT DRAX ANGELA

GUARDIANS OF THE GALAXY / ALL-NEW X-MEN

THE TRIAL OF JEAN GREY

WRITER: **BRIAN MICHAEL BENDIS**

GUARDIANS OF THE GALAXY #11-13

ARTISTS: **SARA PICHELLI** WITH **STUART IMMONEN** (#12) & **DAVID MARQUEZ** (#13)
ADDITIONAL INKS, #12: **WADE VON GRAWBADGER** COLORIST: **JUSTIN PONSOR**
LETTERER: **VC'S CORY PETIT** COVER ART: **SARA PICHELLI & JUSTIN PONSOR**
EDITORS: **ELLIE PYLE** & **STEPHEN WACKER**

ALL-NEW X-MEN #22-24

PENCILER: **STUART IMMONEN** INKER: **WADE VON GRAWBADGER**
COLORIST: **MARTE GRACIA** LETTERER: **VC'S CORY PETIT**
COVER ART: **STUART IMMONEN, WADE VON GRAWBADGER & MARTE GRACIA**
ASSISTANT EDITOR: **XANDER JAROWEY** ASSOCIATE EDITOR: **JORDAN D. WHITE** EDITOR: **NICK LOWE**

COLLECTION EDITOR: **JENNIFER GRÜNWALD** ASSISTANT EDITOR: **SARAH BRUNSTAD**
ASSOCIATE MANAGING EDITOR: **ALEX STARBUCK** EDITOR, SPECIAL PROJECTS: **MARK D. BEAZLEY**
SENIOR EDITOR, SPECIAL PROJECTS: **JEFF YOUNGQUIST** SVP PRINT, SALES & MARKETING: **DAVID GABRIEL**

EDITOR IN CHIEF: **AXEL ALONSO** CHIEF CREATIVE OFFICER: **JOE QUESADA**
PUBLISHER: **DAN BUCKLEY** EXECUTIVE PRODUCER: **ALAN FINE**

CYCLOPS MARVEL GIRL ICEMAN BEAST ANGEL KITTY PRYDE X-23

PREVIOUSLY IN GUARDIANS OF THE GALAXY...

PETER QUILL'S ESTRANGED FATHER, THE KING OF SPARTAX, TRIED TO CAPTURE THE GUARDIANS FOR DISOBEYING HIS NEW RULE THAT NO ALIEN HAND MAY TOUCH THE PLANET EARTH. IN RETURN, PETER SHAMED HIM WITH SOME COLORFUL PUBLIC DEFIANCE.

THE HUNTER/WARRIOR ANGELA HAS COME TO THIS GALAXY BECAUSE OF A TIME-SPACE CONTINUUM ACCIDENT. SHE IS TRYING TO FIGURE OUT HER PLACE IN THE GALAXY.

THANOS' ARMY CAME VERY CLOSE TO TAKING THE PLANET EARTH, BUT THE GUARDIANS HELPED SAVE THE PLANET. THE MAD TITAN HAS DISAPPEARED.

PREVIOUSLY IN ALL-NEW X-MEN...

THE ORIGINAL X-MEN WERE BROUGHT TO THE PRESENT TO HELP SHOW THE PRESENT-DAY X-MEN HOW FAR THEY HAVE STRAYED FROM XAVIER'S DREAM. AFTER LEARNING OF THEIR FUTURE, THE ORIGINAL X-MEN FOUND THEMSELVES IN CONFLICT WITH ONE ANOTHER AS THEY TRIED TO COME TO GRIPS WITH WHAT THEIR DESTINY WILL BRING. THIS ESPECIALLY AFFECTED JEAN GREY AND SCOTT SUMMERS AS THEY LEARNED OF THEIR FUTURE TOGETHER AND JEAN'S SUBSEQUENT DEATHS.

ALTHOUGH THEY HAVE ATTEMPTED TO RETURN TO THEIR OWN TIME, THEY DISCOVERED THAT THEY ARE, IN FACT, STUCK IN THE PRESENT. RECENTLY MOVING FROM WOLVERINE'S JEAN GREY SCHOOL TO PRESENT-DAY CYCLOPS' NEW XAVIER SCHOOL, THEY HAVE BEEN JOINED BY THE NEWLY RESCUED X-23. YET, THIS NEW HOME MAY NOT BE AS SAFE AND SECURE AS THEY HAVE BEEN LED TO BELIEVE.

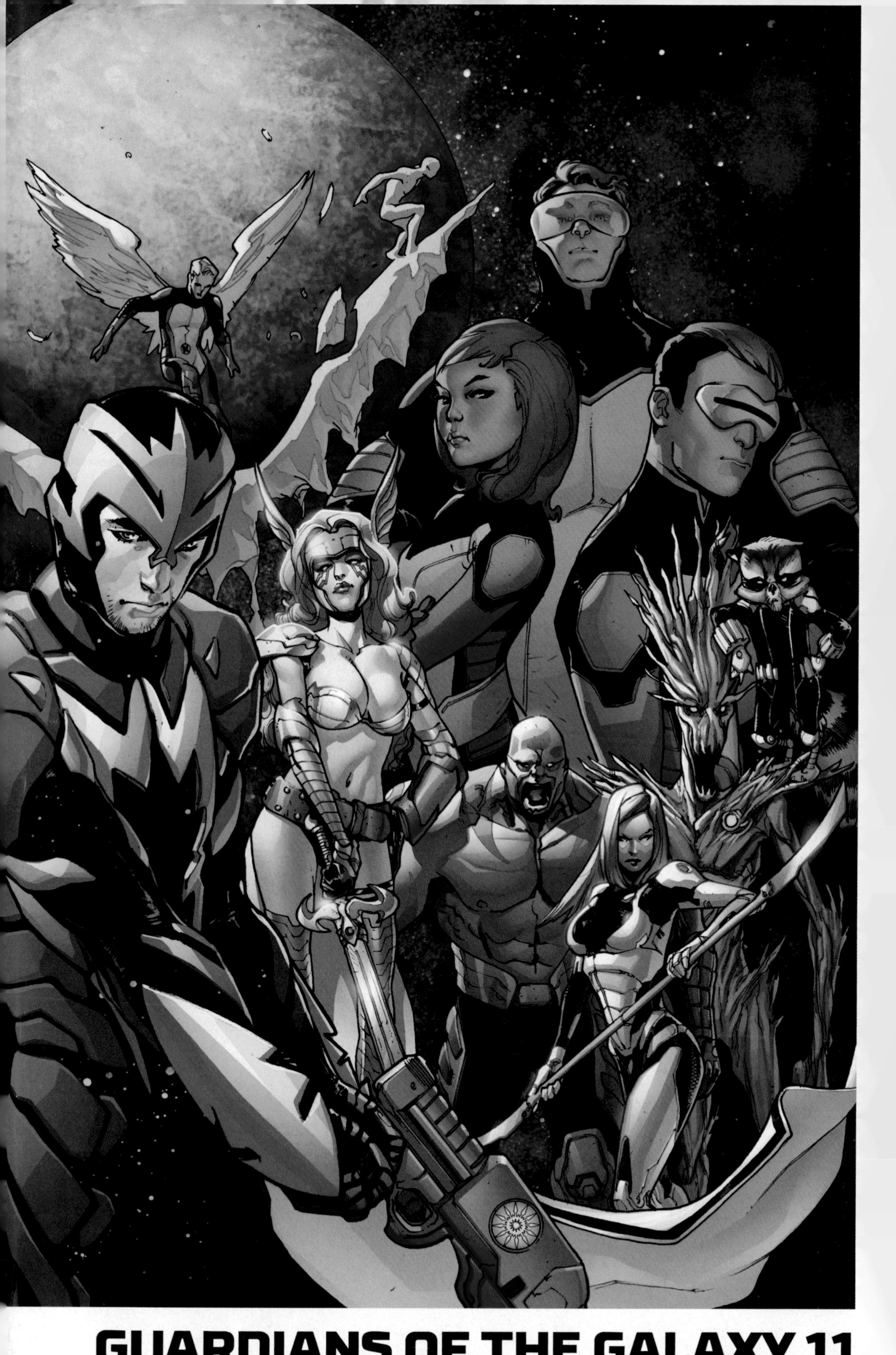

GUARDIANS OF THE GALAXY 11

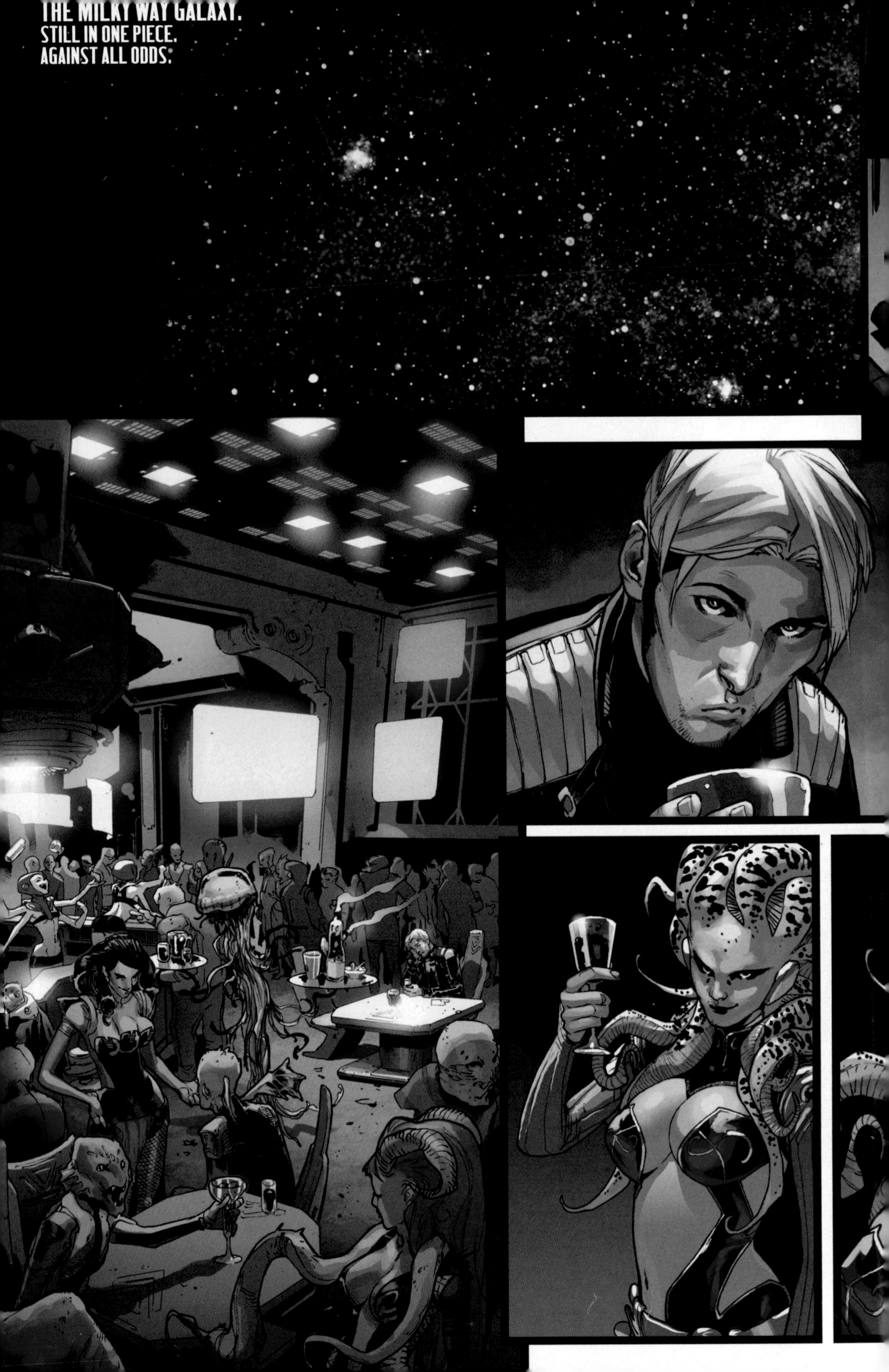
THE MILKY WAY GALAXY.
STILL IN ONE PIECE.
AGAINST ALL ODDS.

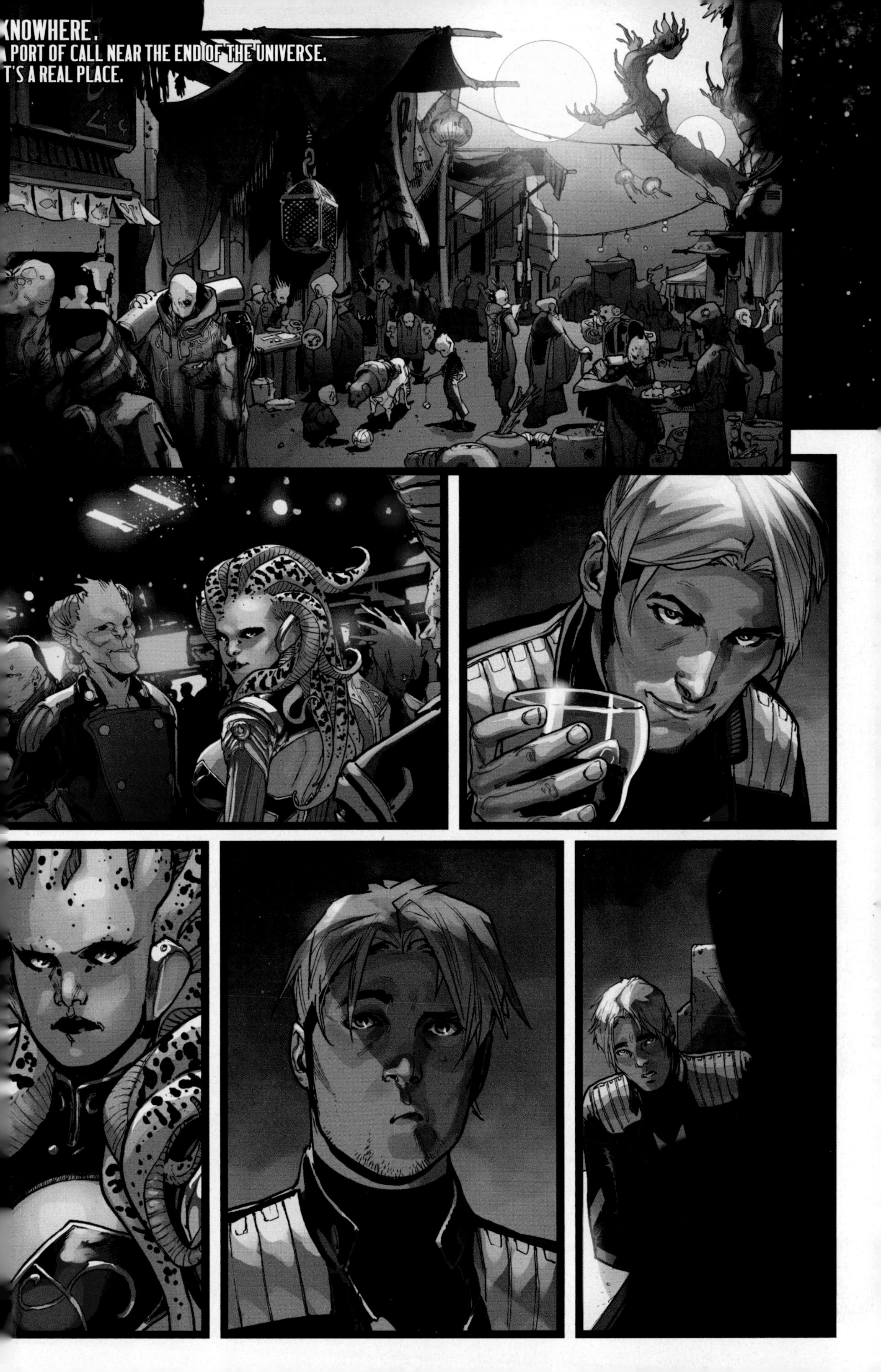
KNOWHERE.
A PORT OF CALL NEAR THE END OF THE UNIVERSE.
IT'S A REAL PLACE.

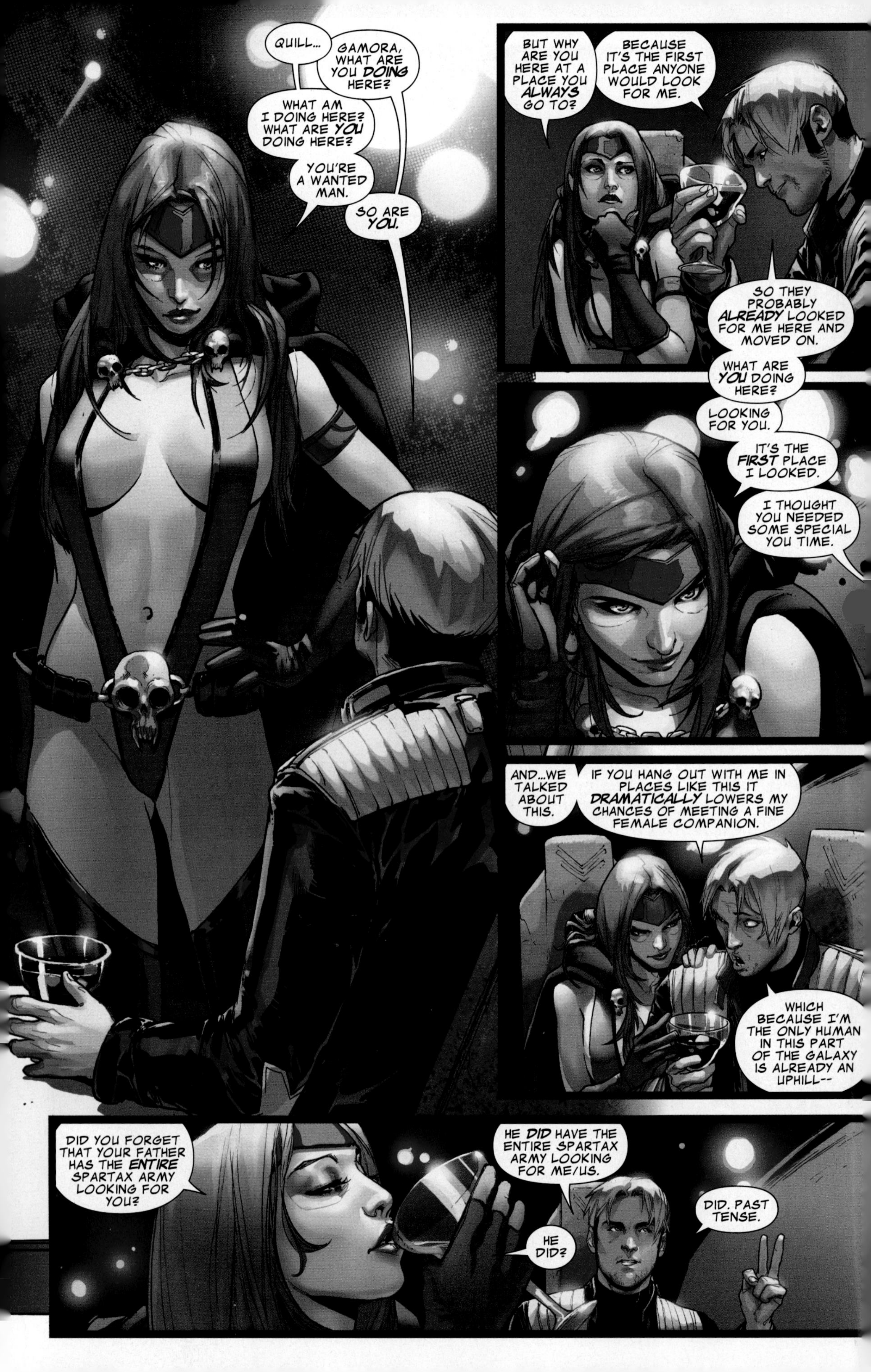
QUILL...
GAMORA, WHAT ARE YOU DOING HERE?
WHAT AM I DOING HERE? WHAT ARE YOU DOING HERE?
YOU'RE A WANTED MAN.
SO ARE YOU.
BUT WHY ARE YOU HERE AT A PLACE YOU ALWAYS GO TO?
BECAUSE IT'S THE FIRST PLACE ANYONE WOULD LOOK FOR ME.
SO THEY PROBABLY ALREADY LOOKED FOR ME HERE AND MOVED ON.
WHAT ARE YOU DOING HERE?
LOOKING FOR YOU.
IT'S THE FIRST PLACE I LOOKED.
I THOUGHT YOU NEEDED SOME SPECIAL YOU TIME.
AND...WE TALKED ABOUT THIS.
IF YOU HANG OUT WITH ME IN PLACES LIKE THIS IT DRAMATICALLY LOWERS MY CHANCES OF MEETING A FINE FEMALE COMPANION.
WHICH BECAUSE I'M THE ONLY HUMAN IN THIS PART OF THE GALAXY IS ALREADY AN UPHILL--
DID YOU FORGET THAT YOUR FATHER HAS THE ENTIRE SPARTAX ARMY LOOKING FOR YOU?
HE DID HAVE THE ENTIRE SPARTAX ARMY LOOKING FOR ME/US.
HE DID?
DID. PAST TENSE.

HE *DID* HAVE THE ENTIRE SPARTAX ARMY LOOKING FOR ME AND *NOW* HE HAS THE ENTIRE SPARTAX ARMY LOOKING FOR *THANOS.*

HE DIDN'T FORGET ABOUT YOU.

I *AM* HARD TO FORGET.

SO WHAT'S THE PLAN?

PLAN?

WHAT ARE WE GOING TO DO NEXT?

WHAT ARE WE GOING TO DO NEXT?

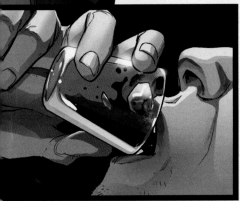

FIRST *YOU* ARE GOING TO LOOK DOWN AT YOUR BELLY BUTTON...

AND YOU'RE GOING TO SEE THAT MY ONE-OF-A-KIND ELEMENTAL GUN IS POINTED RIGHT AT IT.

THEN YOU ARE GOING TO TELL ME WHO YOU *REALLY* ARE.

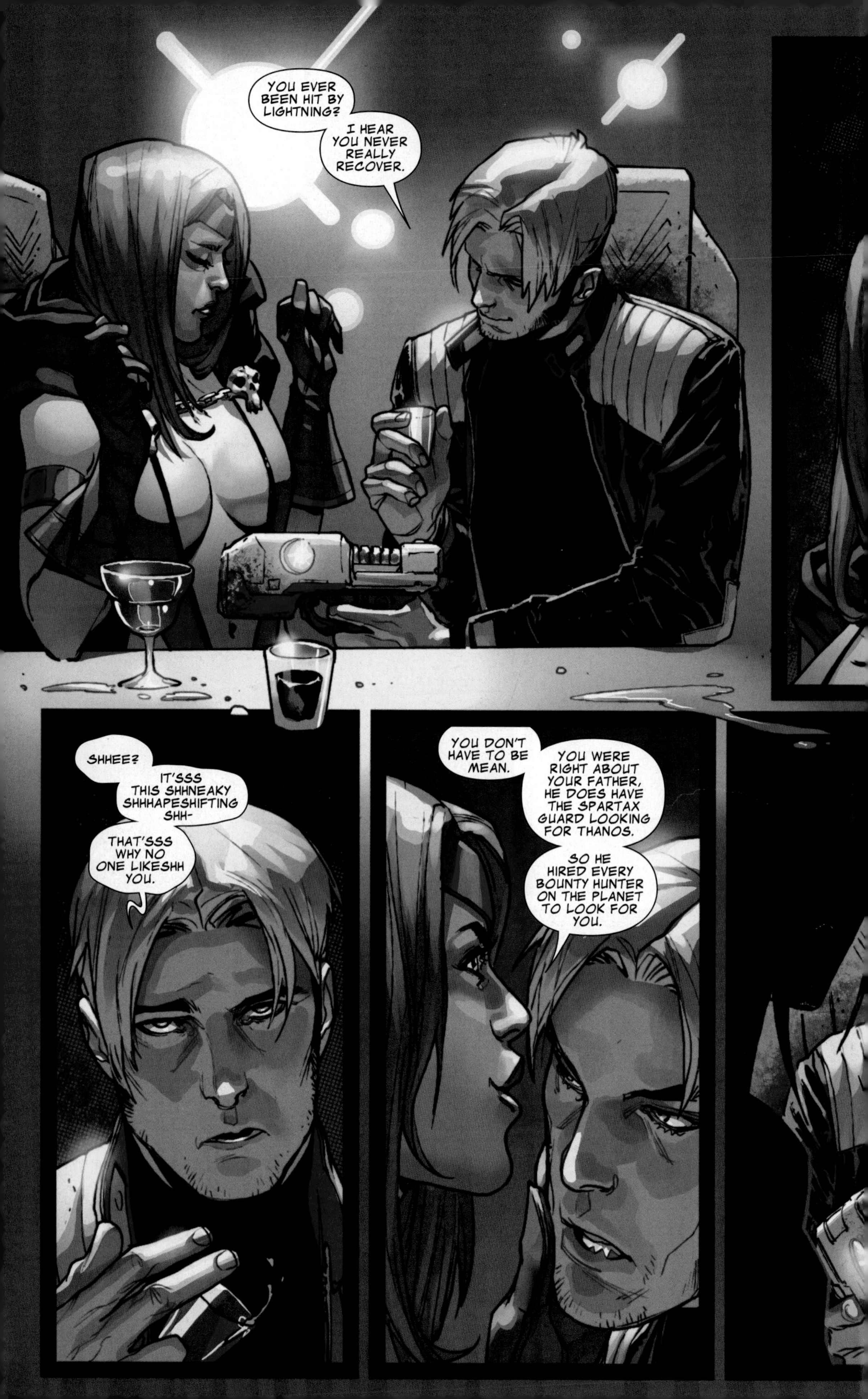
YOU EVER BEEN HIT BY LIGHTNING?
I HEAR YOU NEVER REALLY RECOVER.
SHHEE?
IT'SSS THIS SHHNEAKY SHHHAPESHIFTING SHH-
THAT'SSS WHY NO ONE LIKESHH YOU.
YOU DON'T HAVE TO BE MEAN.
YOU WERE RIGHT ABOUT YOUR FATHER, HE DOES HAVE THE SPARTAX GUARD LOOKING FOR THANOS.
SO HE HIRED EVERY BOUNTY HUNTER ON THE PLANET TO LOOK FOR YOU.

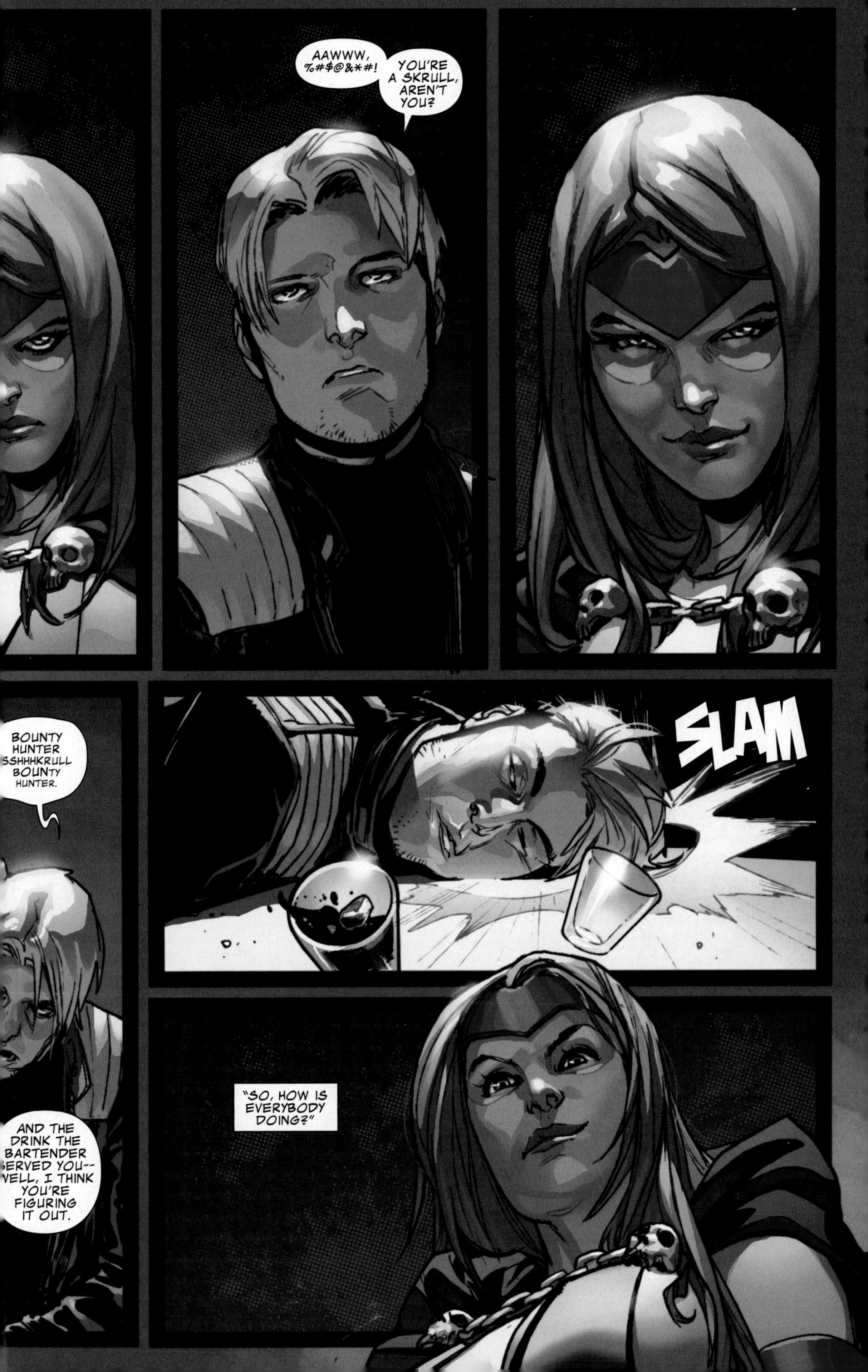
AAWWW, %#$@&**#!
YOU'RE A SKRULL, AREN'T YOU?
SLAM
BOUNTY HUNTER SSHHHKRULL BOUNty HUNTER.
"SO, HOW IS EVERYBODY DOING?"
AND THE DRINK THE BARTENDER SERVED YOU-- WELL, I THINK YOU'RE FIGURING IT OUT.

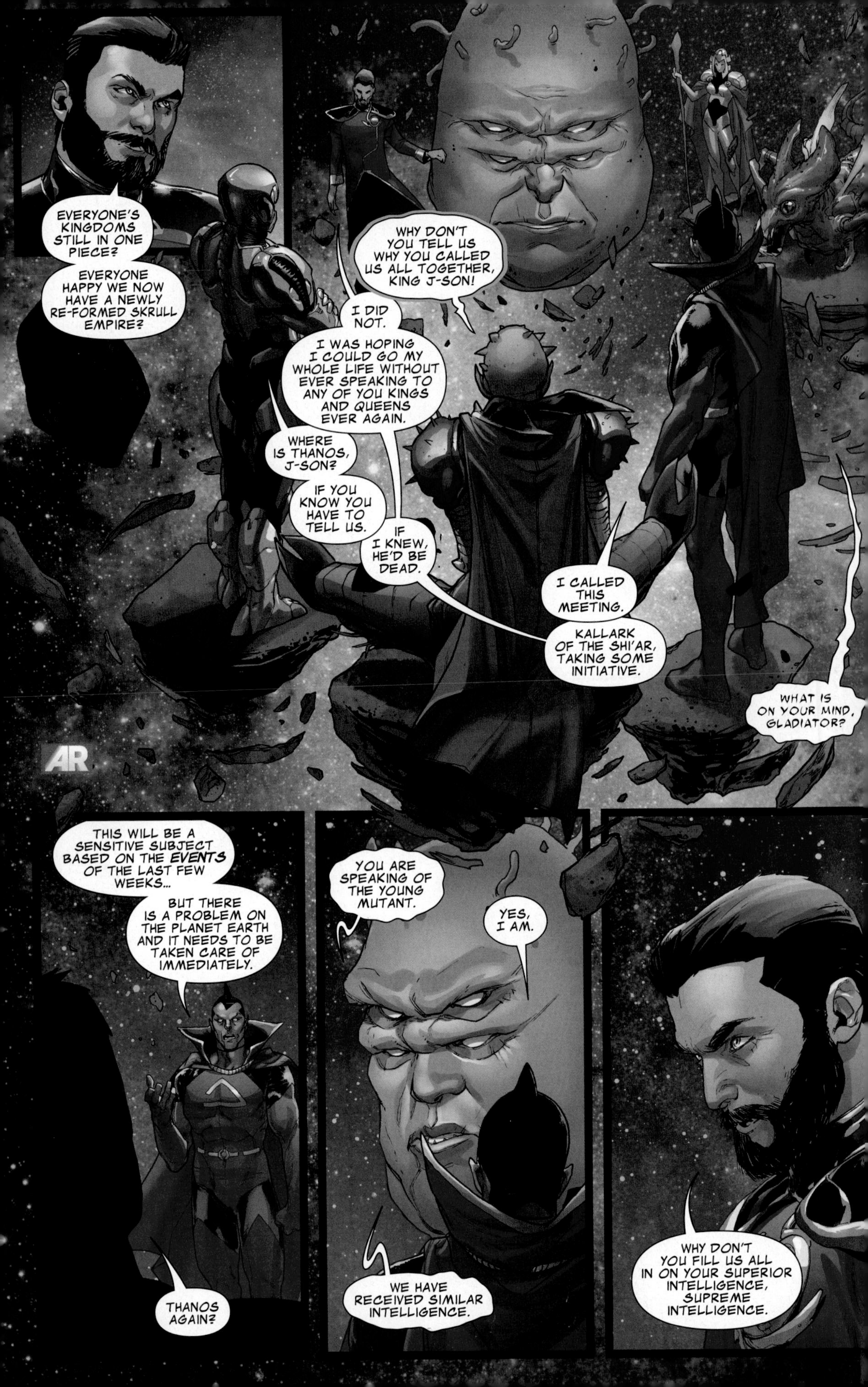
EVERYONE'S KINGDOMS STILL IN ONE PIECE?
EVERYONE HAPPY WE NOW HAVE A NEWLY RE-FORMED SKRULL EMPIRE?
WHY DON'T YOU TELL US WHY YOU CALLED US ALL TOGETHER, KING J-SON!
I DID NOT.
I WAS HOPING I COULD GO MY WHOLE LIFE WITHOUT EVER SPEAKING TO ANY OF YOU KINGS AND QUEENS EVER AGAIN.
WHERE IS THANOS, J-SON?
IF YOU KNOW YOU HAVE TO TELL US.
IF I KNEW, HE'D BE DEAD.
I CALLED THIS MEETING.
KALLARK OF THE SHI'AR, TAKING SOME INITIATIVE.
WHAT IS ON YOUR MIND, GLADIATOR?
THIS WILL BE A SENSITIVE SUBJECT BASED ON THE *EVENTS* OF THE LAST FEW WEEKS...
BUT THERE IS A PROBLEM ON THE PLANET EARTH AND IT NEEDS TO BE TAKEN CARE OF IMMEDIATELY.
THANOS AGAIN?
YOU ARE SPEAKING OF THE YOUNG MUTANT.
YES, I AM.
WE HAVE RECEIVED SIMILAR INTELLIGENCE.
WHY DON'T YOU FILL US ALL IN ON YOUR SUPERIOR INTELLIGENCE, SUPREME INTELLIGENCE.

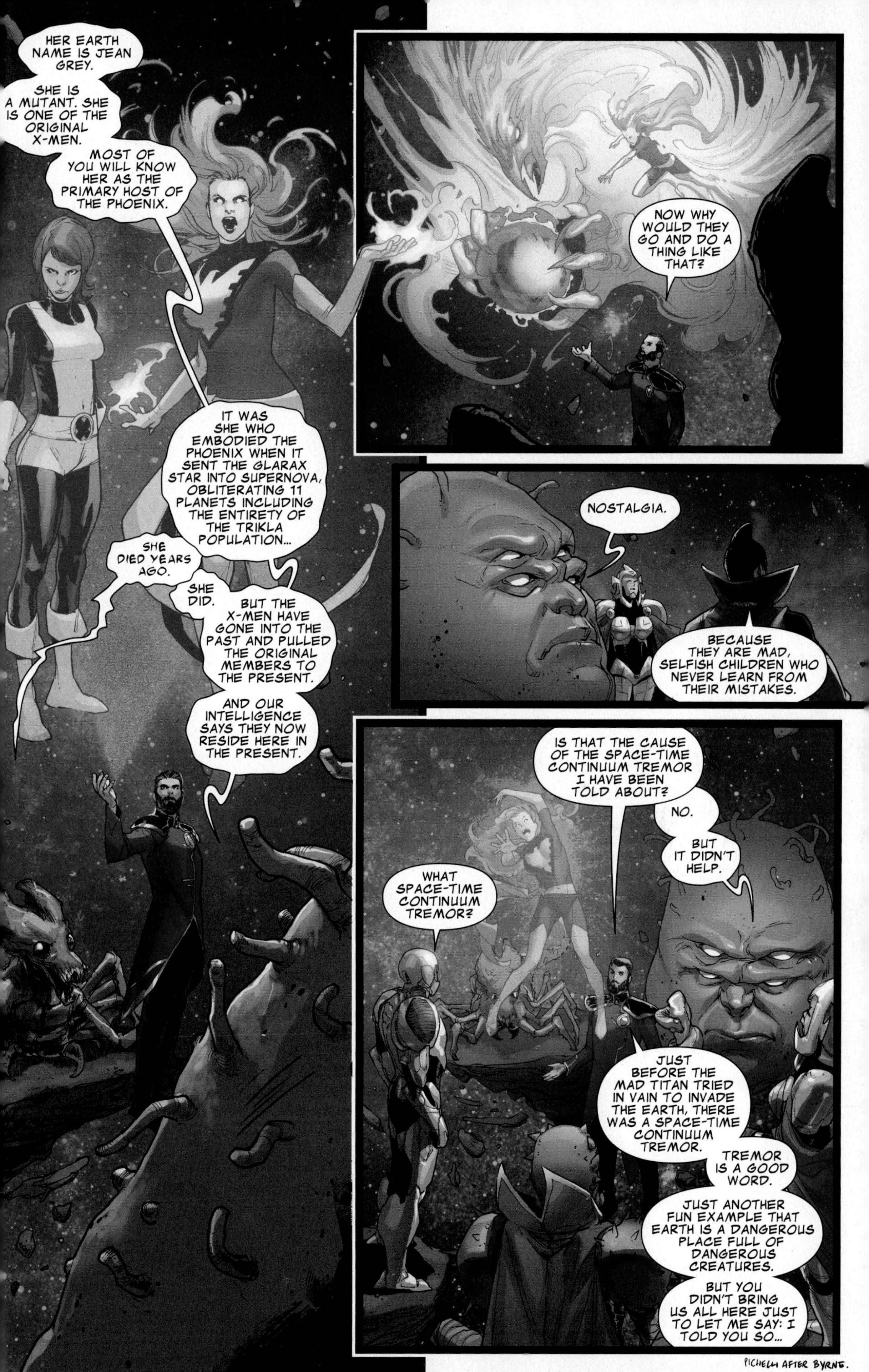
HER EARTH NAME IS JEAN GREY.
SHE IS A MUTANT. SHE IS ONE OF THE ORIGINAL X-MEN.
MOST OF YOU WILL KNOW HER AS THE PRIMARY HOST OF THE PHOENIX.
IT WAS SHE WHO EMBODIED THE PHOENIX WHEN IT SENT THE GLARAX STAR INTO SUPERNOVA, OBLITERATING 11 PLANETS INCLUDING THE ENTIRETY OF THE TRIKLA POPULATION...
SHE DIED YEARS AGO.
SHE DID.
BUT THE X-MEN HAVE GONE INTO THE PAST AND PULLED THE ORIGINAL MEMBERS TO THE PRESENT.
AND OUR INTELLIGENCE SAYS THEY NOW RESIDE HERE IN THE PRESENT.
NOW WHY WOULD THEY GO AND DO A THING LIKE THAT?
NOSTALGIA.
BECAUSE THEY ARE MAD, SELFISH CHILDREN WHO NEVER LEARN FROM THEIR MISTAKES.
IS THAT THE CAUSE OF THE SPACE-TIME CONTINUUM TREMOR I HAVE BEEN TOLD ABOUT?
NO.
BUT IT DIDN'T HELP.
WHAT SPACE-TIME CONTINUUM TREMOR?
JUST BEFORE THE MAD TITAN TRIED IN VAIN TO INVADE THE EARTH, THERE WAS A SPACE-TIME CONTINUUM TREMOR.
TREMOR IS A GOOD WORD.
JUST ANOTHER FUN EXAMPLE THAT EARTH IS A DANGEROUS PLACE FULL OF DANGEROUS CREATURES.
BUT YOU DIDN'T BRING US ALL HERE JUST TO LET ME SAY: I TOLD YOU SO...

PICHELLI AFTER BYRNE.

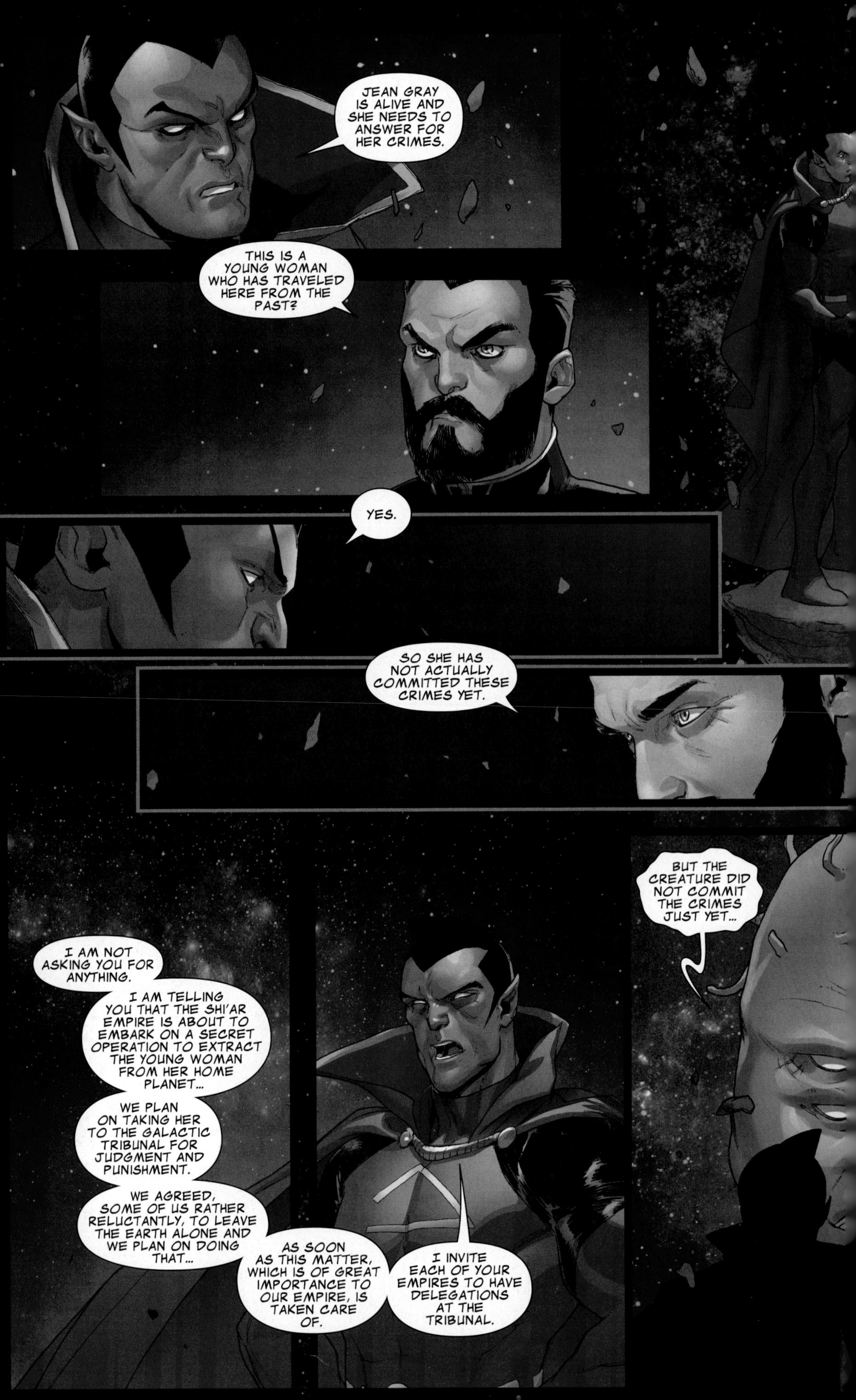
JEAN GRAY IS ALIVE AND SHE NEEDS TO ANSWER FOR HER CRIMES.
THIS IS A YOUNG WOMAN WHO HAS TRAVELED HERE FROM THE PAST?
YES.
SO SHE HAS NOT ACTUALLY COMMITTED THESE CRIMES YET.
BUT THE CREATURE DID NOT COMMIT THE CRIMES JUST YET...
I AM NOT ASKING YOU FOR ANYTHING.
I AM TELLING YOU THAT THE SHI'AR EMPIRE IS ABOUT TO EMBARK ON A SECRET OPERATION TO EXTRACT THE YOUNG WOMAN FROM HER HOME PLANET...
WE PLAN ON TAKING HER TO THE GALACTIC TRIBUNAL FOR JUDGMENT AND PUNISHMENT.
WE AGREED, SOME OF US RATHER RELUCTANTLY, TO LEAVE THE EARTH ALONE AND WE PLAN ON DOING THAT...
AS SOON AS THIS MATTER, WHICH IS OF GREAT IMPORTANCE TO OUR EMPIRE, IS TAKEN CARE OF.
I INVITE EACH OF YOUR EMPIRES TO HAVE DELEGATIONS AT THE TRIBUNAL.

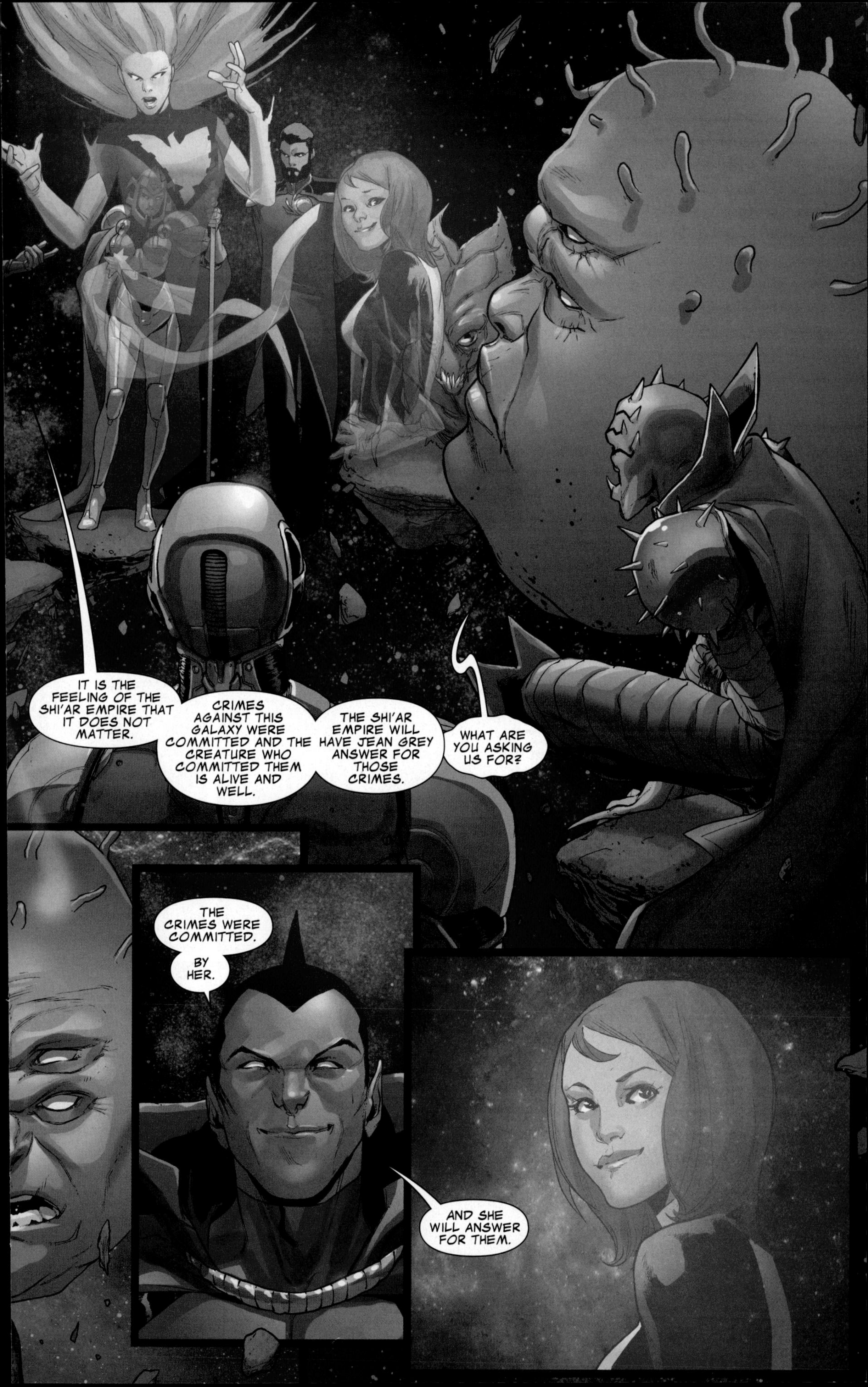
IT IS THE FEELING OF THE SHI'AR EMPIRE THAT IT DOES NOT MATTER.
CRIMES AGAINST THIS GALAXY WERE COMMITTED AND THE CREATURE WHO COMMITTED THEM IS ALIVE AND WELL.
THE SHI'AR EMPIRE WILL HAVE JEAN GREY ANSWER FOR THOSE CRIMES.
WHAT ARE YOU ASKING US FOR?
THE CRIMES WERE COMMITTED.
BY HER.
AND SHE WILL ANSWER FOR THEM.

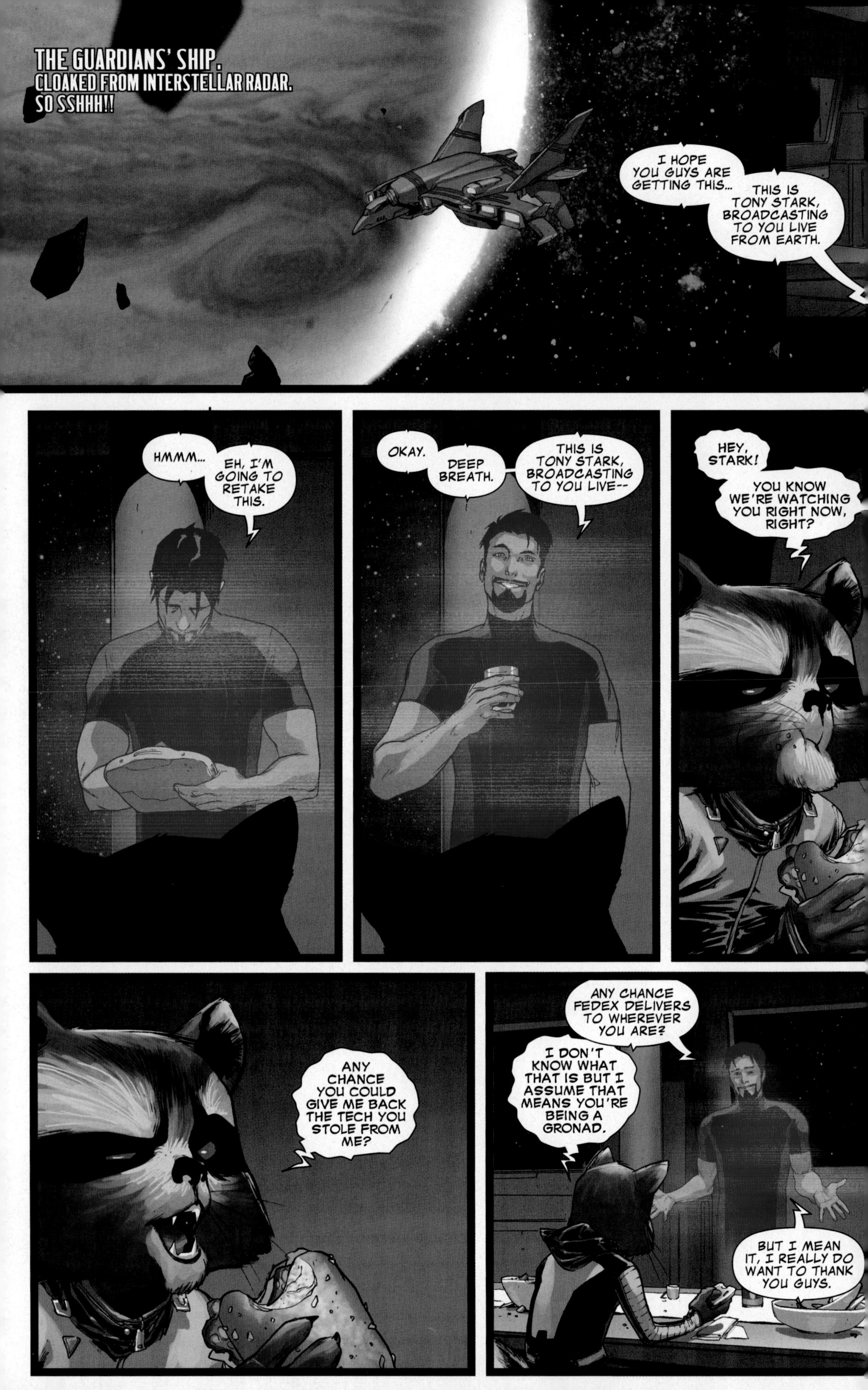
THE GUARDIANS' SHIP.
CLOAKED FROM INTERSTELLAR RADAR.
SO SSHHH!!
I HOPE YOU GUYS ARE GETTING THIS...
THIS IS TONY STARK, BROADCASTING TO YOU LIVE FROM EARTH.
HMMM...
EH, I'M GOING TO RETAKE THIS.
OKAY.
DEEP BREATH.
THIS IS TONY STARK, BROADCASTING TO YOU LIVE--
HEY, STARK!
YOU KNOW WE'RE WATCHING YOU RIGHT NOW, RIGHT?
ANY CHANCE YOU COULD GIVE ME BACK THE TECH YOU STOLE FROM ME?
ANY CHANCE FEDEX DELIVERS TO WHEREVER YOU ARE?
I DON'T KNOW WHAT THAT IS BUT I ASSUME THAT MEANS YOU'RE BEING A GRONAD.
BUT I MEAN IT, I REALLY DO WANT TO THANK YOU GUYS.

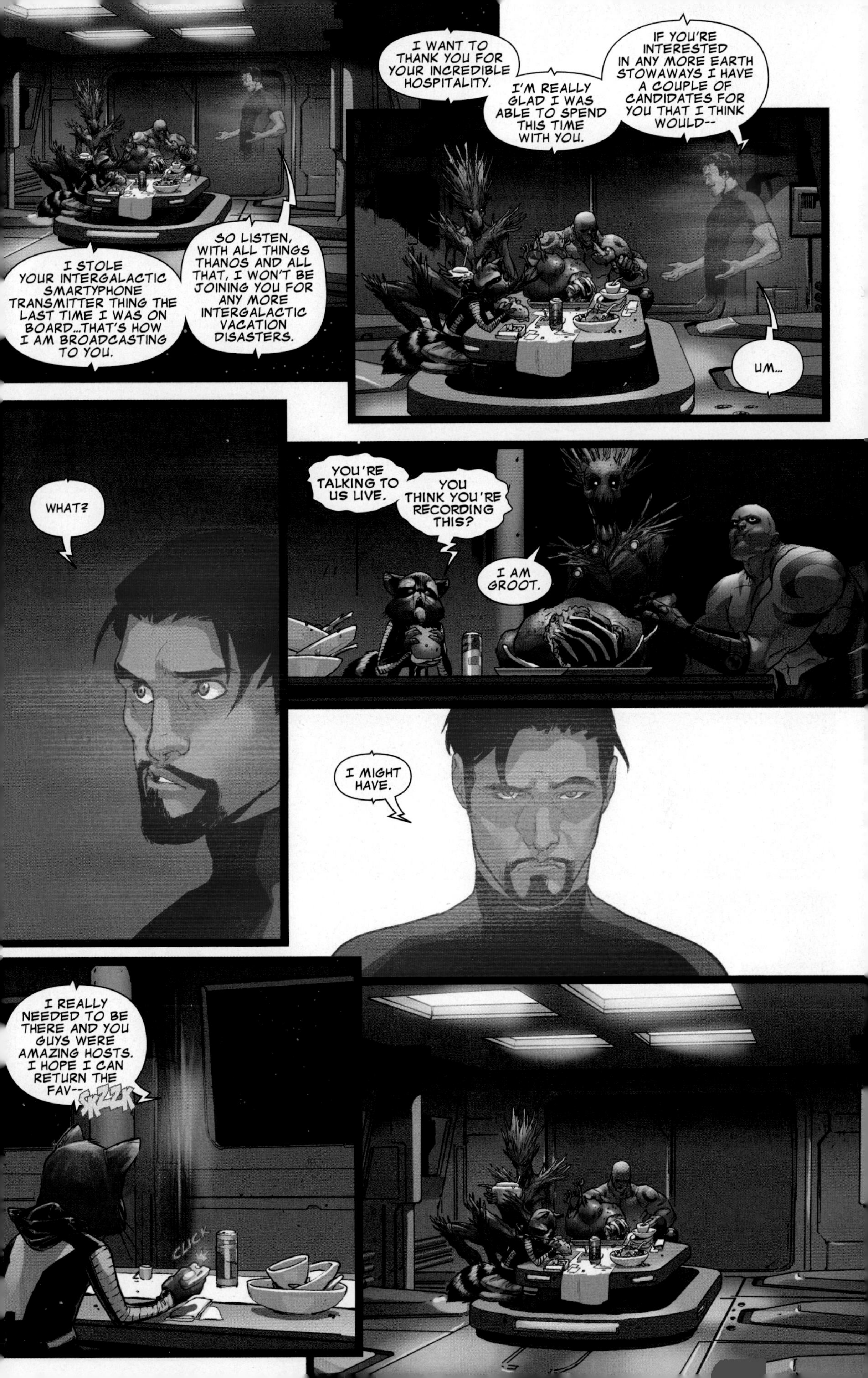
I STOLE YOUR INTERGALACTIC SMARTYPHONE TRANSMITTER THING THE LAST TIME I WAS ON BOARD...THAT'S HOW I AM BROADCASTING TO YOU.
SO LISTEN, WITH ALL THINGS THANOS AND ALL THAT, I WON'T BE JOINING YOU FOR ANY MORE INTERGALACTIC VACATION DISASTERS.
I WANT TO THANK YOU FOR YOUR INCREDIBLE HOSPITALITY.
I'M REALLY GLAD I WAS ABLE TO SPEND THIS TIME WITH YOU.
IF YOU'RE INTERESTED IN ANY MORE EARTH STOWAWAYS I HAVE A COUPLE OF CANDIDATES FOR YOU THAT I THINK WOULD--
UM...
WHAT?
YOU'RE TALKING TO US LIVE.
YOU THINK YOU'RE RECORDING THIS?
I AM GROOT.
I MIGHT HAVE.
I REALLY NEEDED TO BE THERE AND YOU GUYS WERE AMAZING HOSTS. I HOPE I CAN RETURN THE FAV--
SKZZK
CLICK

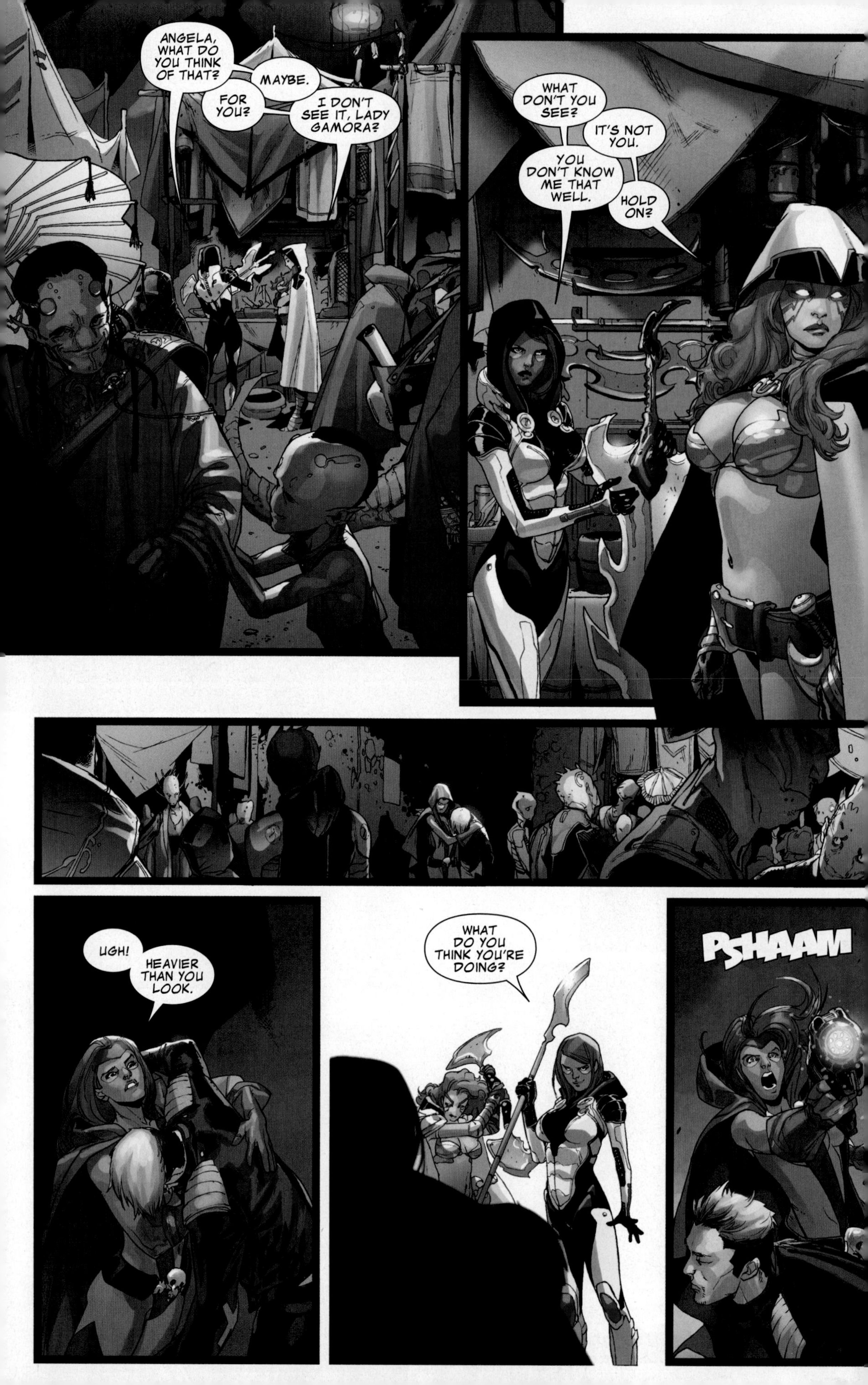
ANGELA, WHAT DO YOU THINK OF THAT?
MAYBE.
FOR YOU?
I DON'T SEE IT, LADY GAMORA?
WHAT DON'T YOU SEE?
IT'S NOT YOU.
YOU DON'T KNOW ME THAT WELL.
HOLD ON?
UGH!
HEAVIER THAN YOU LOOK.
WHAT DO YOU THINK YOU'RE DOING?
PSHAAM

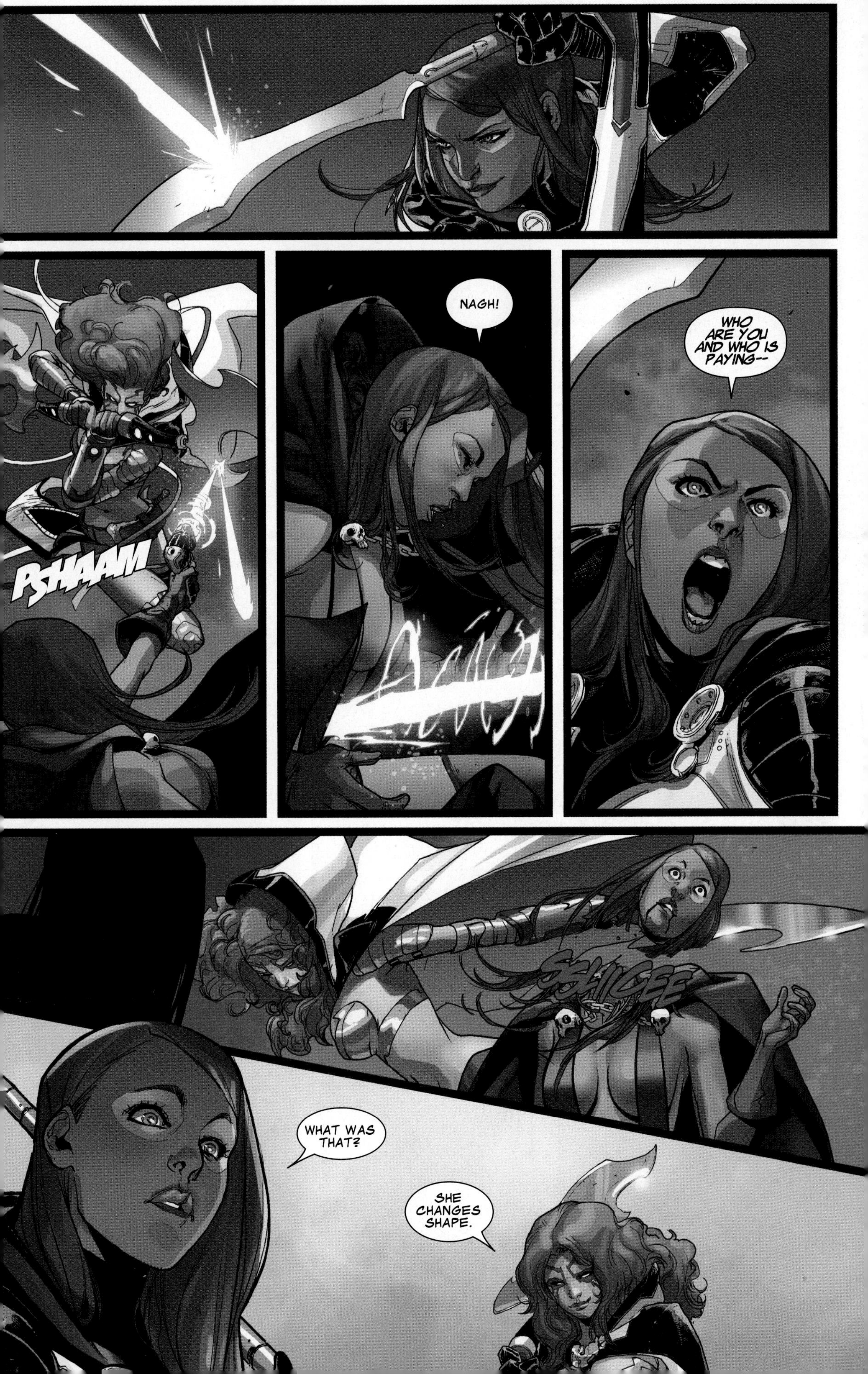
PSHAAM
NAGH!
WHO ARE YOU AND WHO IS PAYING--
SSLICEE
WHAT WAS THAT?
SHE CHANGES SHAPE.

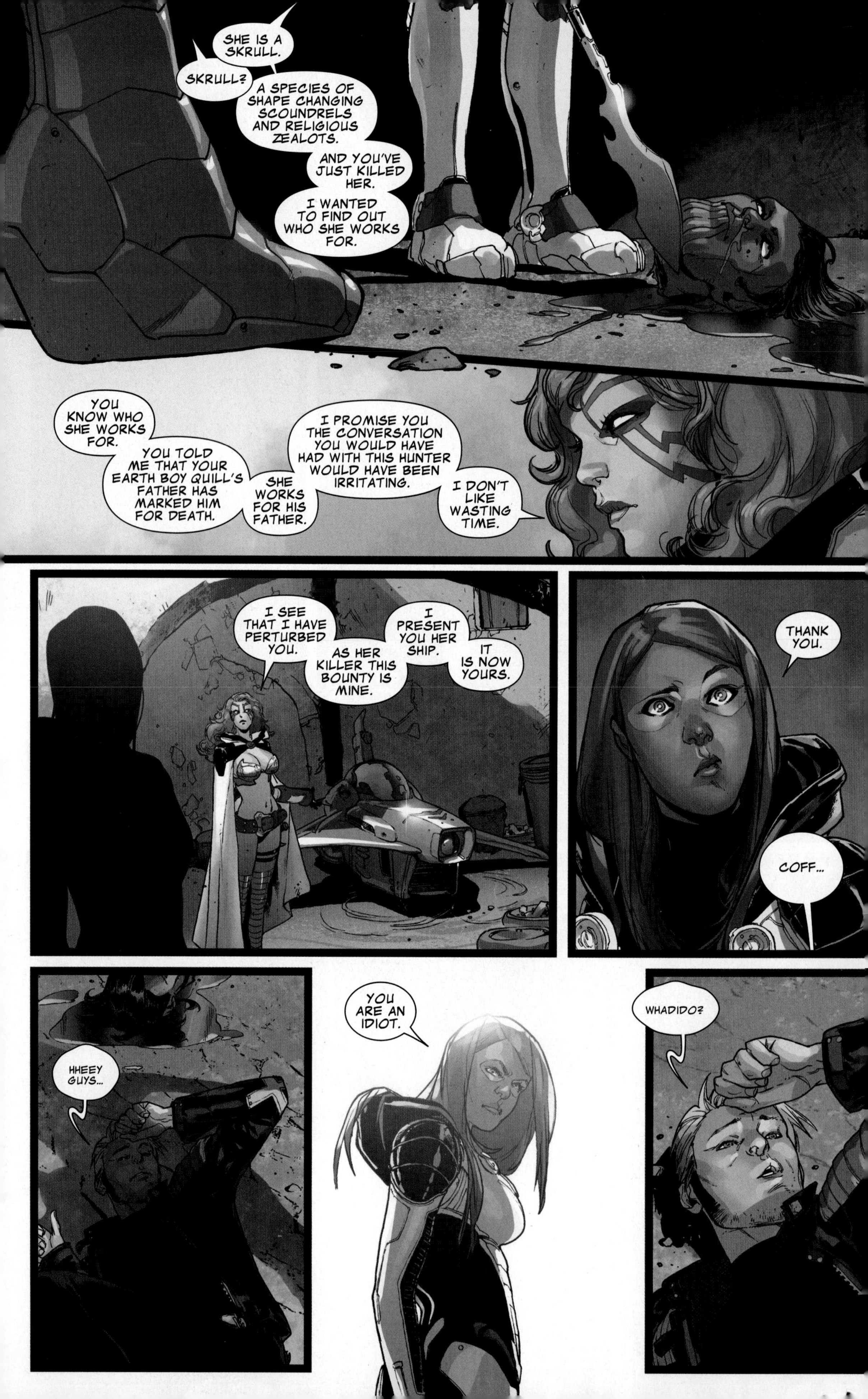
SHE IS A SKRULL.
SKRULL?
A SPECIES OF SHAPE CHANGING SCOUNDRELS AND RELIGIOUS ZEALOTS.
AND YOU'VE JUST KILLED HER.
I WANTED TO FIND OUT WHO SHE WORKS FOR.
YOU KNOW WHO SHE WORKS FOR.
YOU TOLD ME THAT YOUR EARTH BOY QUILL'S FATHER HAS MARKED HIM FOR DEATH.
SHE WORKS FOR HIS FATHER.
I PROMISE YOU THE CONVERSATION YOU WOULD HAVE HAD WITH THIS HUNTER WOULD HAVE BEEN IRRITATING.
I DON'T LIKE WASTING TIME.
I SEE THAT I HAVE PERTURBED YOU.
AS HER KILLER THIS BOUNTY IS MINE.
I PRESENT YOU HER SHIP.
IT IS NOW YOURS.
THANK YOU.
COFF...
HHEEY GUYS...
YOU ARE AN IDIOT.
WHADIDO?

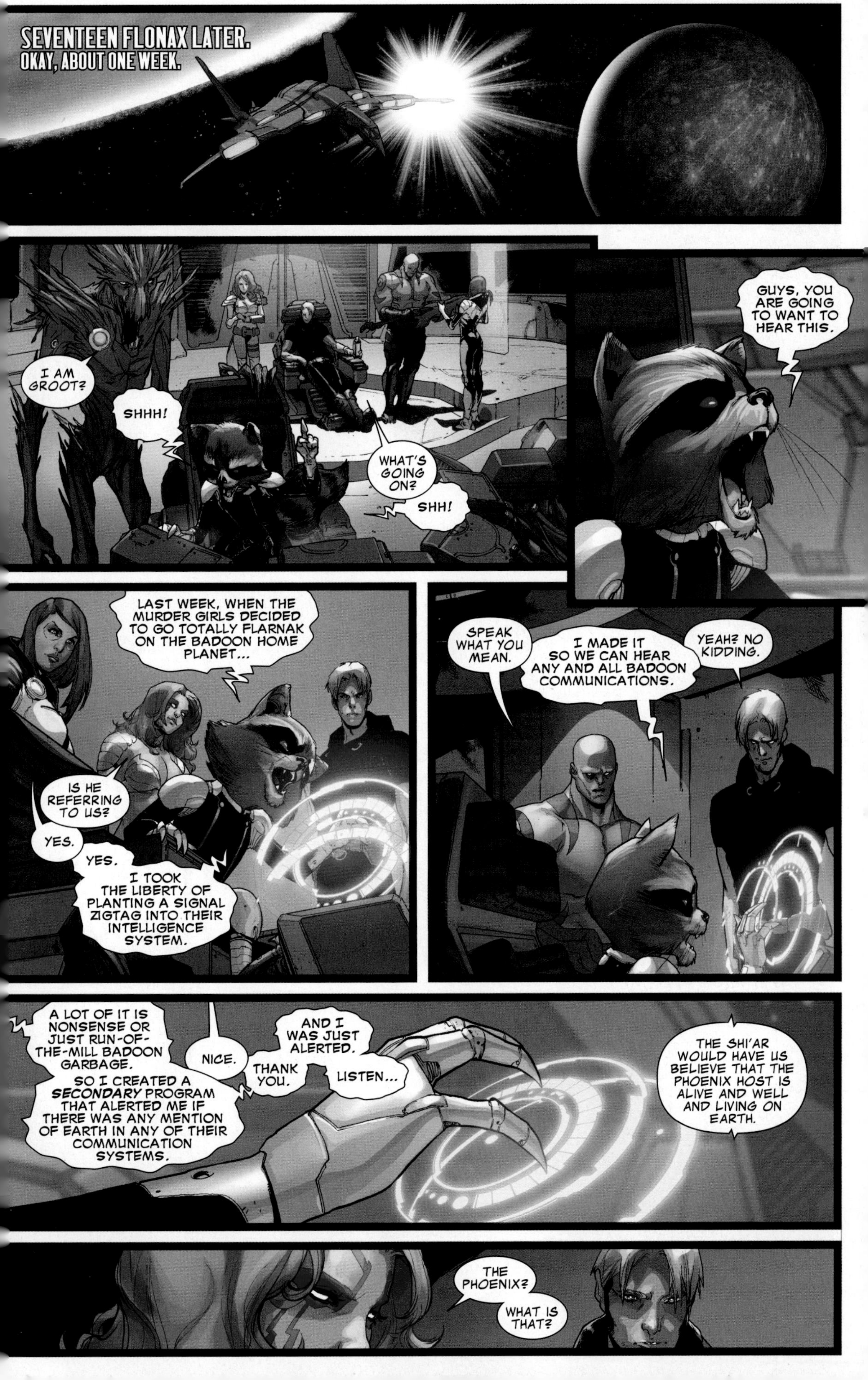

SEVENTEEN FLONAX LATER.
OKAY, ABOUT ONE WEEK.
I AM GROOT?
SHHH!
WHAT'S GOING ON?
SHH!
GUYS, YOU ARE GOING TO WANT TO HEAR THIS.
LAST WEEK, WHEN THE MURDER GIRLS DECIDED TO GO TOTALLY FLARNAK ON THE BADOON HOME PLANET...
IS HE REFERRING TO US?
YES.
YES.
I TOOK THE LIBERTY OF PLANTING A SIGNAL ZIGTAG INTO THEIR INTELLIGENCE SYSTEM.
SPEAK WHAT YOU MEAN.
I MADE IT SO WE CAN HEAR ANY AND ALL BADOON COMMUNICATIONS.
YEAH? NO KIDDING.
A LOT OF IT IS NONSENSE OR JUST RUN-OF-THE-MILL BADOON GARBAGE.
NICE.
SO I CREATED A SECONDARY PROGRAM THAT ALERTED ME IF THERE WAS ANY MENTION OF EARTH IN ANY OF THEIR COMMUNICATION SYSTEMS.
THANK YOU.
AND I WAS JUST ALERTED.
LISTEN...
THE SHI'AR WOULD HAVE US BELIEVE THAT THE PHOENIX HOST IS ALIVE AND WELL AND LIVING ON EARTH.
THE PHOENIX?
WHAT IS THAT?

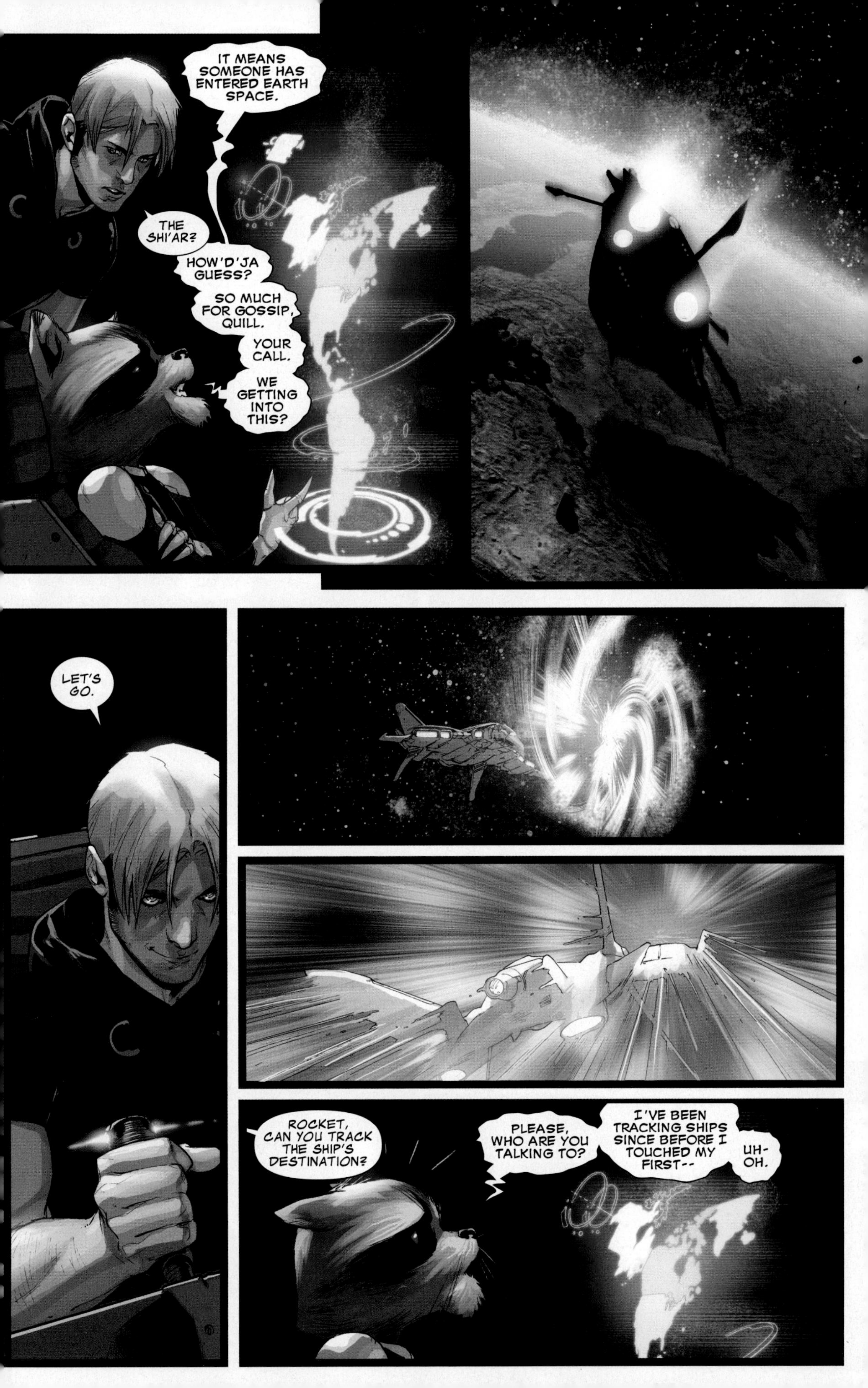
IT MEANS SOMEONE HAS ENTERED EARTH SPACE.
THE SHI'AR?
HOW'D'JA GUESS?
SO MUCH FOR GOSSIP, QUILL.
YOUR CALL.
WE GETTING INTO THIS?
LET'S GO.
ROCKET, CAN YOU TRACK THE SHIP'S DESTINATION?
PLEASE, WHO ARE YOU TALKING TO?
I'VE BEEN TRACKING SHIPS SINCE BEFORE I TOUCHED MY FIRST--
UH-OH.

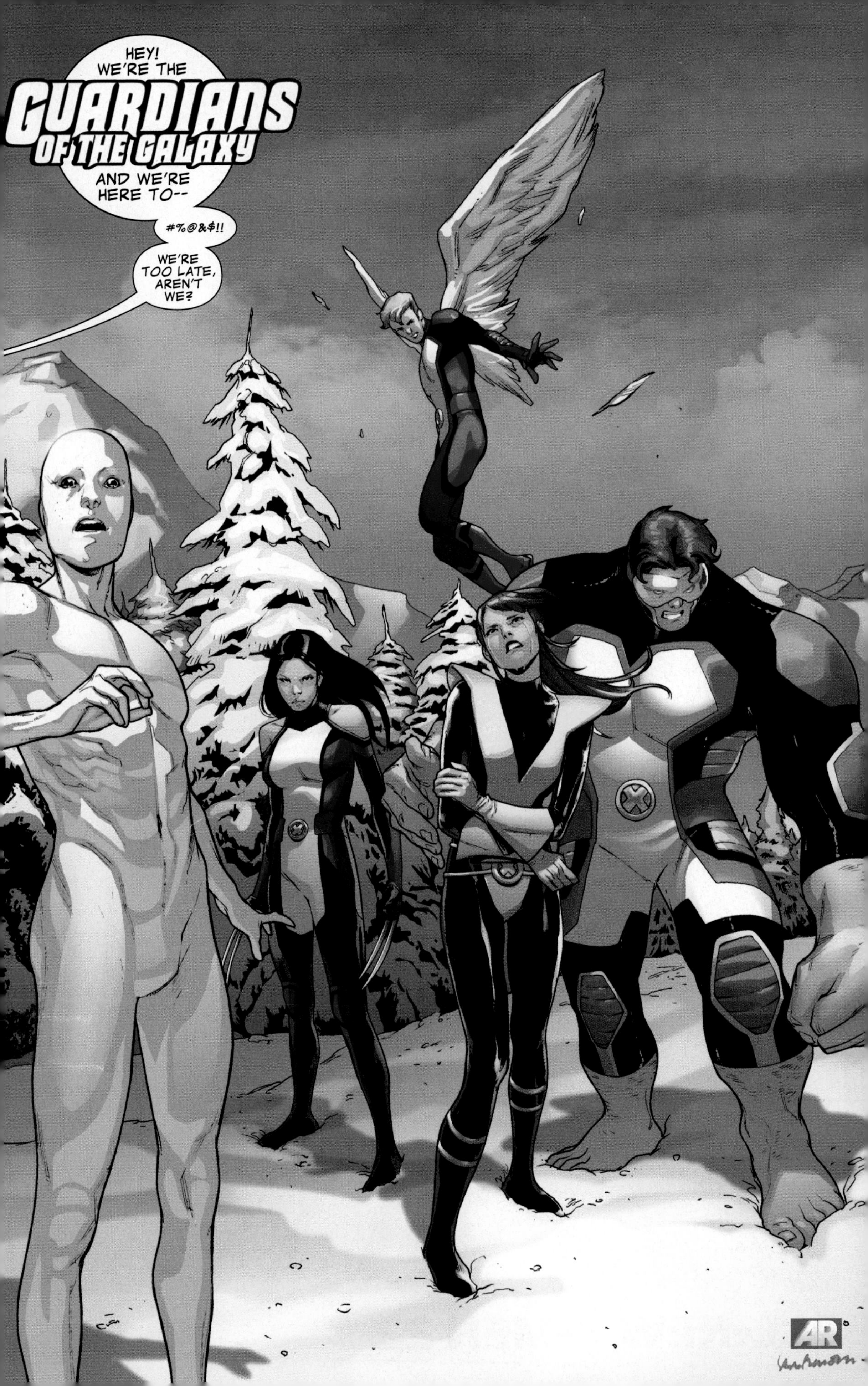
HEY! WE'RE THE GUARDIANS OF THE GALAXY AND WE'RE HERE TO--
#%@&$!!
WE'RE TOO LATE, AREN'T WE?

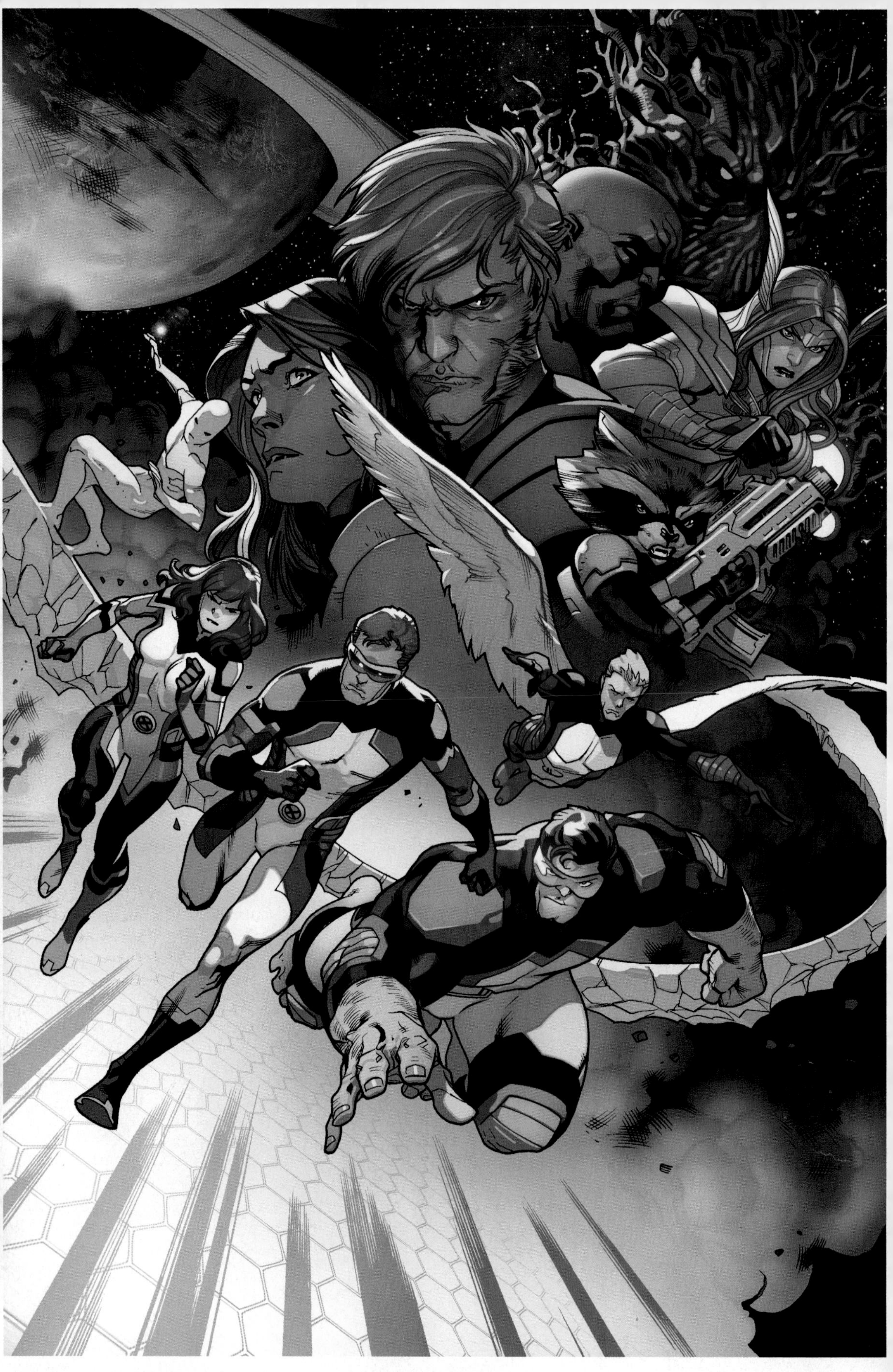

ALL-NEW X-MEN 22

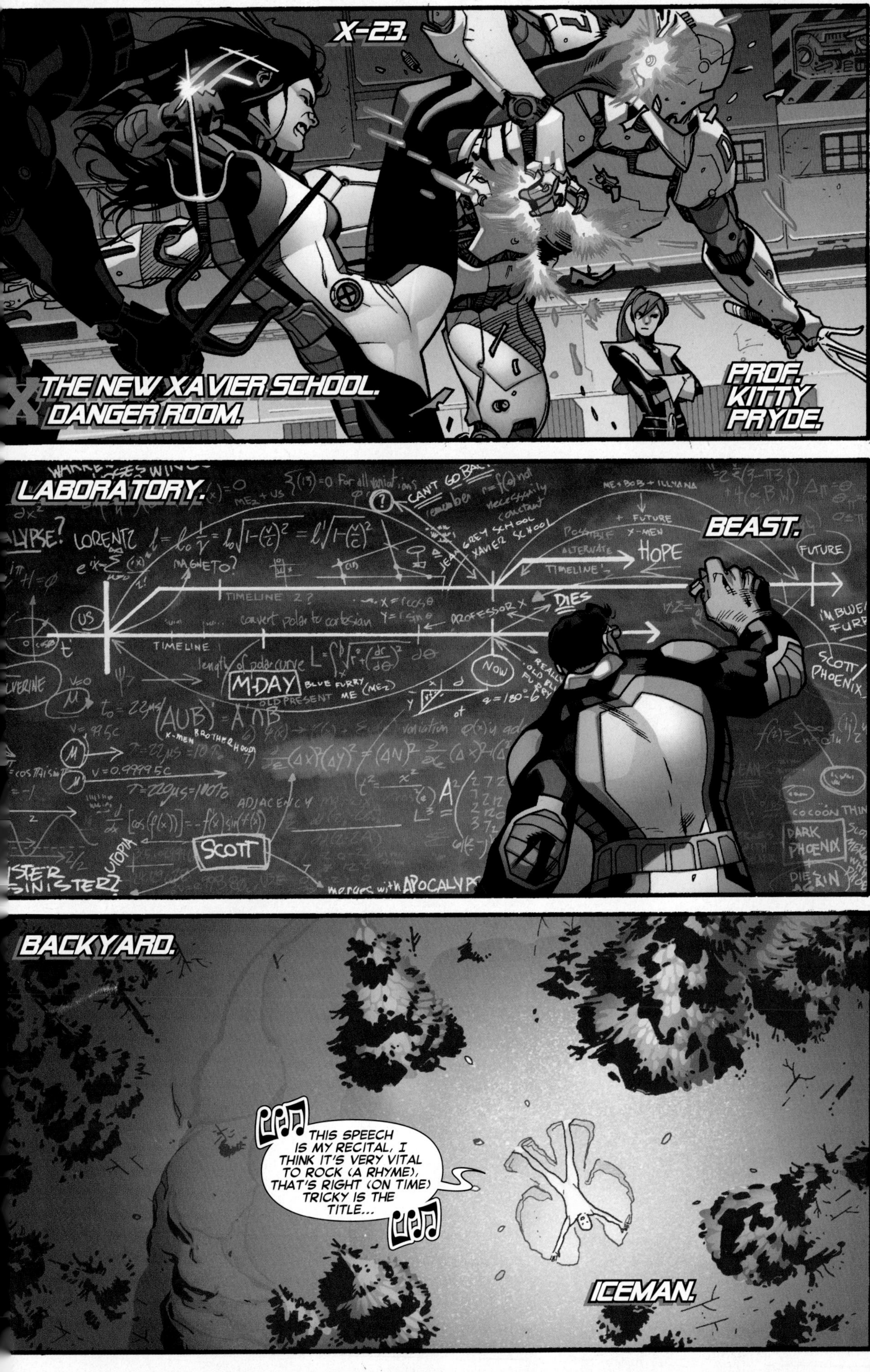
X-23.
THE NEW XAVIER SCHOOL. DANGER ROOM.
PROF. KITTY PRYDE.
LABORATORY.
BEAST.
HOPE
FUTURE
TIMELINE
PROFESSOR X DIES
NOW
M-DAY
SCOTT
DARK PHOENIX
BACKYARD.
THIS SPEECH IS MY RECITAL, I THINK IT'S VERY VITAL TO ROCK (A RHYME), THAT'S RIGHT (ON TIME) TRICKY IS THE TITLE...
ICEMAN.

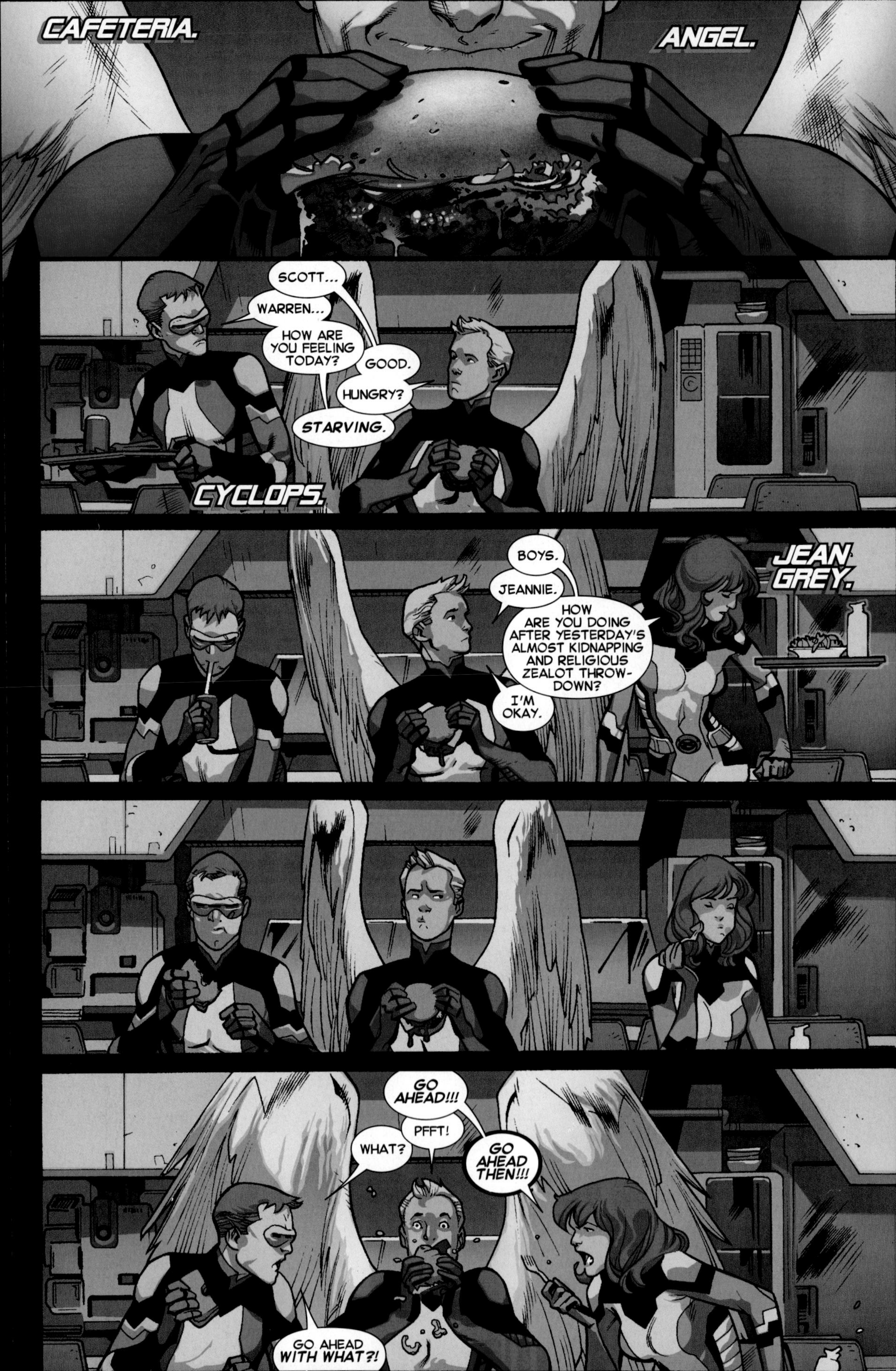
CAFETERIA.
ANGEL.
SCOTT...
WARREN...
HOW ARE YOU FEELING TODAY?
GOOD.
HUNGRY?
STARVING.
CYCLOPS.
BOYS.
JEANNIE.
HOW ARE YOU DOING AFTER YESTERDAY'S ALMOST KIDNAPPING AND RELIGIOUS ZEALOT THROW-DOWN?
JEAN GREY.
I'M OKAY.
GO AHEAD!!!
PFFT!
WHAT?
GO AHEAD THEN!!!
GO AHEAD WITH WHAT?!

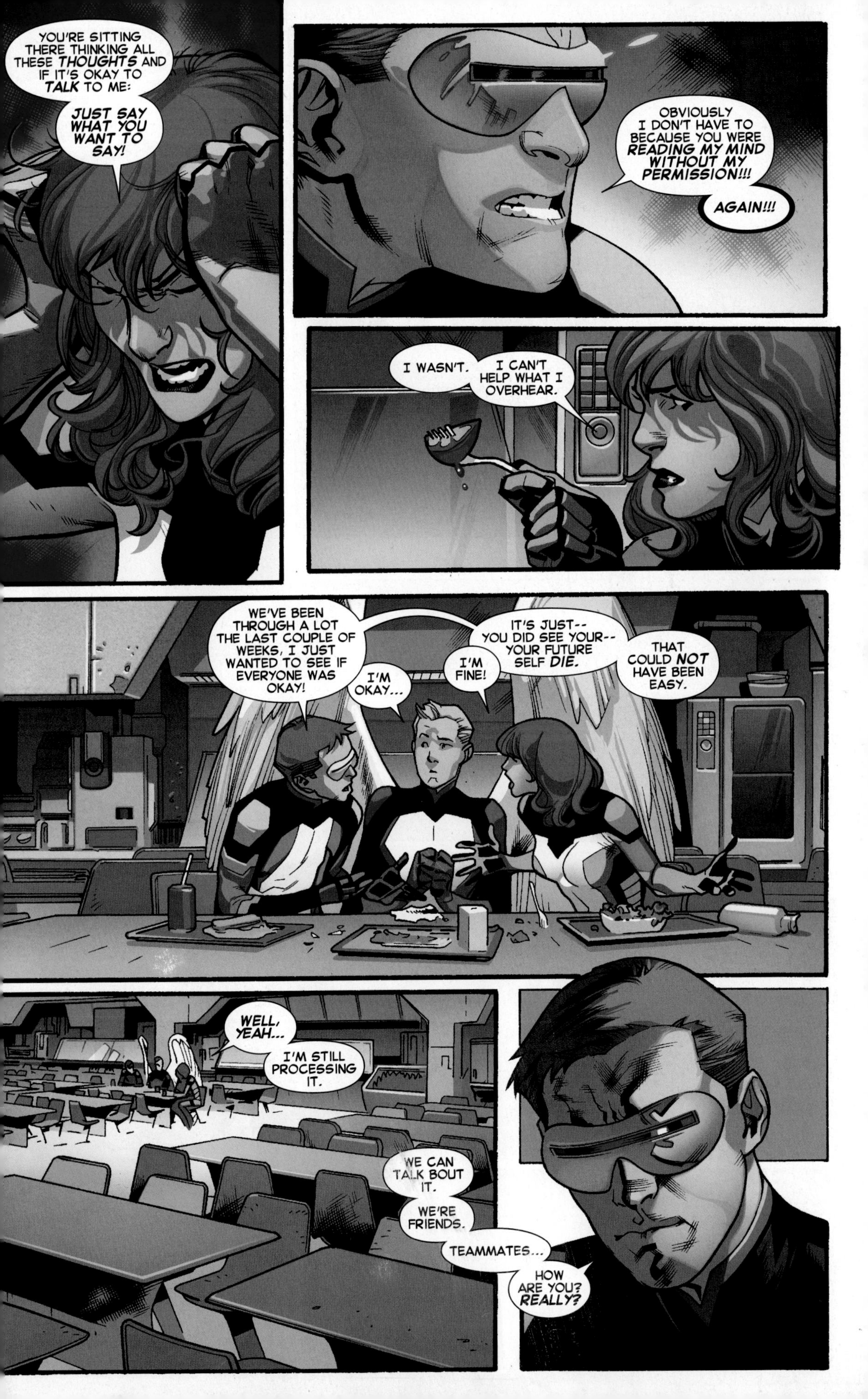
YOU'RE SITTING THERE THINKING ALL THESE *THOUGHTS* AND IF IT'S OKAY TO *TALK* TO ME:
JUST SAY WHAT YOU WANT TO SAY!
OBVIOUSLY I DON'T HAVE TO BECAUSE YOU WERE *READING MY MIND WITHOUT MY PERMISSION!!!*
AGAIN!!!
I WASN'T.
I CAN'T HELP WHAT I OVERHEAR.
WE'VE BEEN THROUGH A LOT THE LAST COUPLE OF WEEKS, I JUST WANTED TO SEE IF EVERYONE WAS OKAY!
I'M OKAY...
I'M FINE!
IT'S JUST-- YOU DID SEE YOUR-- YOUR FUTURE SELF *DIE.*
THAT COULD *NOT* HAVE BEEN EASY.
WELL, YEAH...
I'M STILL PROCESSING IT.
WE CAN TALK BOUT IT.
WE'RE FRIENDS.
TEAMMATES...
HOW ARE YOU? *REALLY?*

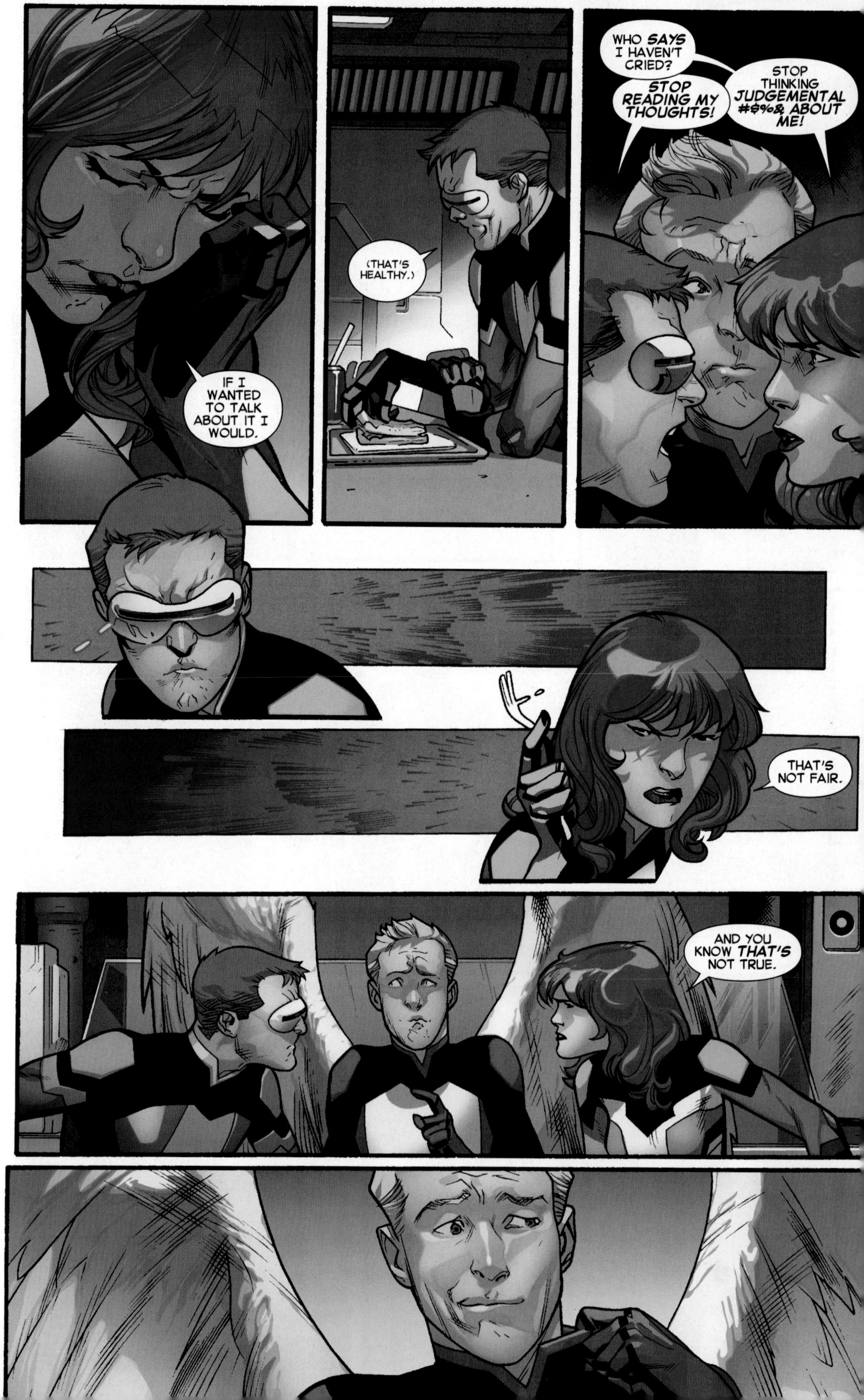
IF I WANTED TO TALK ABOUT IT I WOULD.
(THAT'S HEALTHY.)
WHO SAYS I HAVEN'T CRIED?
STOP READING MY THOUGHTS!
STOP THINKING JUDGEMENTAL #$%& ABOUT ME!
THAT'S NOT FAIR.
AND YOU KNOW THAT'S NOT TRUE.

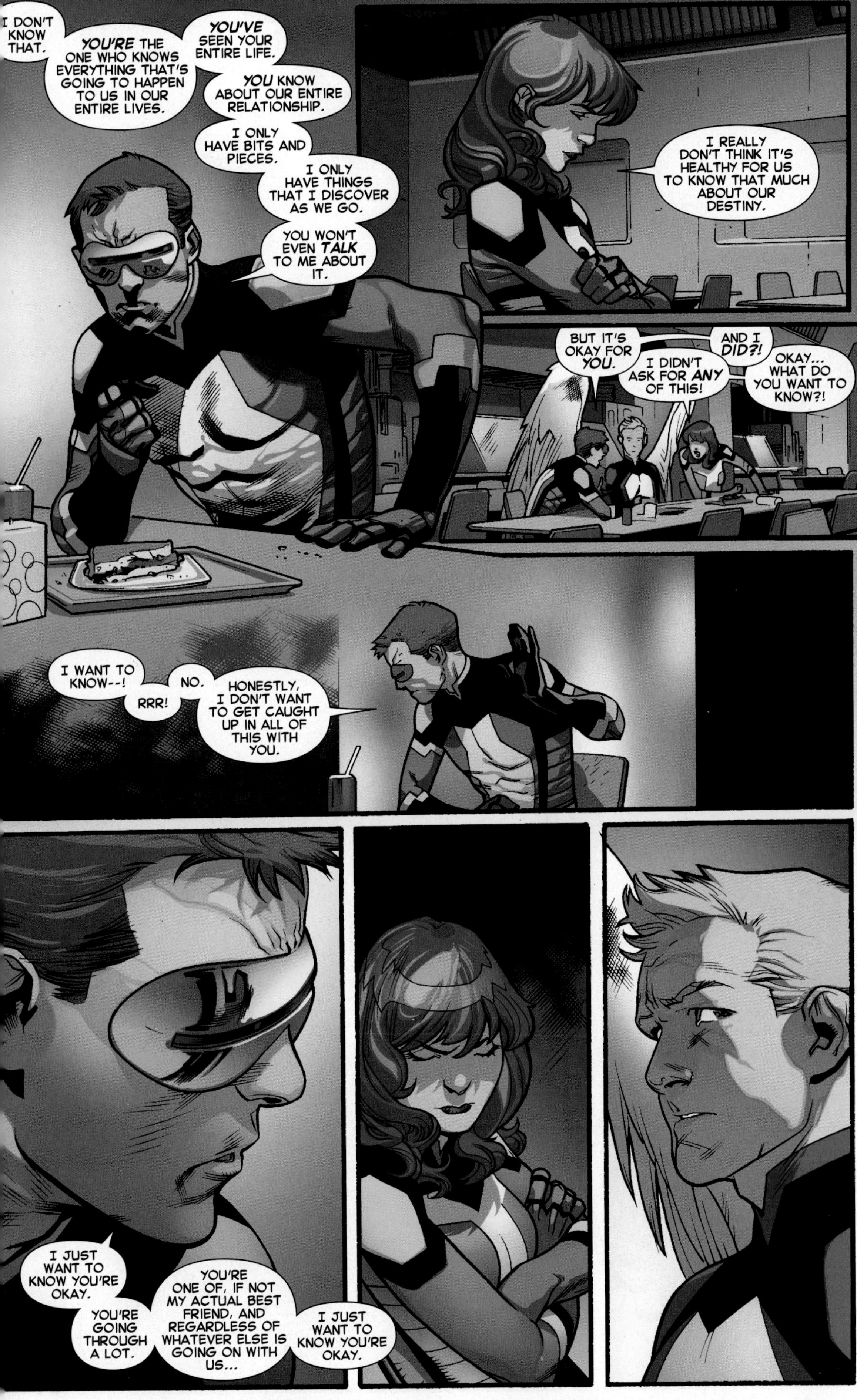

I DON'T KNOW THAT.
YOU'RE THE ONE WHO KNOWS EVERYTHING THAT'S GOING TO HAPPEN TO US IN OUR ENTIRE LIVES.
YOU'VE SEEN YOUR ENTIRE LIFE.
YOU KNOW ABOUT OUR ENTIRE RELATIONSHIP.
I ONLY HAVE BITS AND PIECES.
I ONLY HAVE THINGS THAT I DISCOVER AS WE GO.
YOU WON'T EVEN TALK TO ME ABOUT IT.
I REALLY DON'T THINK IT'S HEALTHY FOR US TO KNOW THAT MUCH ABOUT OUR DESTINY.
BUT IT'S OKAY FOR YOU.
AND I DID?!
I DIDN'T ASK FOR ANY OF THIS!
OKAY... WHAT DO YOU WANT TO KNOW?!
I WANT TO KNOW--!
RRR!
NO.
HONESTLY, I DON'T WANT TO GET CAUGHT UP IN ALL OF THIS WITH YOU.
I JUST WANT TO KNOW YOU'RE OKAY.
YOU'RE GOING THROUGH A LOT.
YOU'RE ONE OF, IF NOT MY ACTUAL BEST FRIEND, AND REGARDLESS OF WHATEVER ELSE IS GOING ON WITH US...
I JUST WANT TO KNOW YOU'RE OKAY.

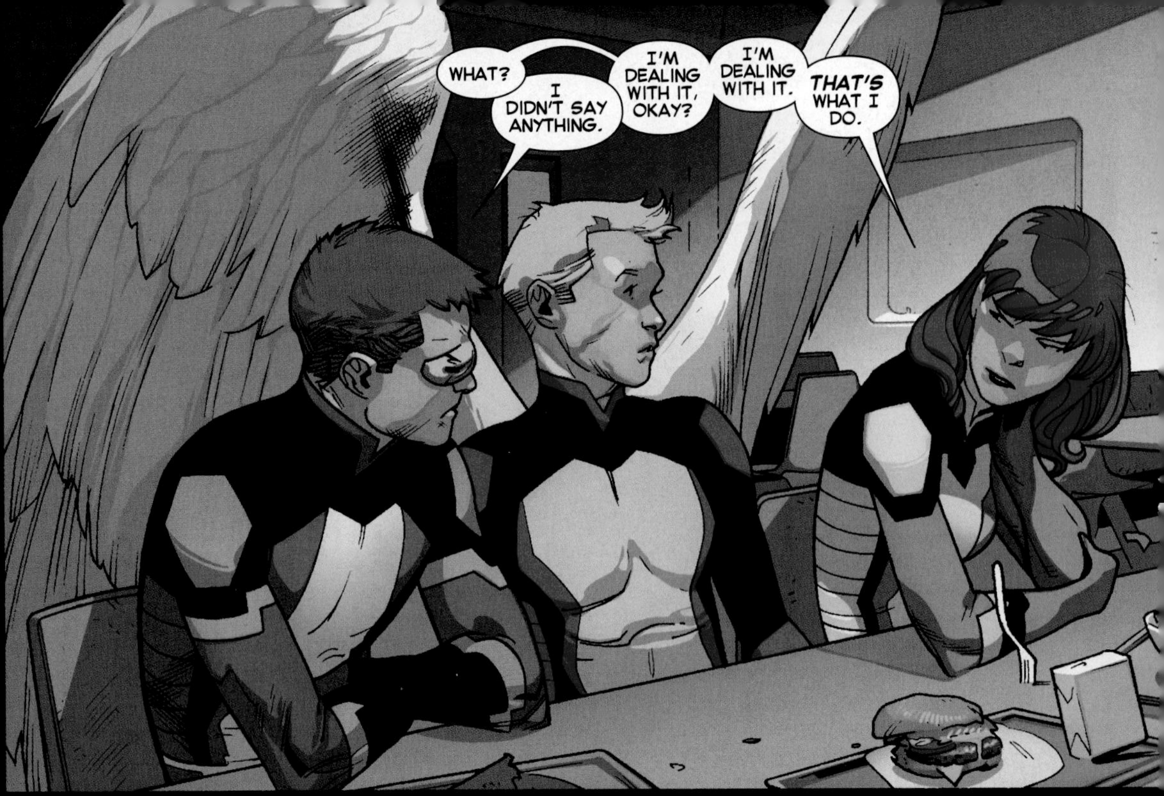
WHAT?
I DIDN'T SAY ANYTHING.
I'M DEALING WITH IT, OKAY?
I'M DEALING WITH IT.
THAT'S WHAT I DO.

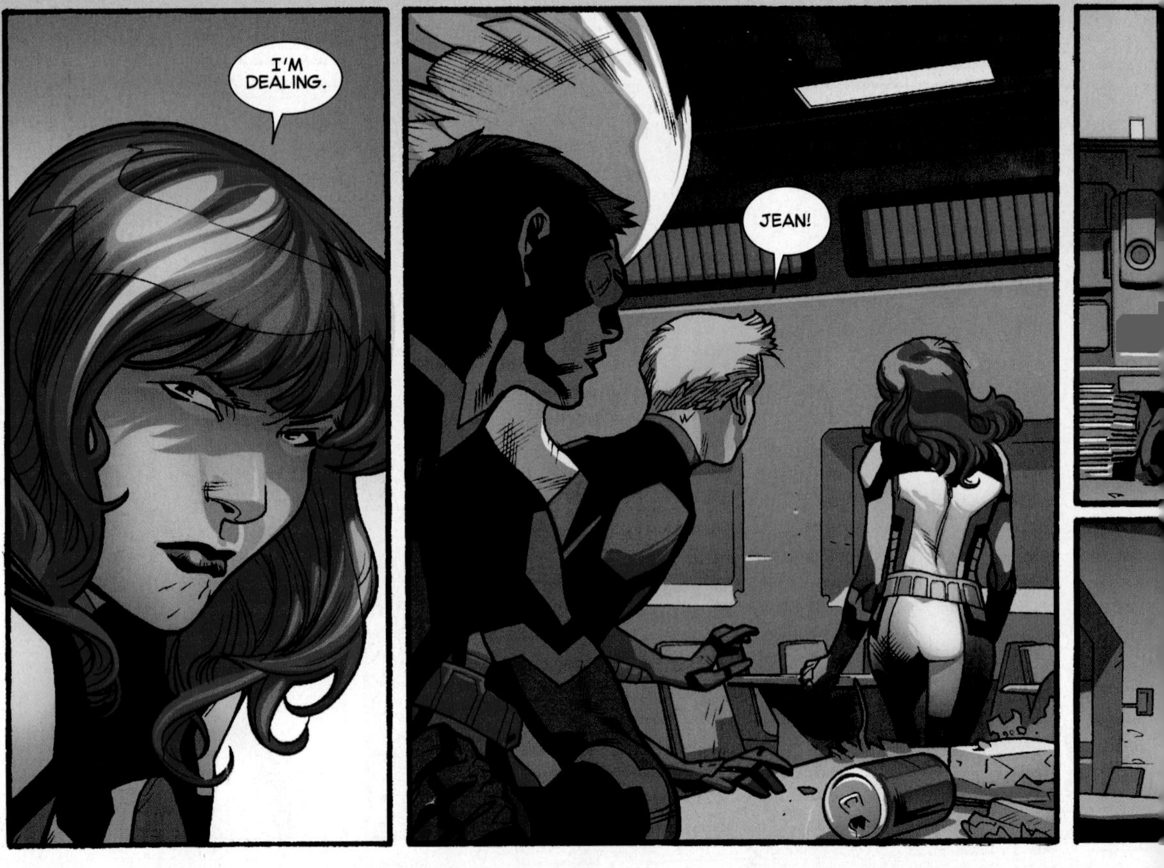
I'M DEALING.
JEAN!

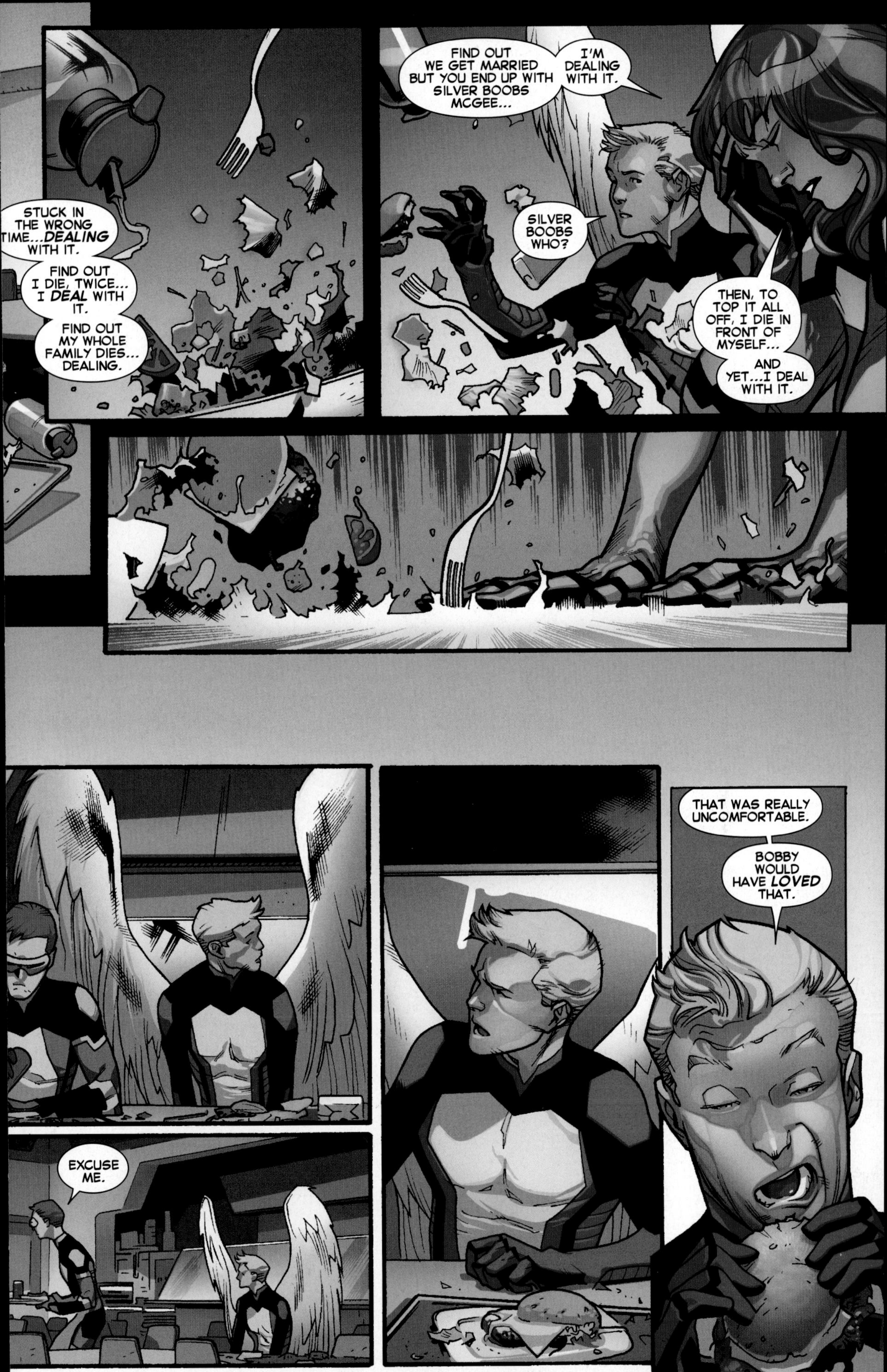
STUCK IN THE WRONG TIME...DEALING WITH IT.
FIND OUT I DIE, TWICE... I DEAL WITH IT.
FIND OUT MY WHOLE FAMILY DIES... DEALING.
FIND OUT WE GET MARRIED BUT YOU END UP WITH SILVER BOOBS MCGEE...
I'M DEALING WITH IT.
SILVER BOOBS WHO?
THEN, TO TOP IT ALL OFF, I DIE IN FRONT OF MYSELF...
AND YET...I DEAL WITH IT.
EXCUSE ME.
THAT WAS REALLY UNCOMFORTABLE.
BOBBY WOULD HAVE LOVED THAT.

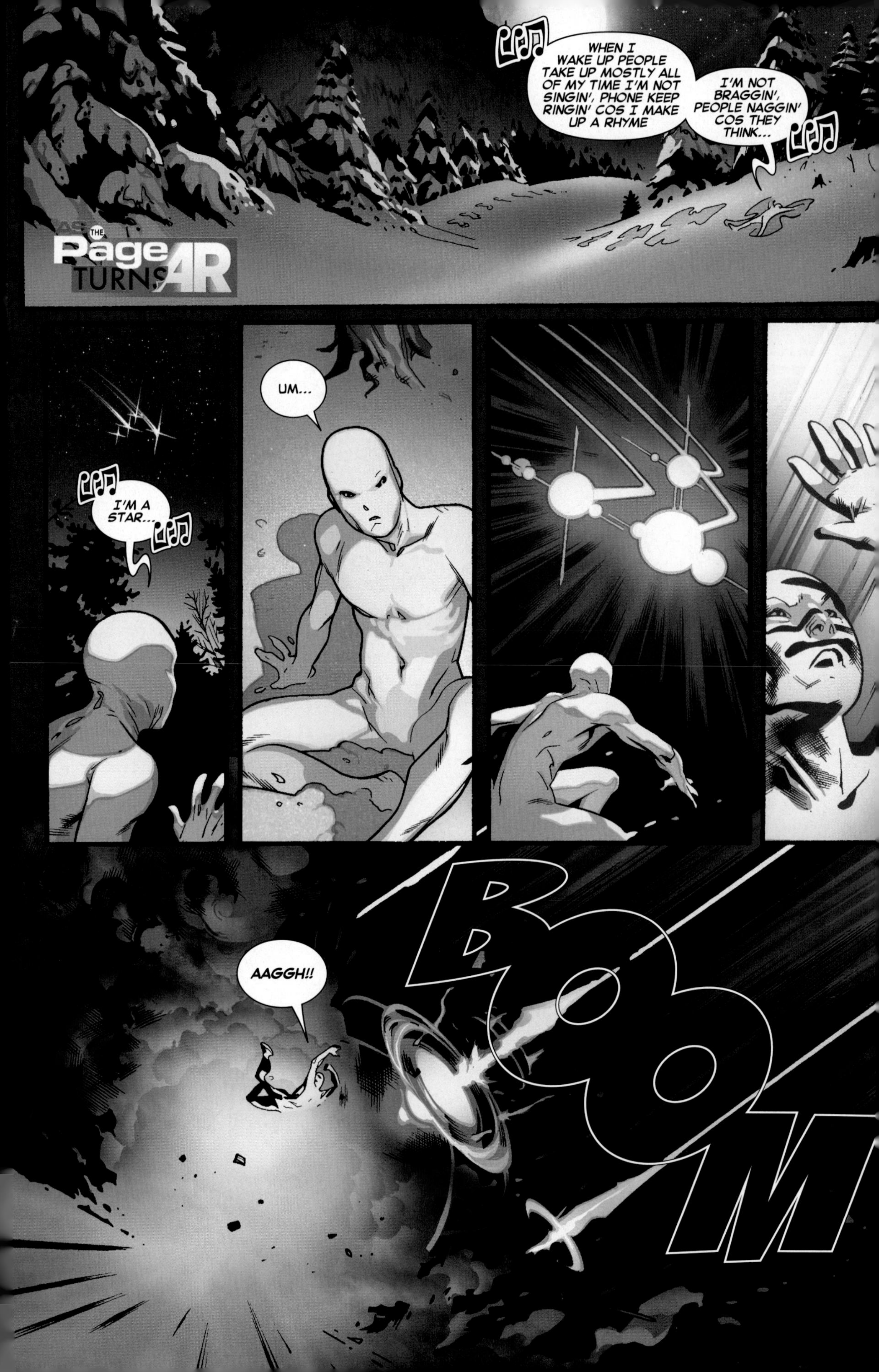
WHEN I WAKE UP PEOPLE TAKE UP MOSTLY ALL OF MY TIME I'M NOT SINGIN', PHONE KEEP RINGIN' COS I MAKE UP A RHYME
I'M NOT BRAGGIN', PEOPLE NAGGIN' COS THEY THINK...
I'M A STAR...
UM...
BOOM
AAGGH!!

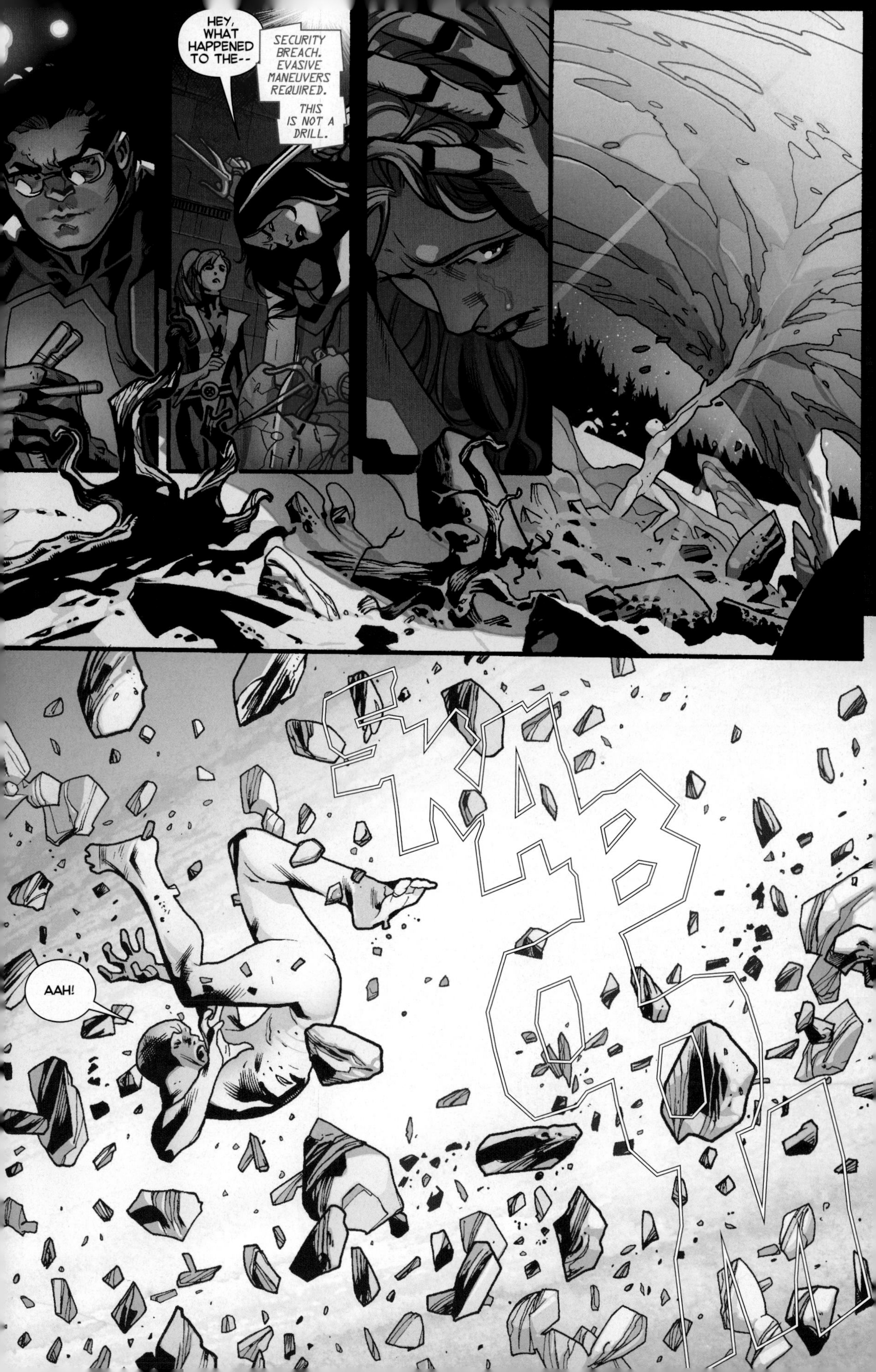
HEY, WHAT HAPPENED TO THE--
SECURITY BREACH. EVASIVE MANEUVERS REQUIRED.
THIS IS NOT A DRILL.
AAH!

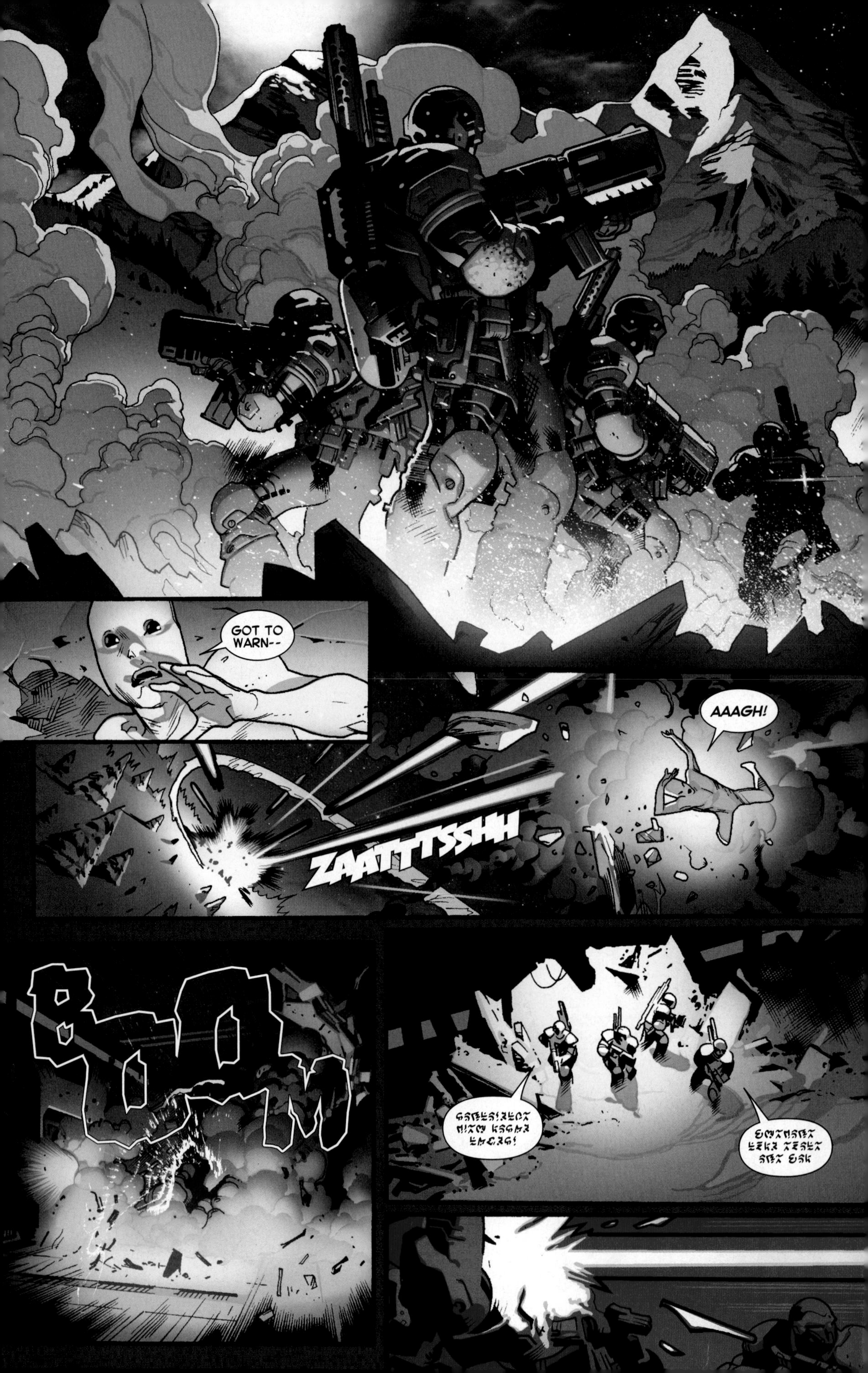

GOT TO WARN--
AAAGH!
ZAATTTSSHH
BOOM

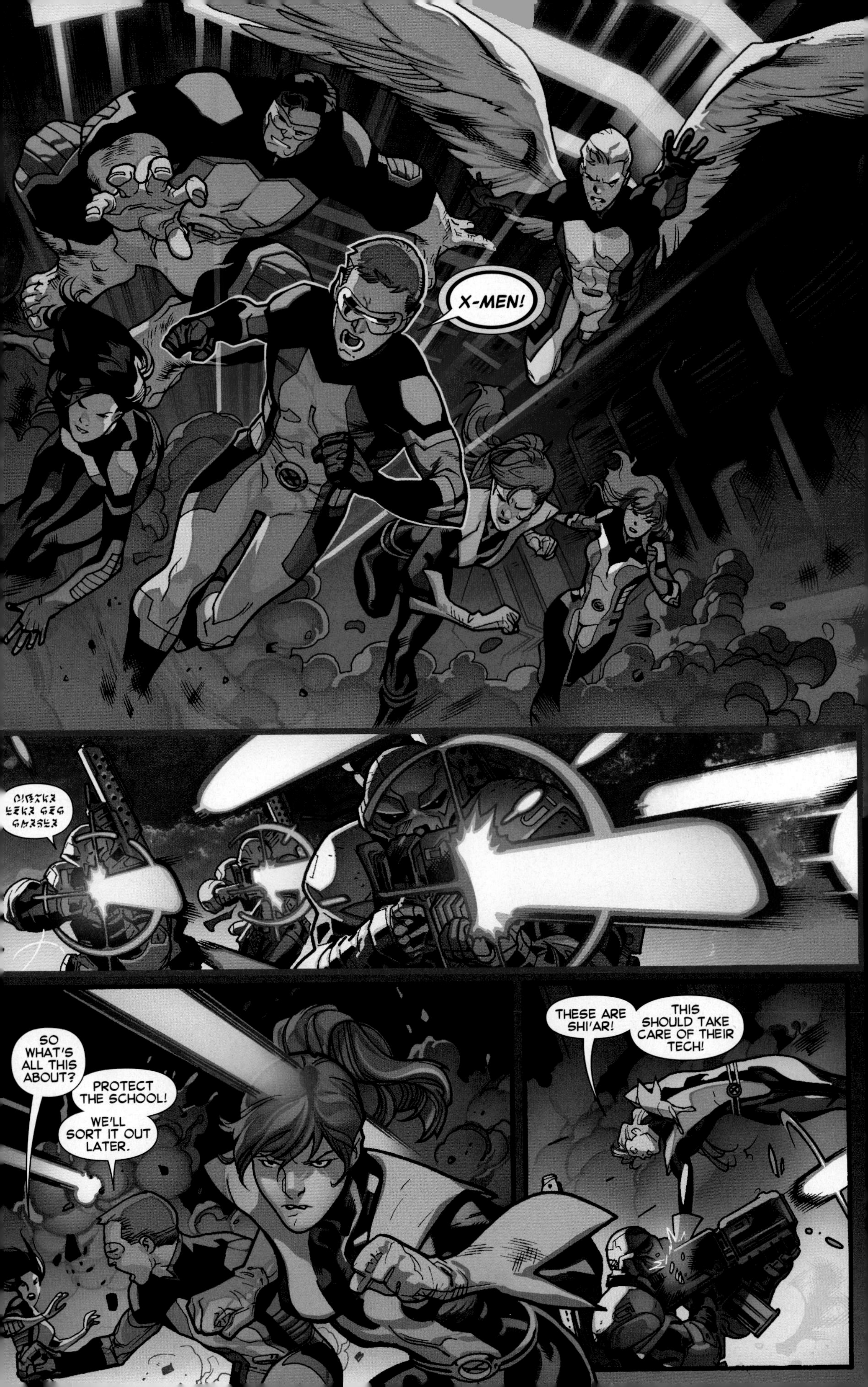
X-MEN!
SO WHAT'S ALL THIS ABOUT?
PROTECT THE SCHOOL!
WE'LL SORT IT OUT LATER.
THESE ARE SHI'AR!
THIS SHOULD TAKE CARE OF THEIR TECH!

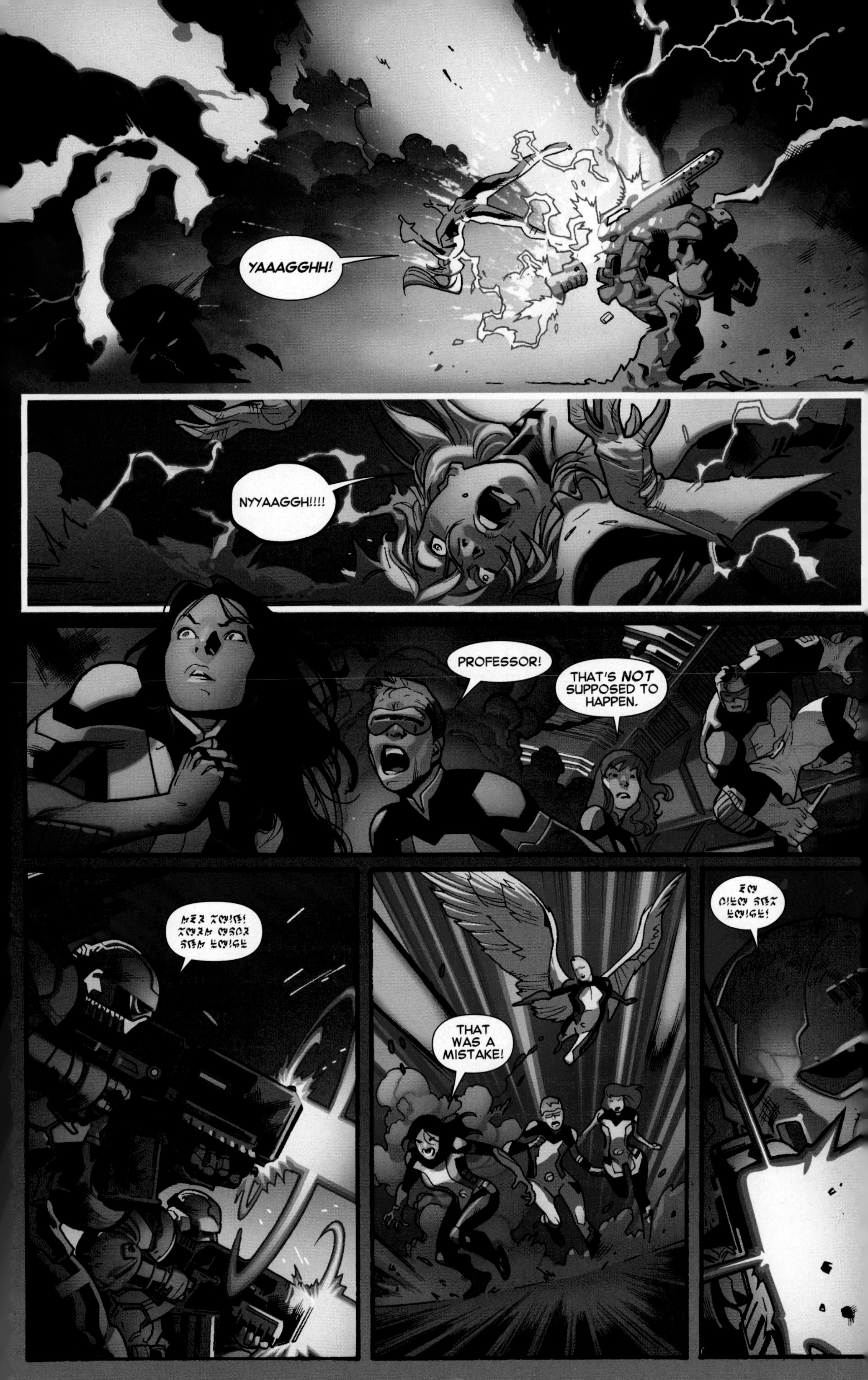
YAAAGGHH!
NYYAAGGH!!!!
PROFESSOR!
THAT'S **NOT** SUPPOSED TO HAPPEN.
THAT WAS A MISTAKE!

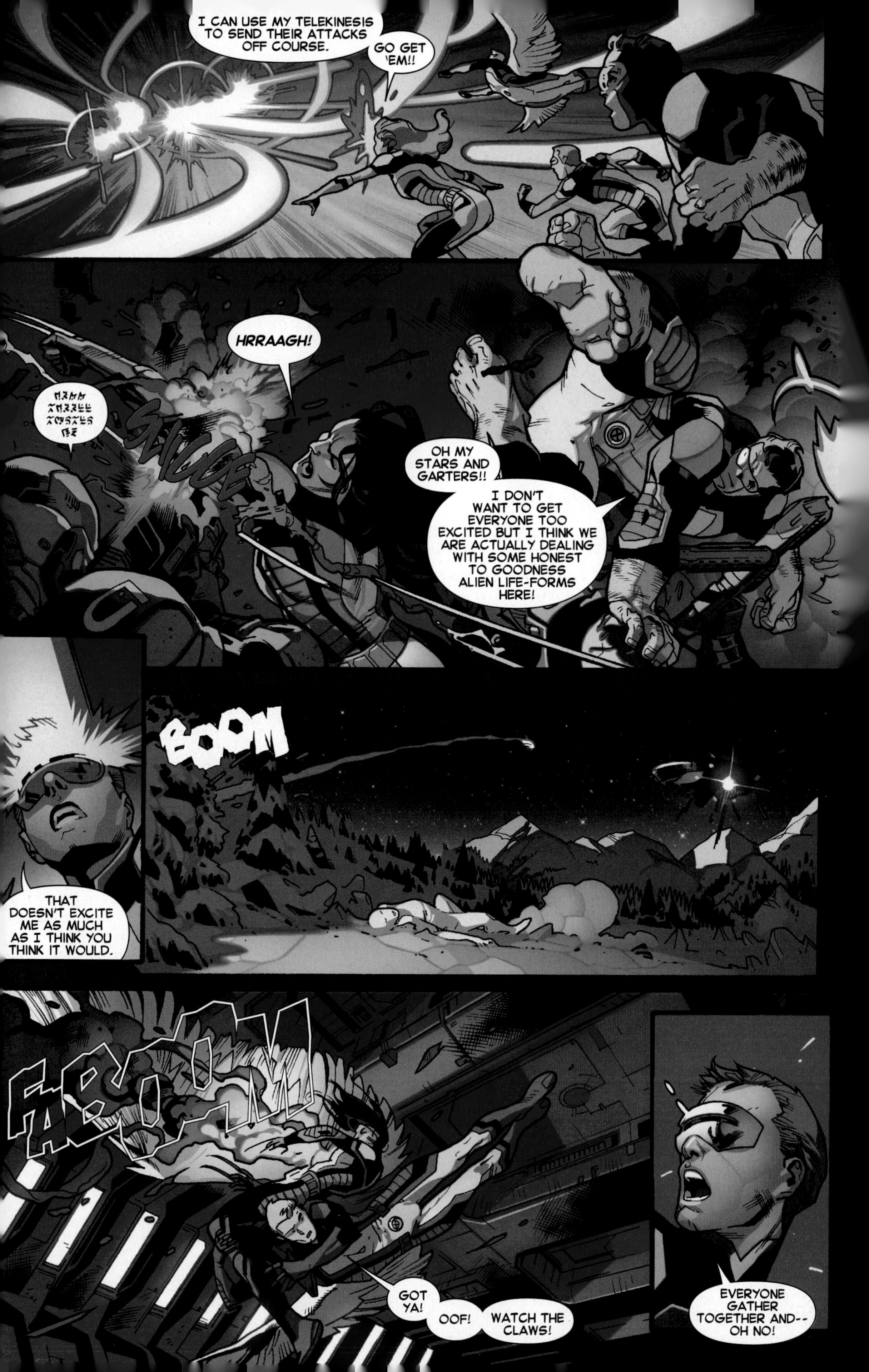
I CAN USE MY TELEKINESIS TO SEND THEIR ATTACKS OFF COURSE.
GO GET 'EM!!
HRRAAGH!
OH MY STARS AND GARTERS!!
I DON'T WANT TO GET EVERYONE TOO EXCITED BUT I THINK WE ARE ACTUALLY DEALING WITH SOME HONEST TO GOODNESS ALIEN LIFE-FORMS HERE!
THAT DOESN'T EXCITE ME AS MUCH AS I THINK YOU THINK IT WOULD.
BOOM
GOT YA!
OOF!
WATCH THE CLAWS!
EVERYONE GATHER TOGETHER AND-- OH NO!

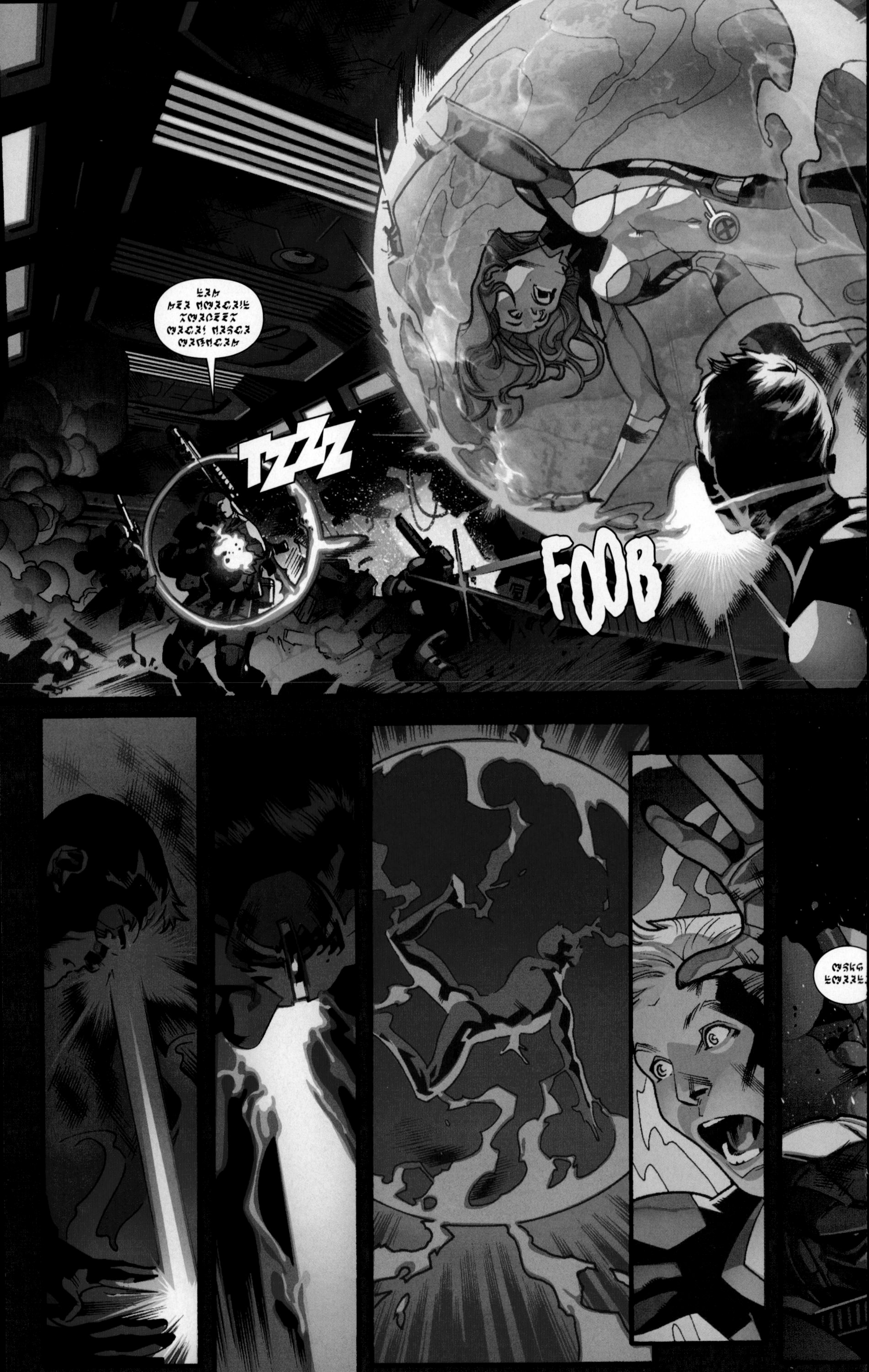
TZZZ
FOOB

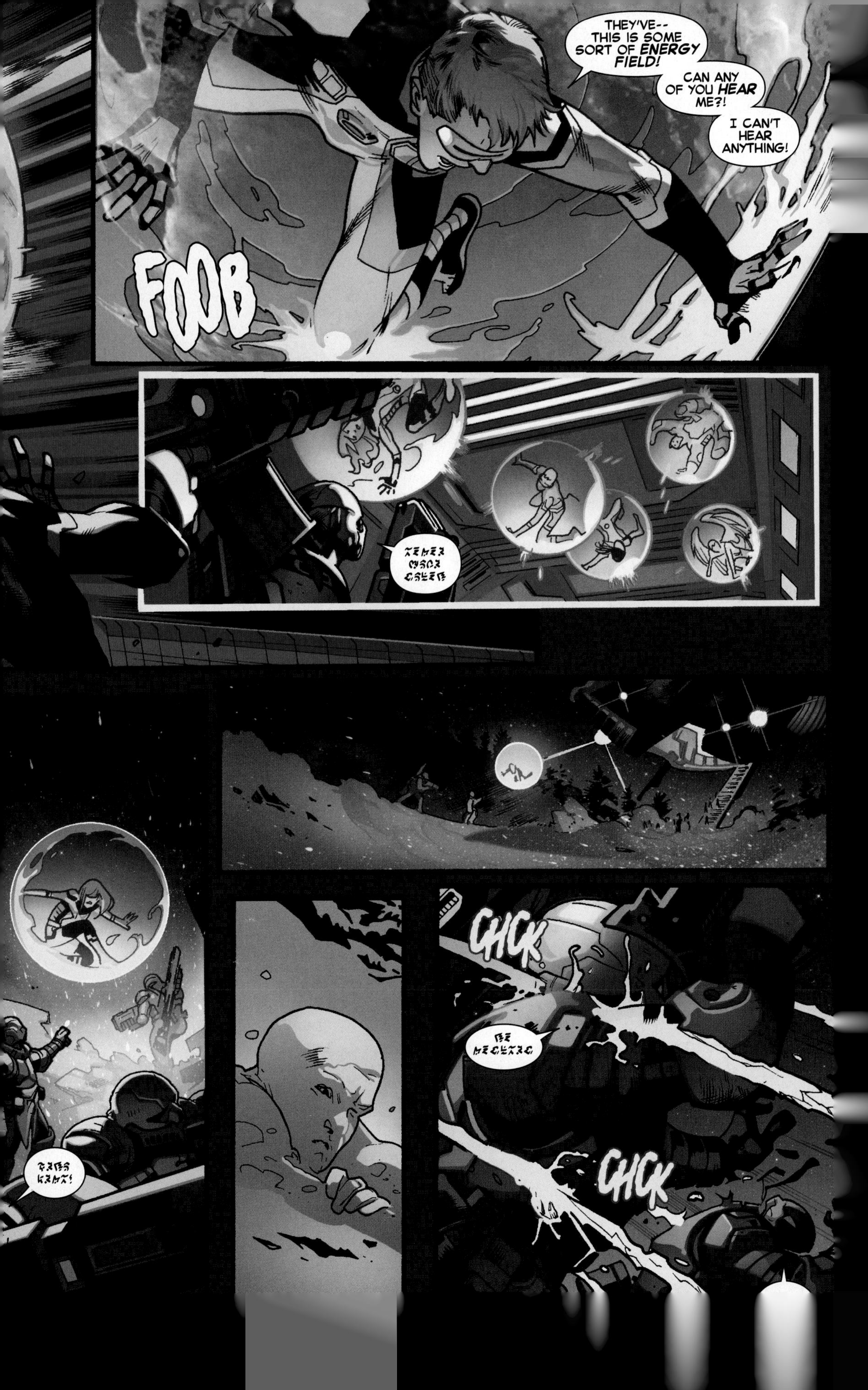
THEY'VE-- THIS IS SOME SORT OF ENERGY FIELD!
CAN ANY OF YOU HEAR ME?!
I CAN'T HEAR ANYTHING!
FOOB
CHCK
CHCK

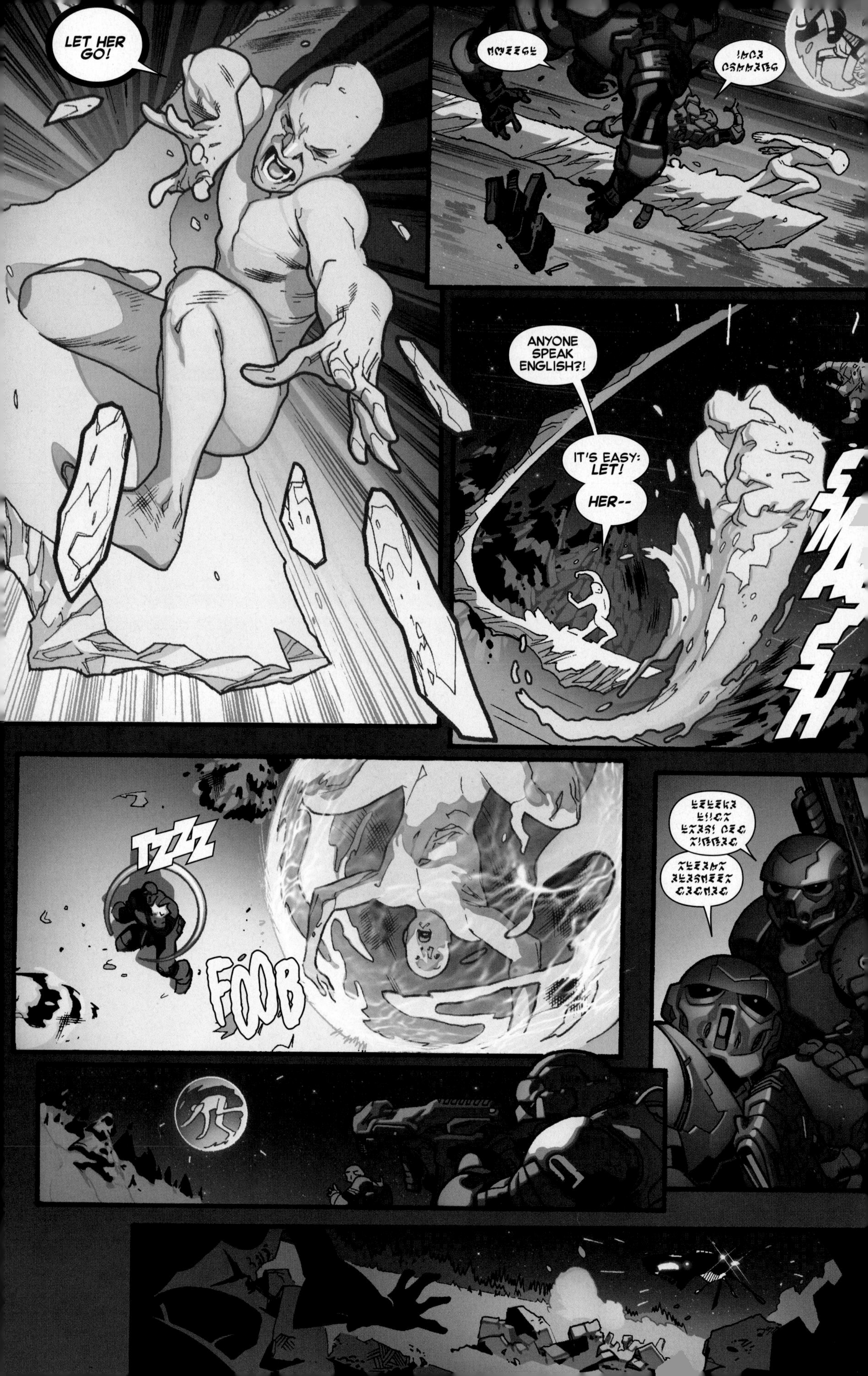
LET HER GO!
ANYONE SPEAK ENGLISH?!
IT'S EASY: LET!
HER--
SMASH
TZZZ
FOOB

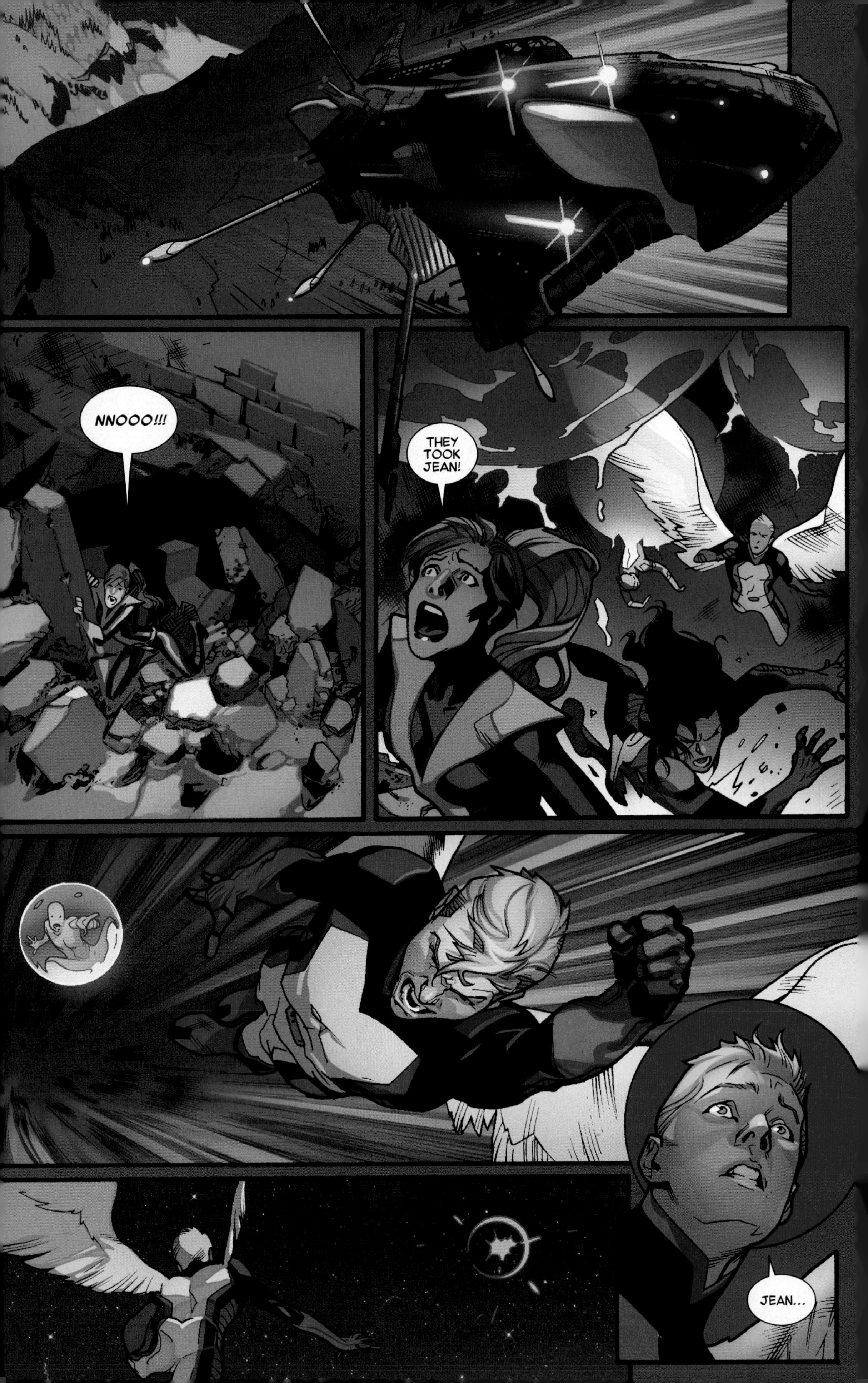
NNOOO!!!
THEY TOOK JEAN!
JEAN...

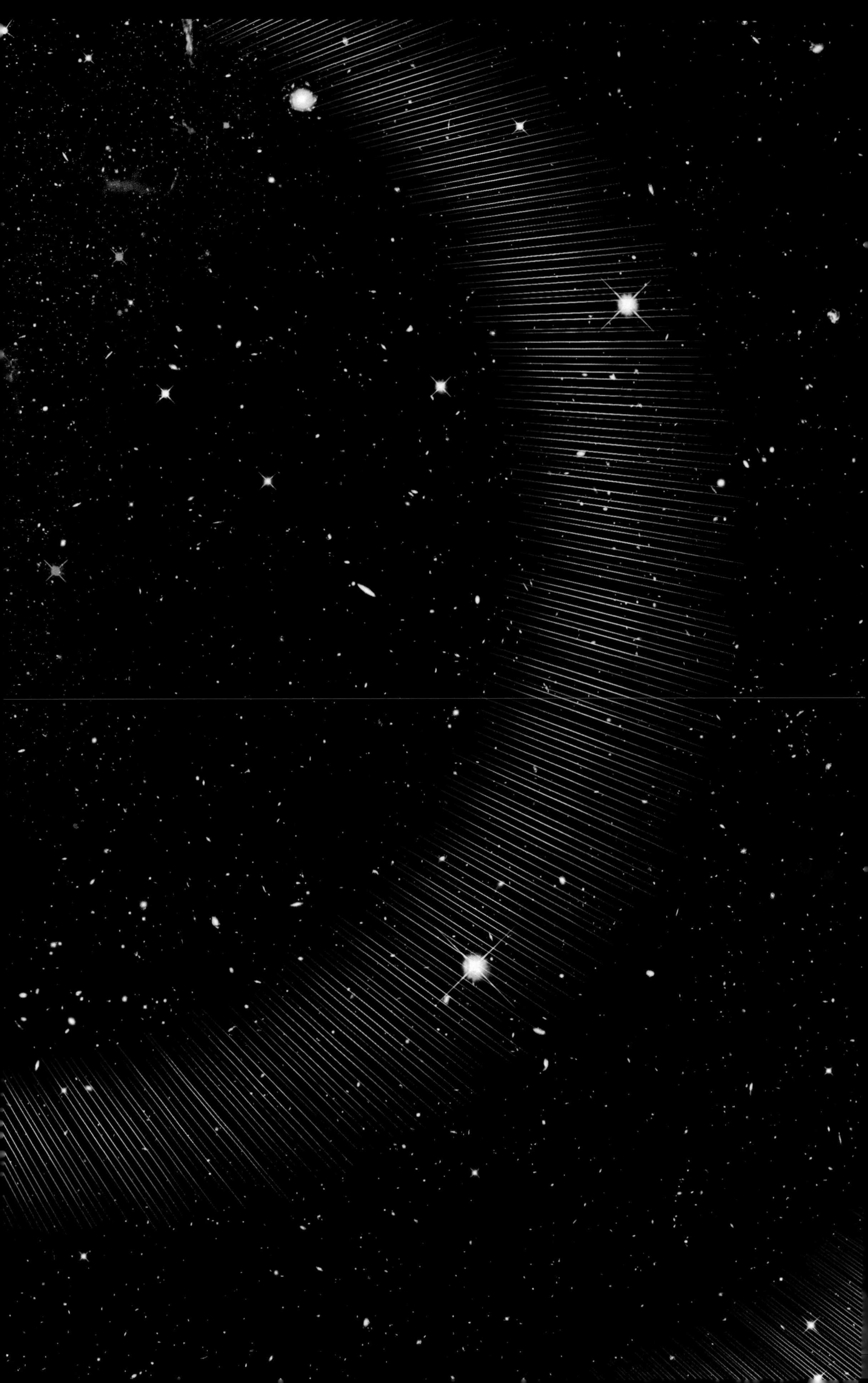

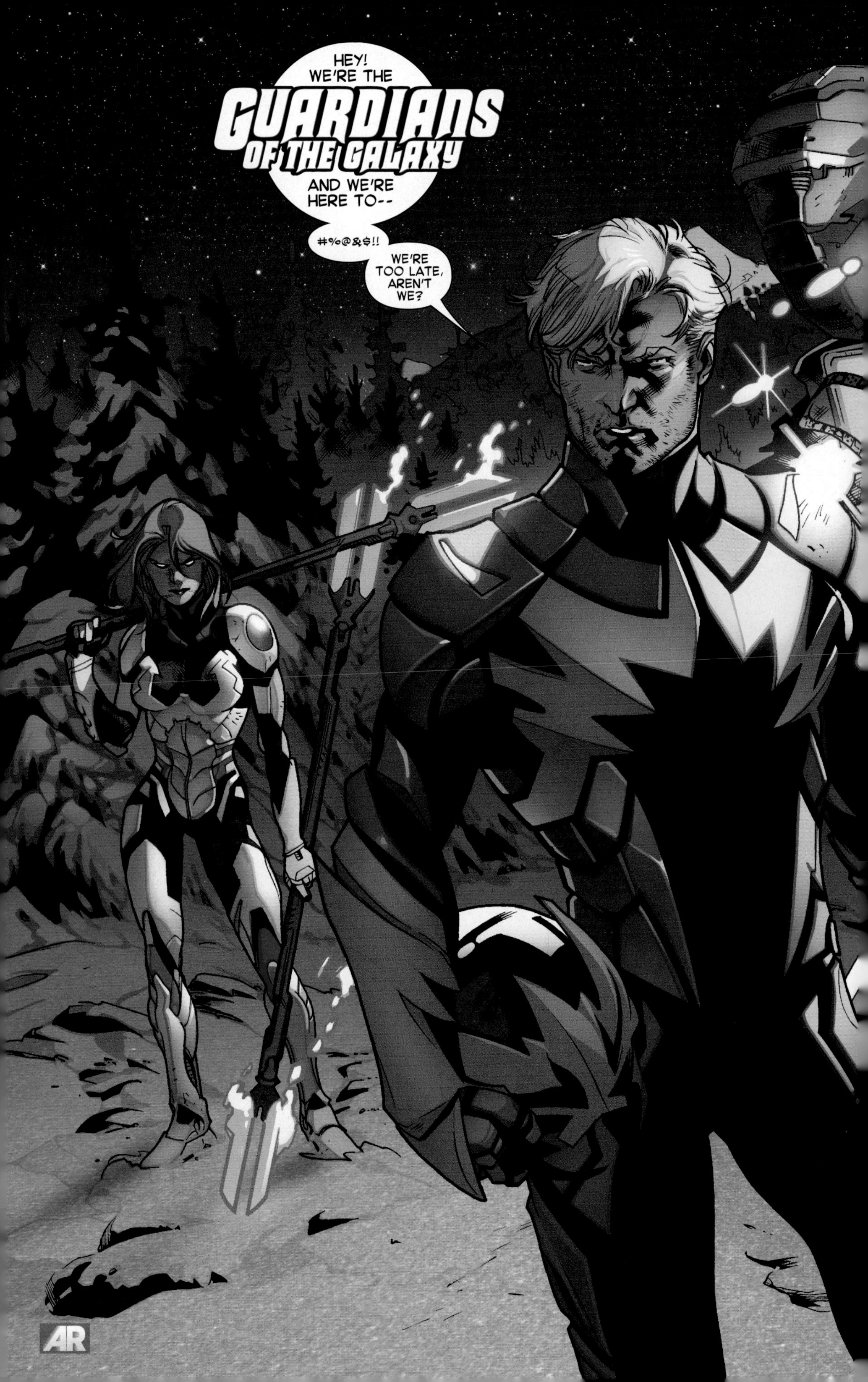
HEY! WE'RE THE GUARDIANS OF THE GALAXY AND WE'RE HERE TO--
#%@&$!!
WE'RE TOO LATE, AREN'T WE?
AR

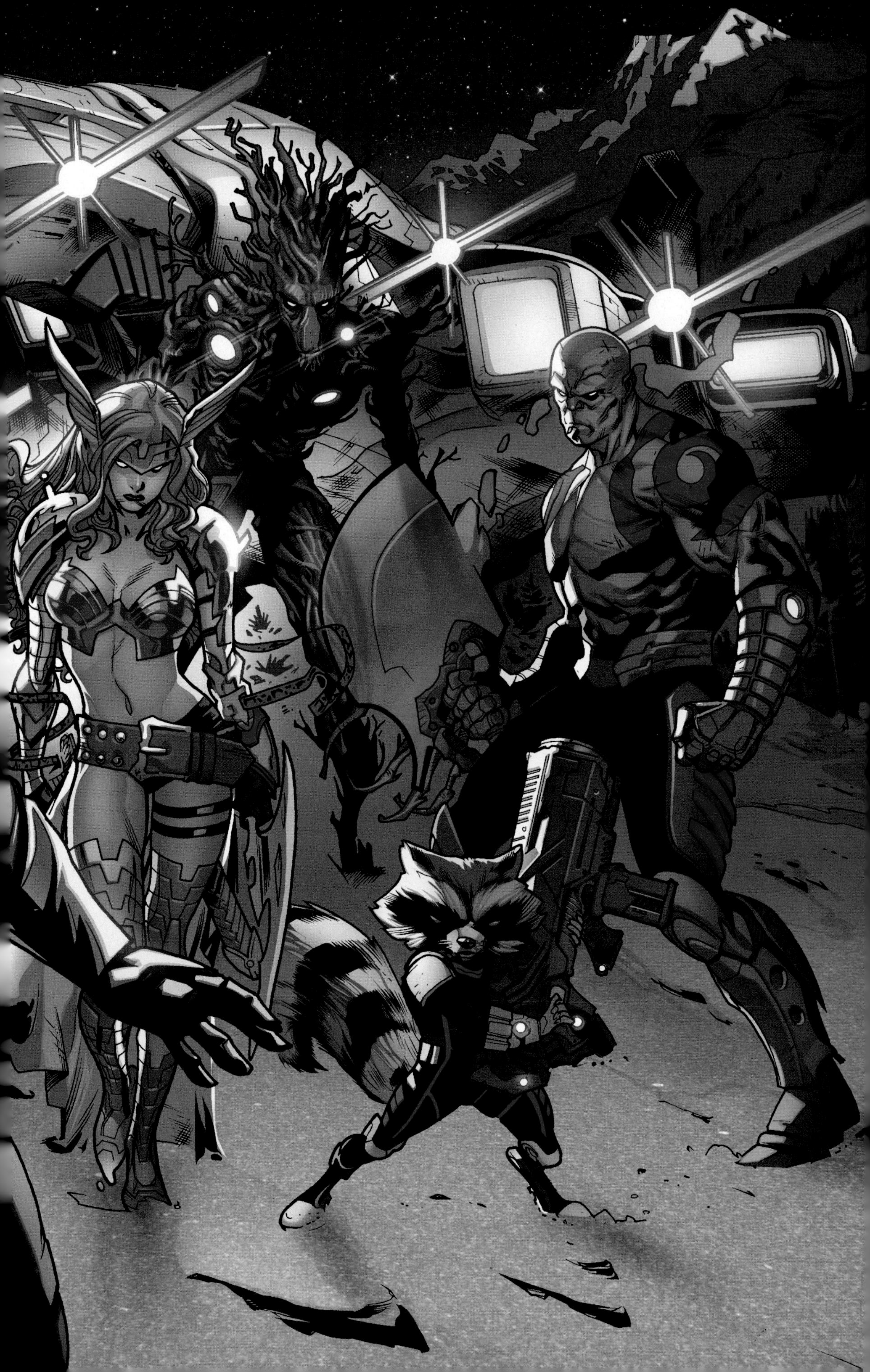

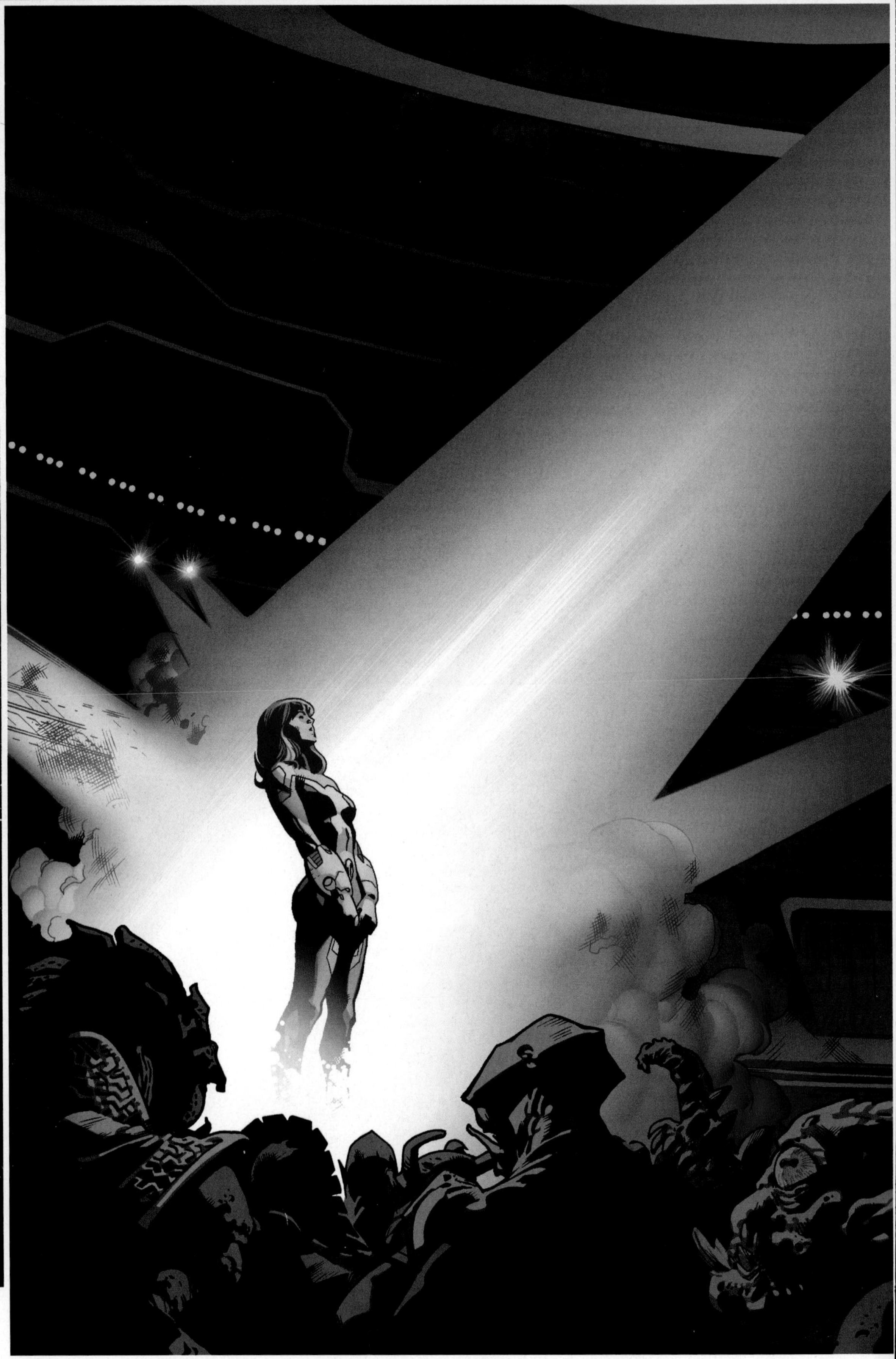

ALL-NEW X-MEN 23

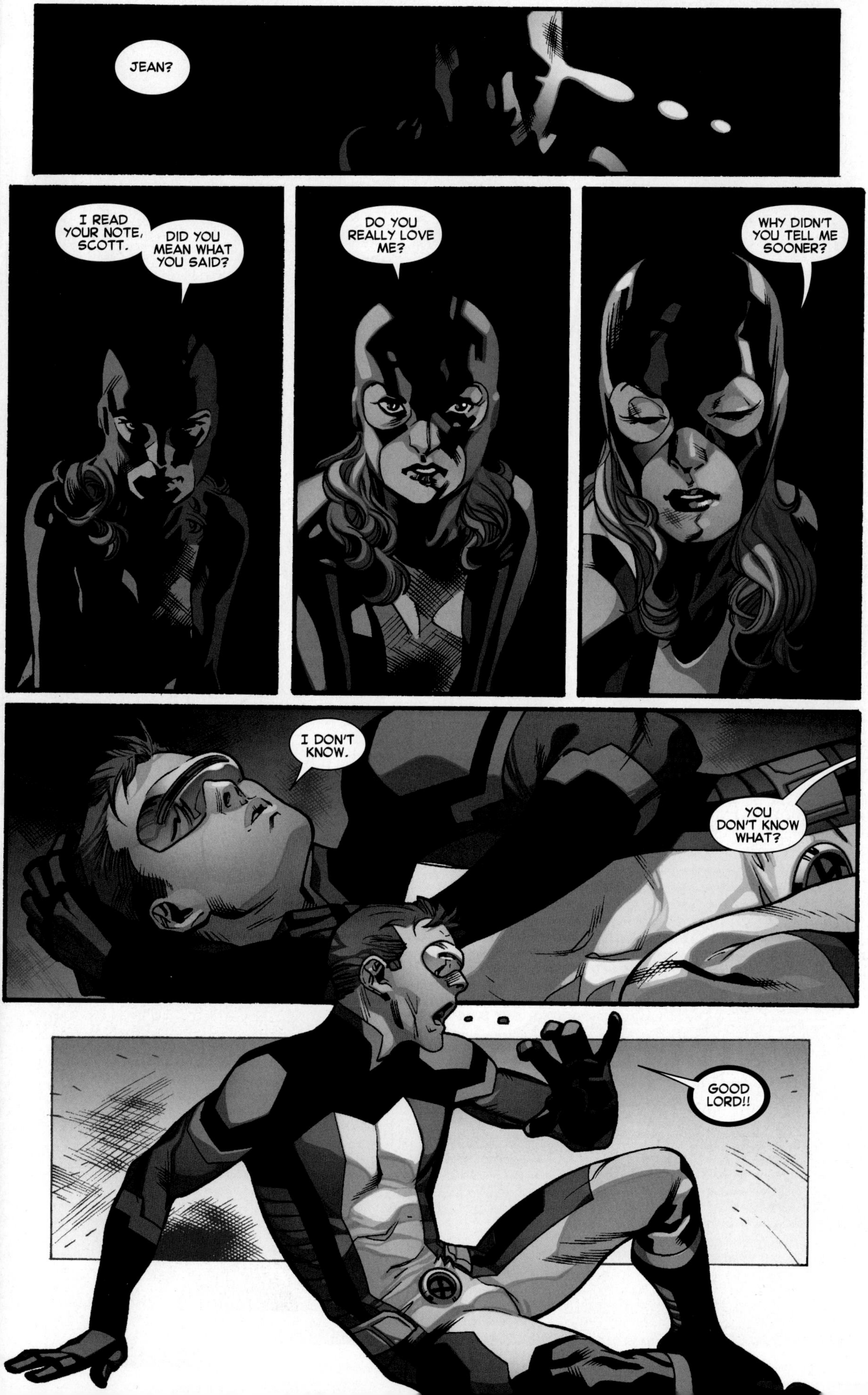
JEAN?
I READ YOUR NOTE, SCOTT.
DID YOU MEAN WHAT YOU SAID?
DO YOU REALLY LOVE ME?
WHY DIDN'T YOU TELL ME SOONER?
I DON'T KNOW.
YOU DON'T KNOW WHAT?
GOOD LORD!!

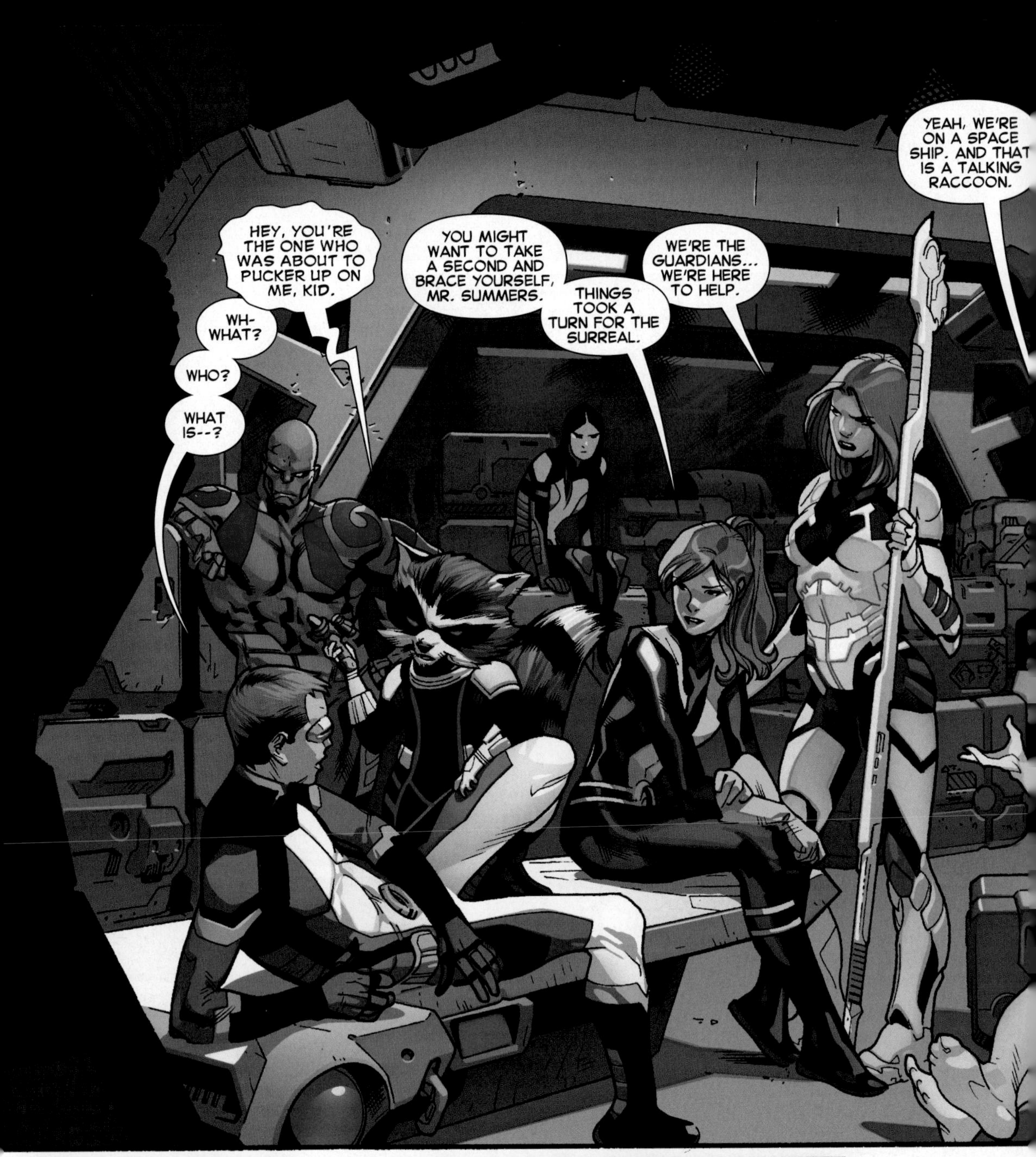
HEY, YOU'RE THE ONE WHO WAS ABOUT TO PUCKER UP ON ME, KID.
WH-WHAT?
WHO?
WHAT IS--?
YOU MIGHT WANT TO TAKE A SECOND AND BRACE YOURSELF, MR. SUMMERS.
THINGS TOOK A TURN FOR THE SURREAL.
WE'RE THE GUARDIANS... WE'RE HERE TO HELP.
YEAH, WE'RE ON A SPACE SHIP. AND THAT IS A TALKING RACCOON.

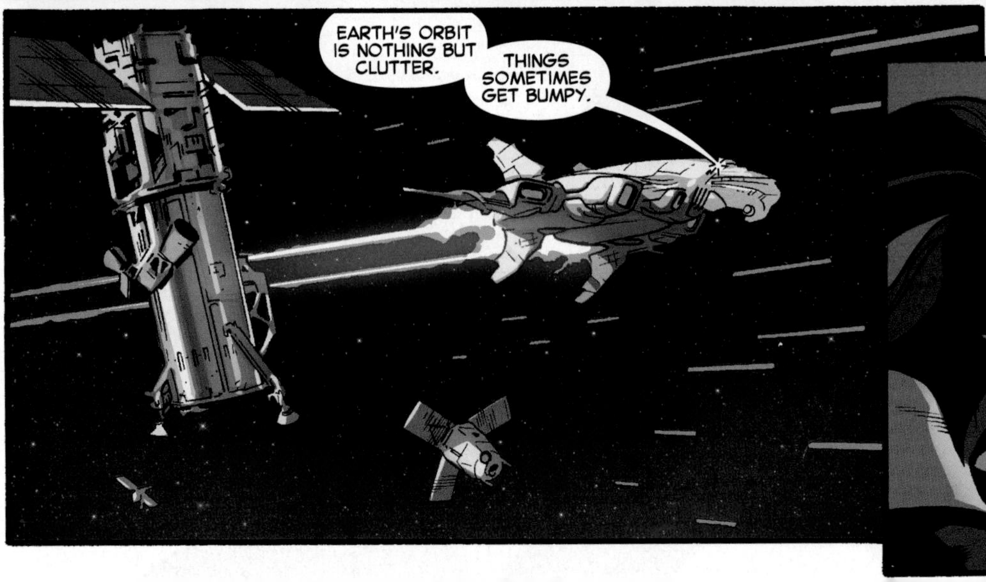
EARTH'S ORBIT IS NOTHING BUT CLUTTER.
THINGS SOMETIMES GET BUMPY.

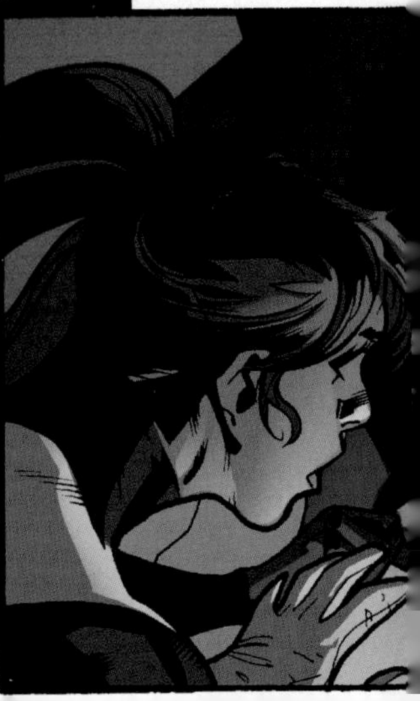

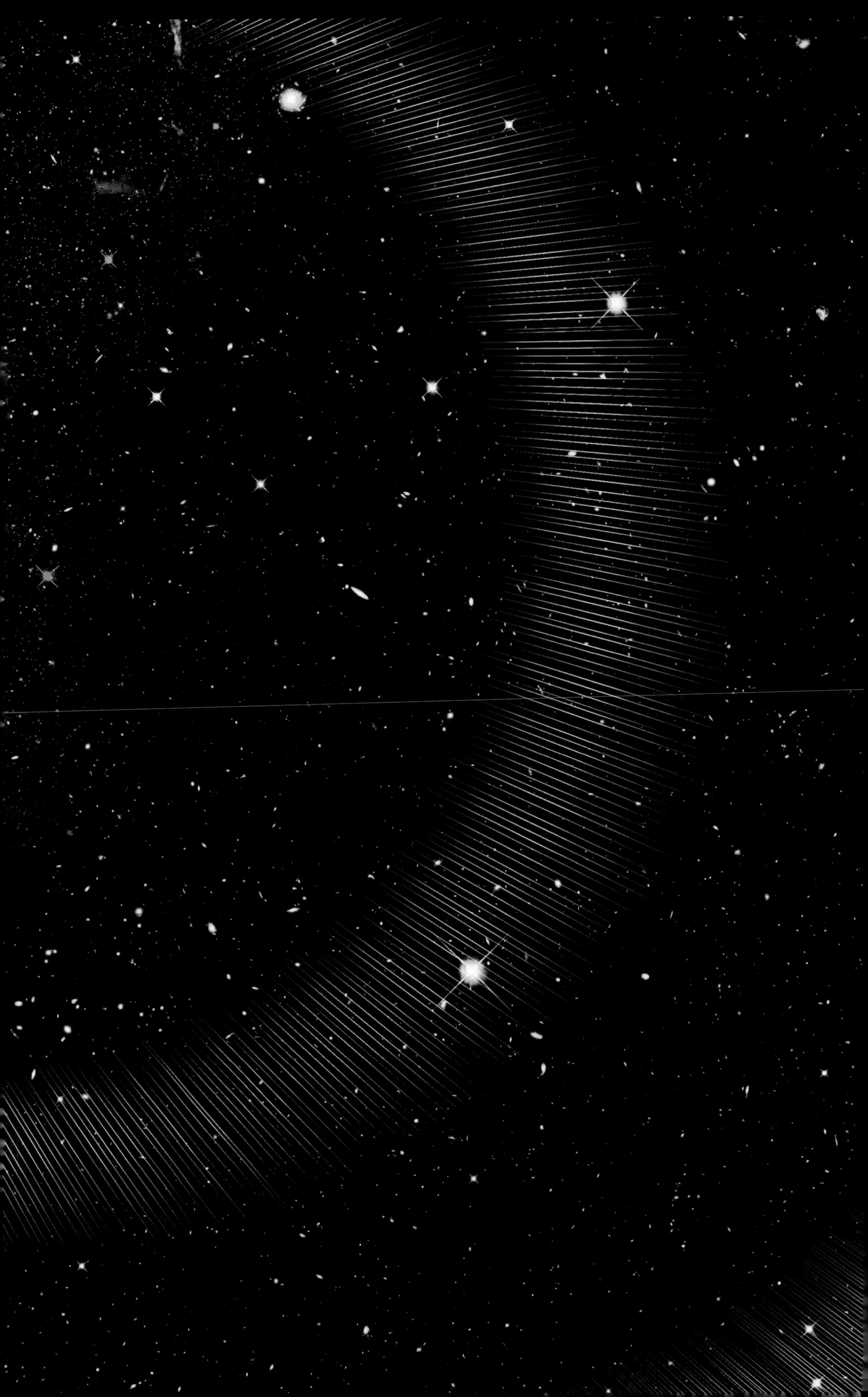

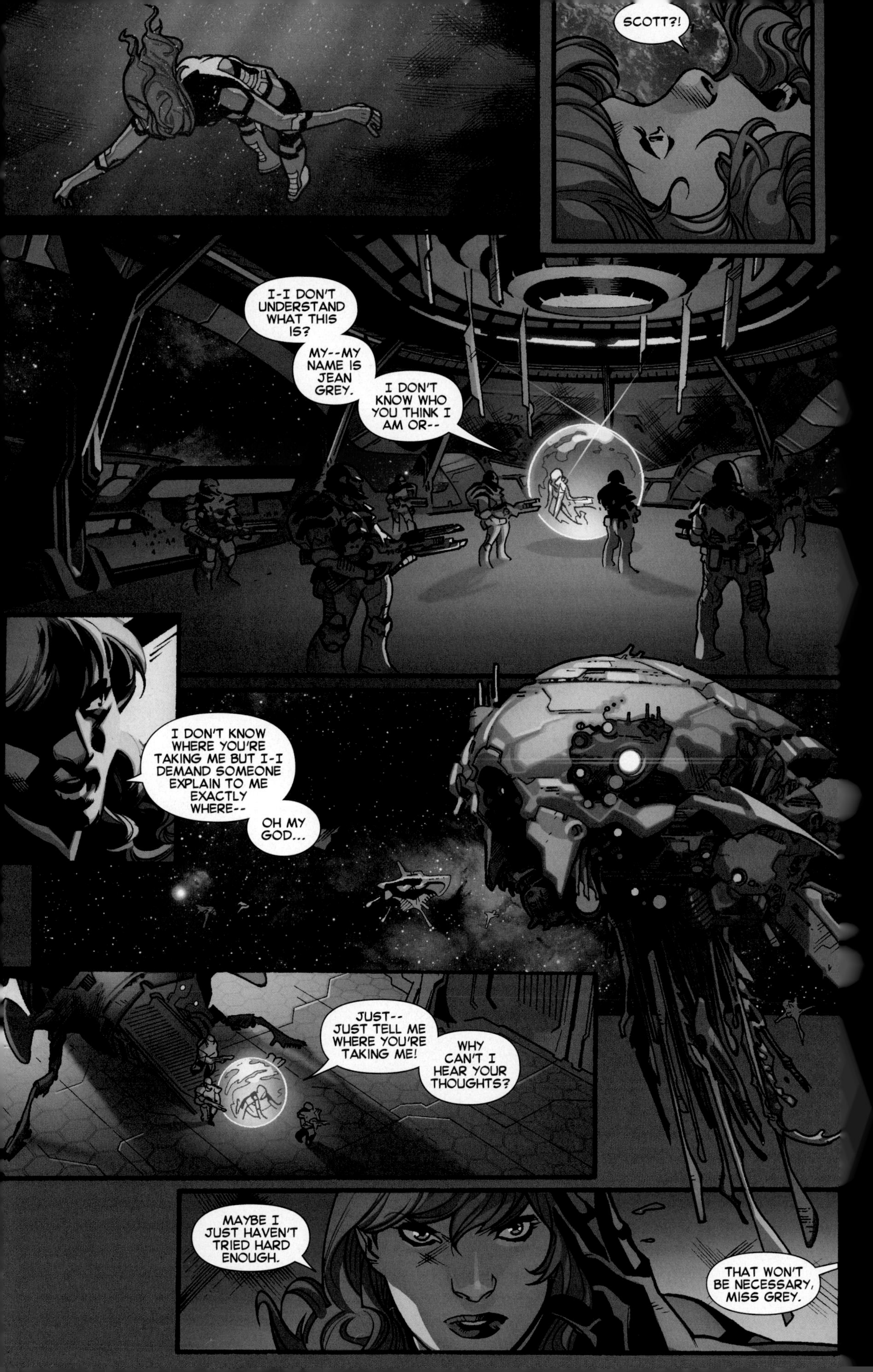
SCOTT?!
I-I DON'T UNDERSTAND WHAT THIS IS?
MY--MY NAME IS JEAN GREY.
I DON'T KNOW WHO YOU THINK I AM OR--
I DON'T KNOW WHERE YOU'RE TAKING ME BUT I-I DEMAND SOMEONE EXPLAIN TO ME EXACTLY WHERE--
OH MY GOD...
JUST-- JUST TELL ME WHERE YOU'RE TAKING ME!
WHY CAN'T I HEAR YOUR THOUGHTS?
MAYBE I JUST HAVEN'T TRIED HARD ENOUGH.
THAT WON'T BE NECESSARY, MISS GREY.

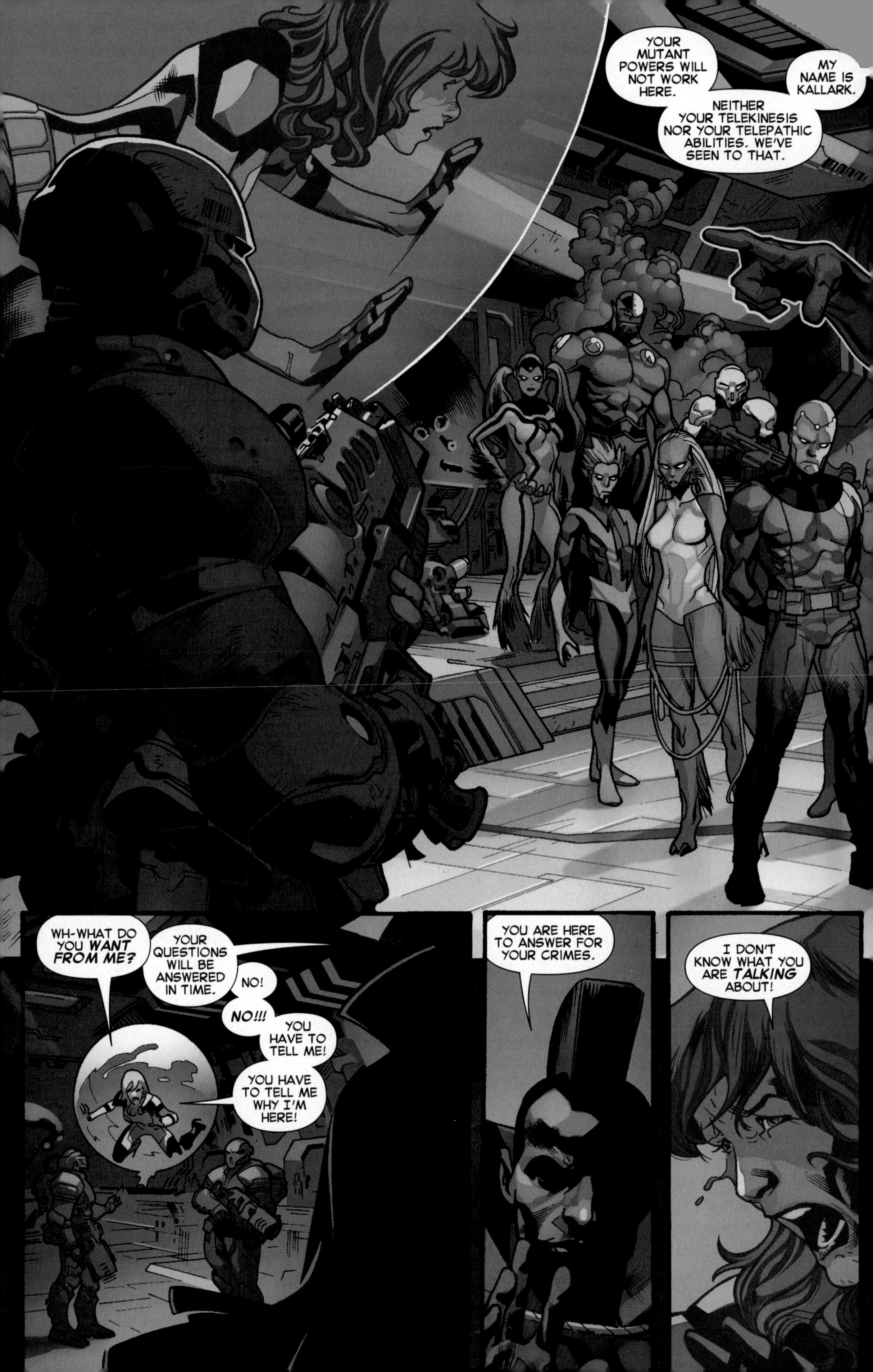
YOUR MUTANT POWERS WILL NOT WORK HERE.
MY NAME IS KALLARK.
NEITHER YOUR TELEKINESIS NOR YOUR TELEPATHIC ABILITIES. WE'VE SEEN TO THAT.
WH-WHAT DO YOU WANT FROM ME?
YOUR QUESTIONS WILL BE ANSWERED IN TIME.
NO!
NO!!!
YOU HAVE TO TELL ME!
YOU HAVE TO TELL ME WHY I'M HERE!
YOU ARE HERE TO ANSWER FOR YOUR CRIMES.
I DON'T KNOW WHAT YOU ARE TALKING ABOUT!

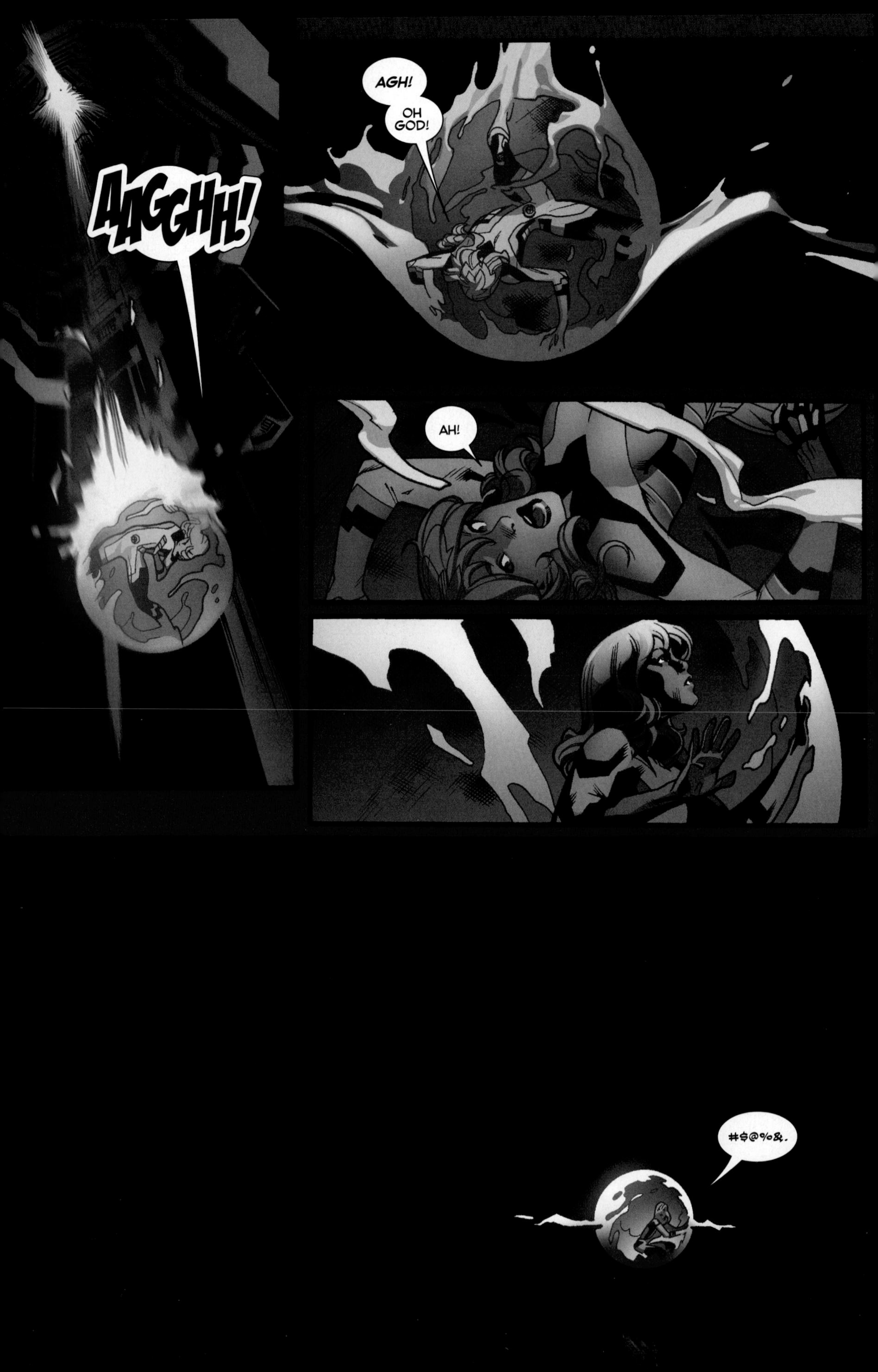
AAGGHH!
AGH!
OH GOD!
AH!
#$@%&.

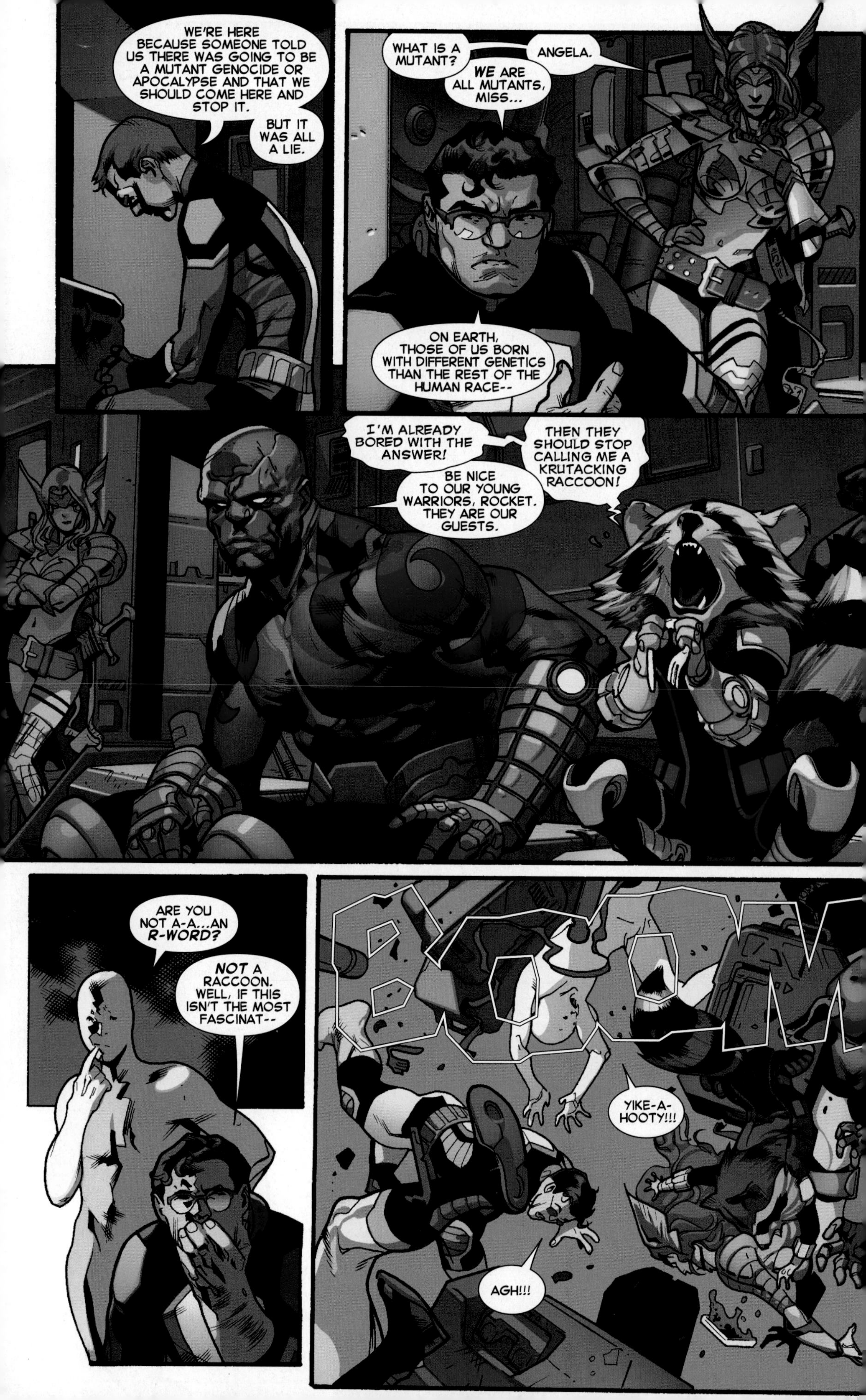
WE'RE HERE BECAUSE SOMEONE TOLD US THERE WAS GOING TO BE A MUTANT GENOCIDE OR APOCALYPSE AND THAT WE SHOULD COME HERE AND STOP IT.
BUT IT WAS ALL A LIE.
WHAT IS A MUTANT?
ANGELA.
WE ARE ALL MUTANTS, MISS...
ON EARTH, THOSE OF US BORN WITH DIFFERENT GENETICS THAN THE REST OF THE HUMAN RACE--
I'M ALREADY BORED WITH THE ANSWER!
THEN THEY SHOULD STOP CALLING ME A KRUTACKING RACCOON!
BE NICE TO OUR YOUNG WARRIORS, ROCKET. THEY ARE OUR GUESTS.
ARE YOU NOT A-A...AN R-WORD?
NOT A RACCOON. WELL, IF THIS ISN'T THE MOST FASCINAT--
BOOM
YIKE-A-HOOTY!!!
AGH!!!

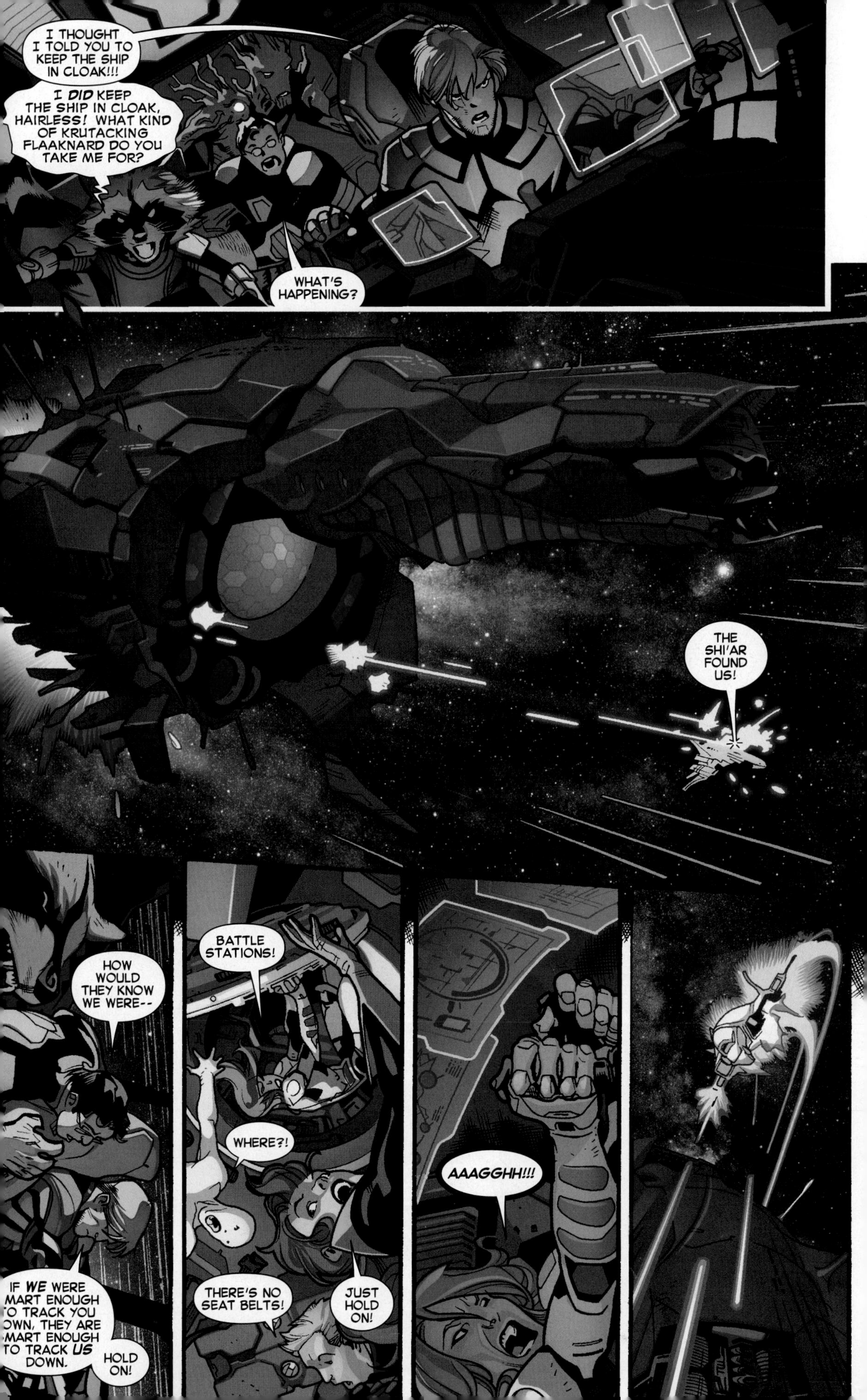
I THOUGHT I TOLD YOU TO KEEP THE SHIP IN CLOAK!!!
I DID KEEP THE SHIP IN CLOAK, HAIRLESS! WHAT KIND OF KRUTACKING FLAAKNARD DO YOU TAKE ME FOR?
WHAT'S HAPPENING?
THE SHI'AR FOUND US!
HOW WOULD THEY KNOW WE WERE--
IF WE WERE MART ENOUGH TO TRACK YOU OWN, THEY ARE MART ENOUGH TO TRACK US DOWN.
HOLD ON!
BATTLE STATIONS!
WHERE?!
THERE'S NO SEAT BELTS!
JUST HOLD ON!
AAAGGHH!!!

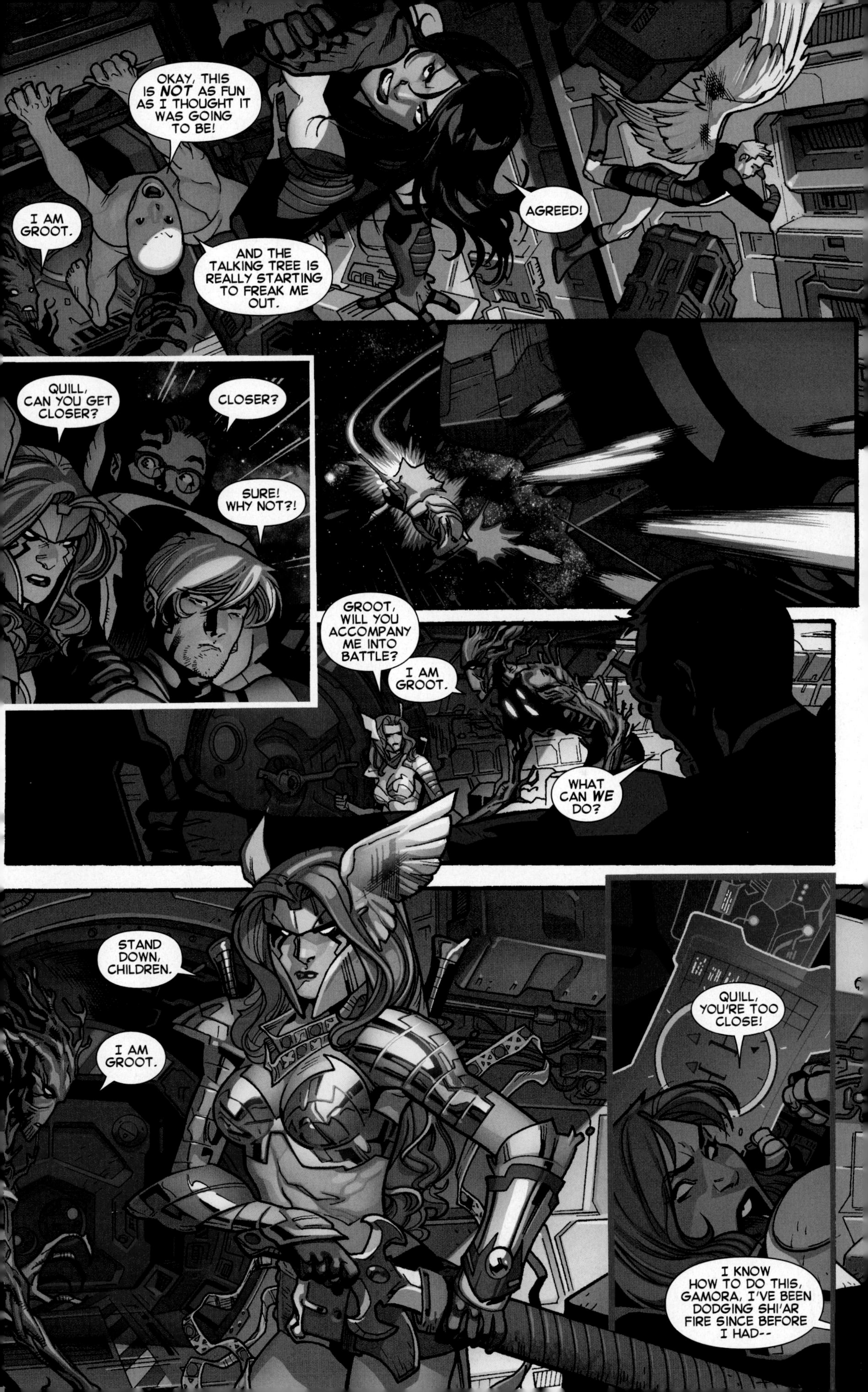

OKAY, THIS IS NOT AS FUN AS I THOUGHT IT WAS GOING TO BE!
I AM GROOT.
AND THE TALKING TREE IS REALLY STARTING TO FREAK ME OUT.
AGREED!
QUILL, CAN YOU GET CLOSER?
CLOSER?
SURE! WHY NOT?!
GROOT, WILL YOU ACCOMPANY ME INTO BATTLE?
I AM GROOT.
WHAT CAN WE DO?
STAND DOWN, CHILDREN.
I AM GROOT.
QUILL, YOU'RE TOO CLOSE!
I KNOW HOW TO DO THIS, GAMORA, I'VE BEEN DODGING SHI'AR FIRE SINCE BEFORE I HAD--

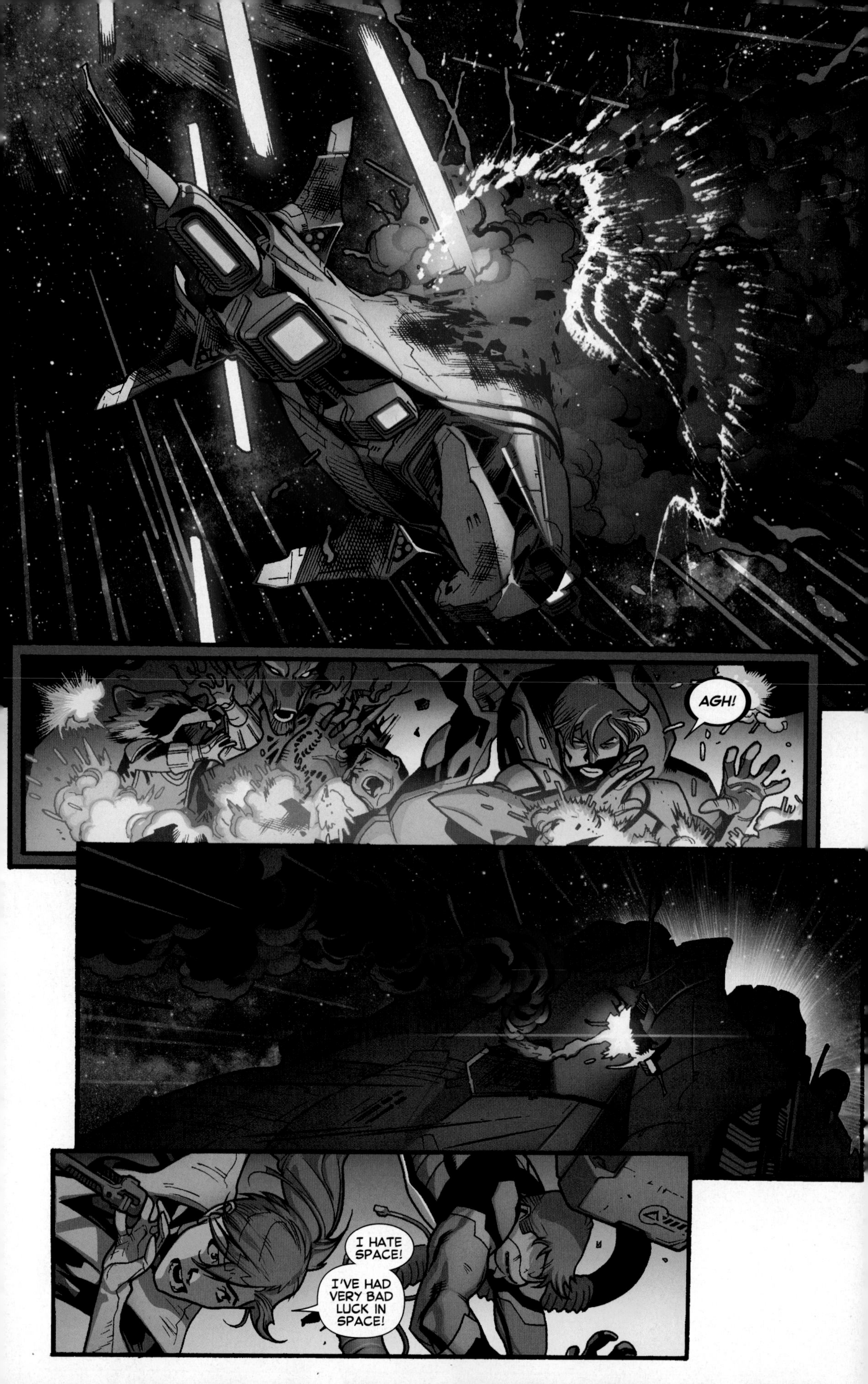
AGH!
I HATE SPACE!
I'VE HAD VERY BAD LUCK IN SPACE!

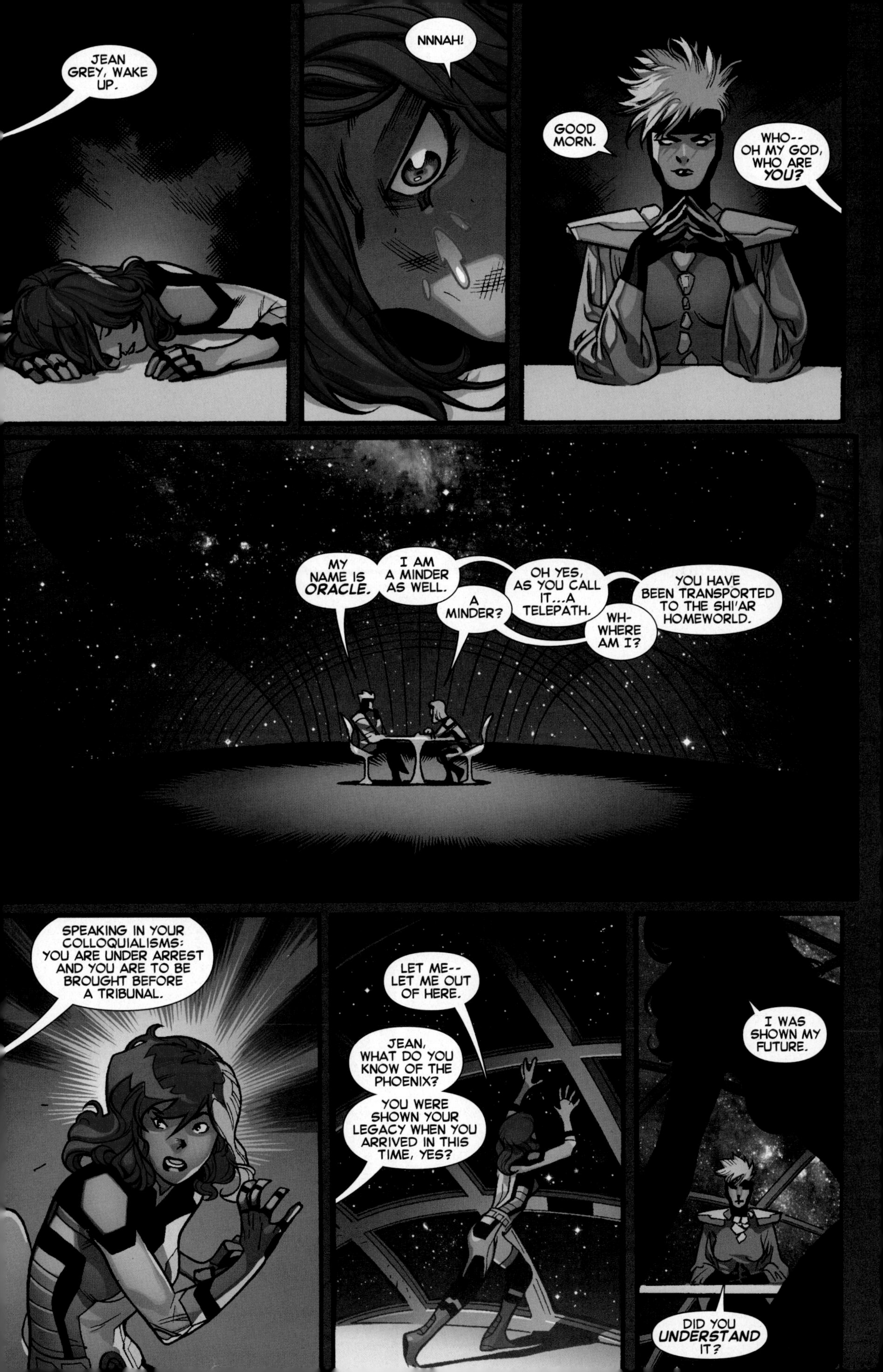

JEAN GREY, WAKE UP.
NNNAH!
GOOD MORN.
WHO-- OH MY GOD, WHO ARE *YOU?*
MY NAME IS *ORACLE.*
I AM A MINDER AS WELL.
A MINDER?
OH YES, AS YOU CALL IT...A TELEPATH.
WH- WHERE AM I?
YOU HAVE BEEN TRANSPORTED TO THE SHI'AR HOMEWORLD.
SPEAKING IN YOUR COLLOQUIALISMS: YOU ARE UNDER ARREST AND YOU ARE TO BE BROUGHT BEFORE A TRIBUNAL.
LET ME-- LET ME OUT OF HERE.
JEAN, WHAT DO YOU KNOW OF THE PHOENIX?
YOU WERE SHOWN YOUR LEGACY WHEN YOU ARRIVED IN THIS TIME, YES?
I WAS SHOWN MY FUTURE.
DID YOU *UNDERSTAND* IT?

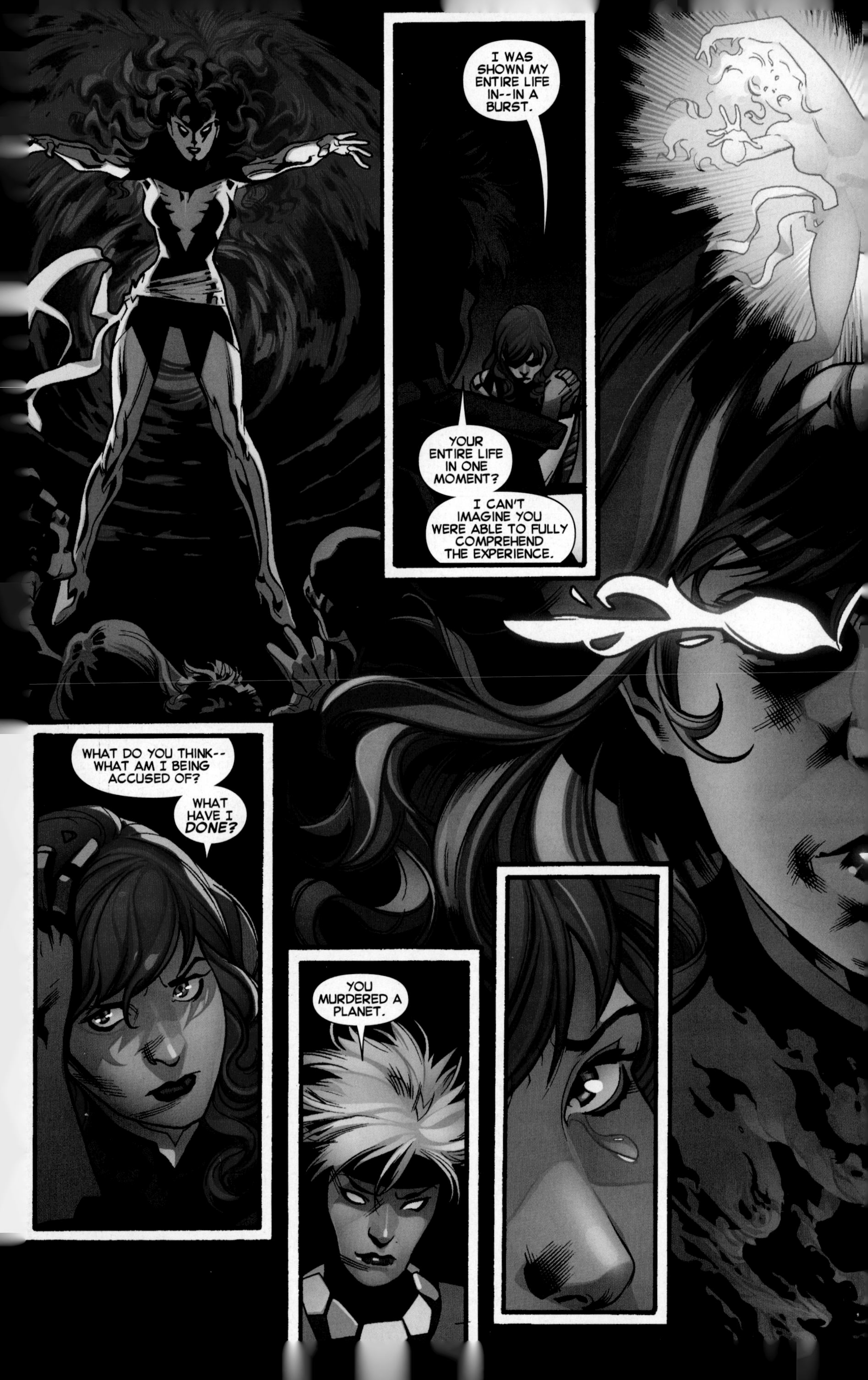
I WAS SHOWN MY ENTIRE LIFE IN--IN A BURST.
YOUR ENTIRE LIFE IN ONE MOMENT?
I CAN'T IMAGINE YOU WERE ABLE TO FULLY COMPREHEND THE EXPERIENCE.
WHAT DO YOU THINK-- WHAT AM I BEING ACCUSED OF?
WHAT HAVE I DONE?
YOU MURDERED A PLANET.

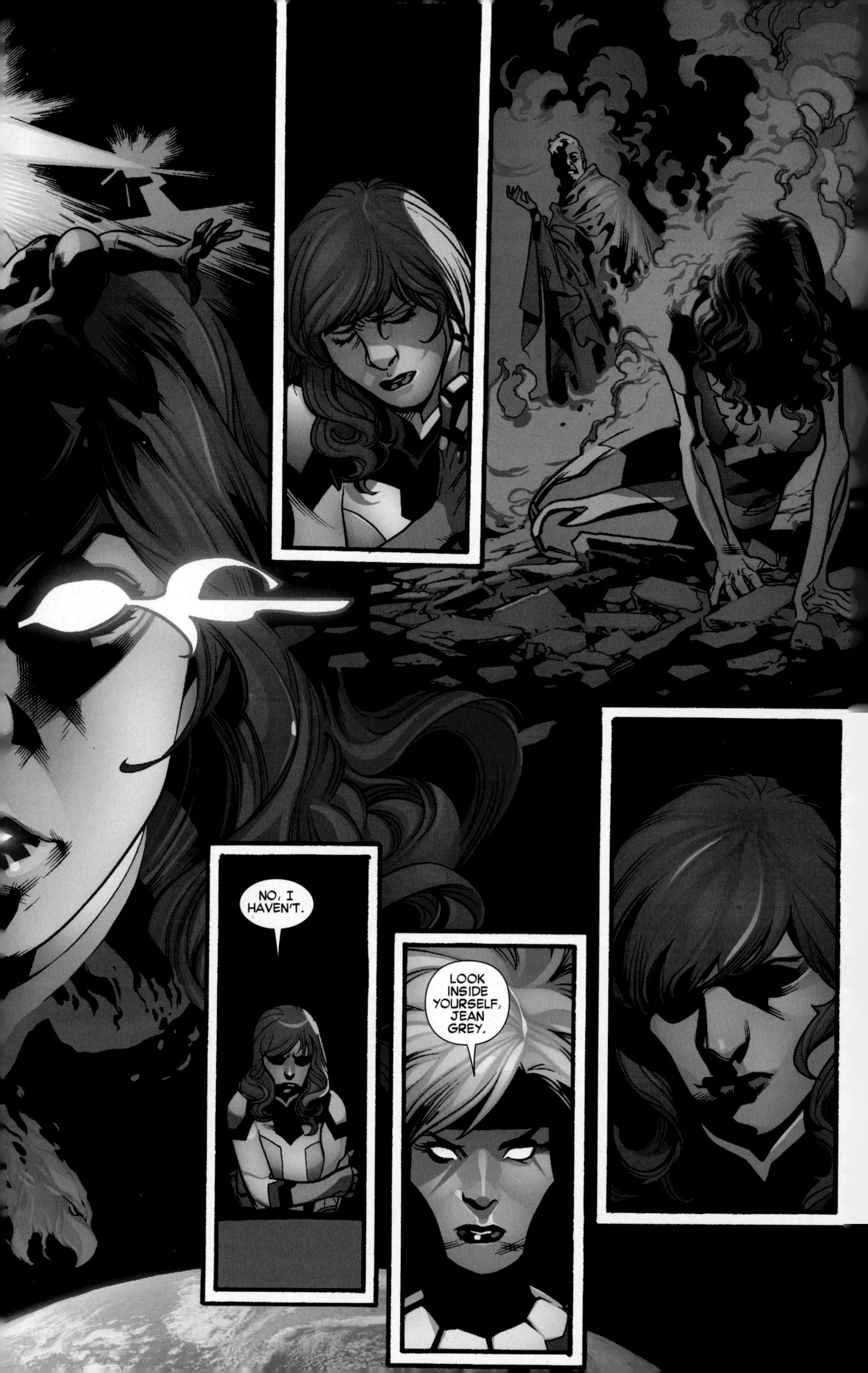
NO, I HAVEN'T.
LOOK INSIDE YOURSELF, JEAN GREY.

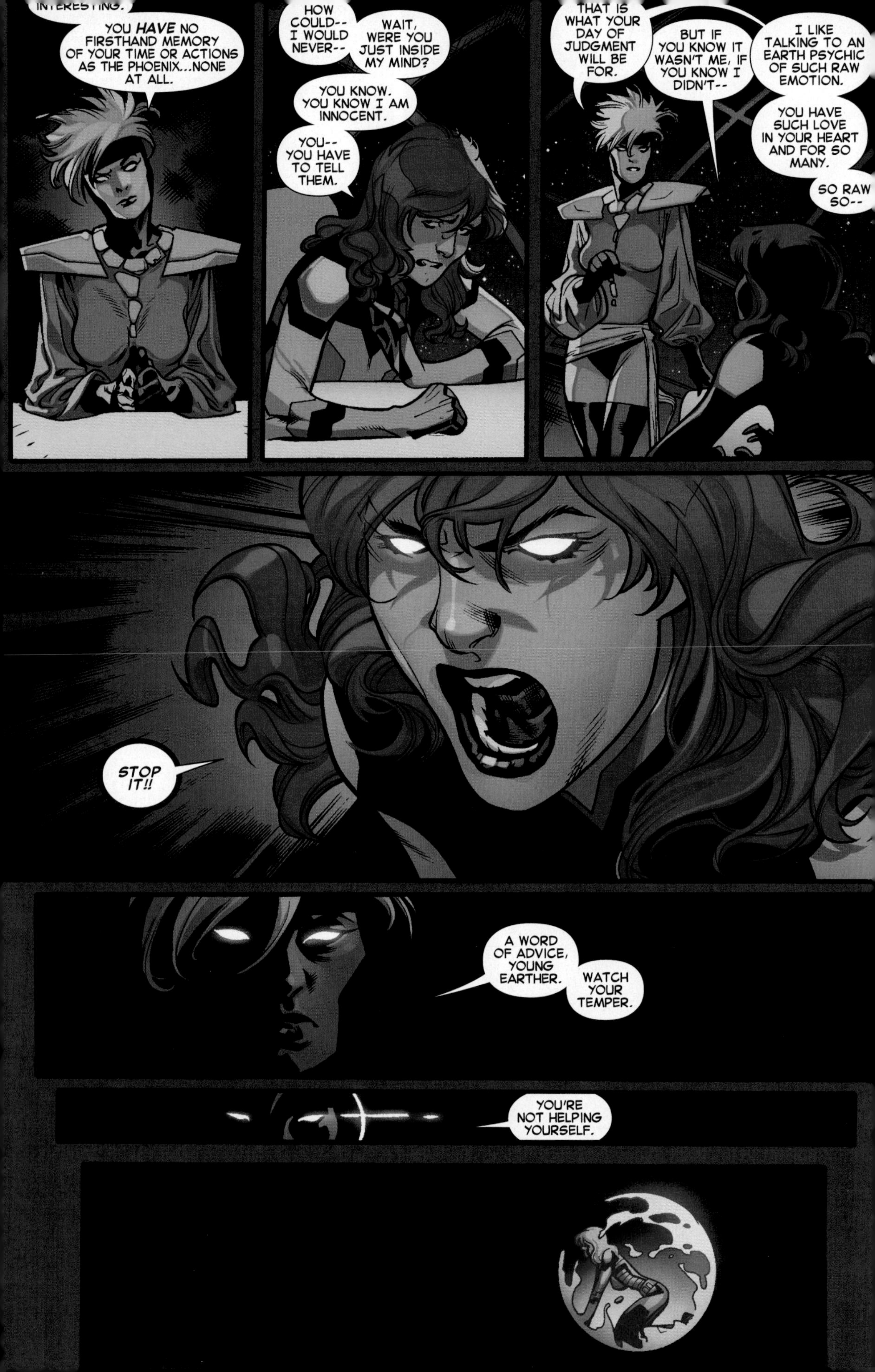
INTERESTING.
YOU HAVE NO FIRSTHAND MEMORY OF YOUR TIME OR ACTIONS AS THE PHOENIX...NONE AT ALL.
HOW COULD-- I WOULD NEVER--
WAIT, WERE YOU JUST INSIDE MY MIND?
YOU KNOW. YOU KNOW I AM INNOCENT.
YOU-- YOU HAVE TO TELL THEM.
THAT IS WHAT YOUR DAY OF JUDGMENT WILL BE FOR.
BUT IF YOU KNOW IT WASN'T ME, IF YOU KNOW I DIDN'T--
I LIKE TALKING TO AN EARTH PSYCHIC OF SUCH RAW EMOTION.
YOU HAVE SUCH LOVE IN YOUR HEART AND FOR SO MANY.
SO RAW SO--
STOP IT!!
A WORD OF ADVICE, YOUNG EARTHER.
WATCH YOUR TEMPER.
YOU'RE NOT HELPING YOURSELF.

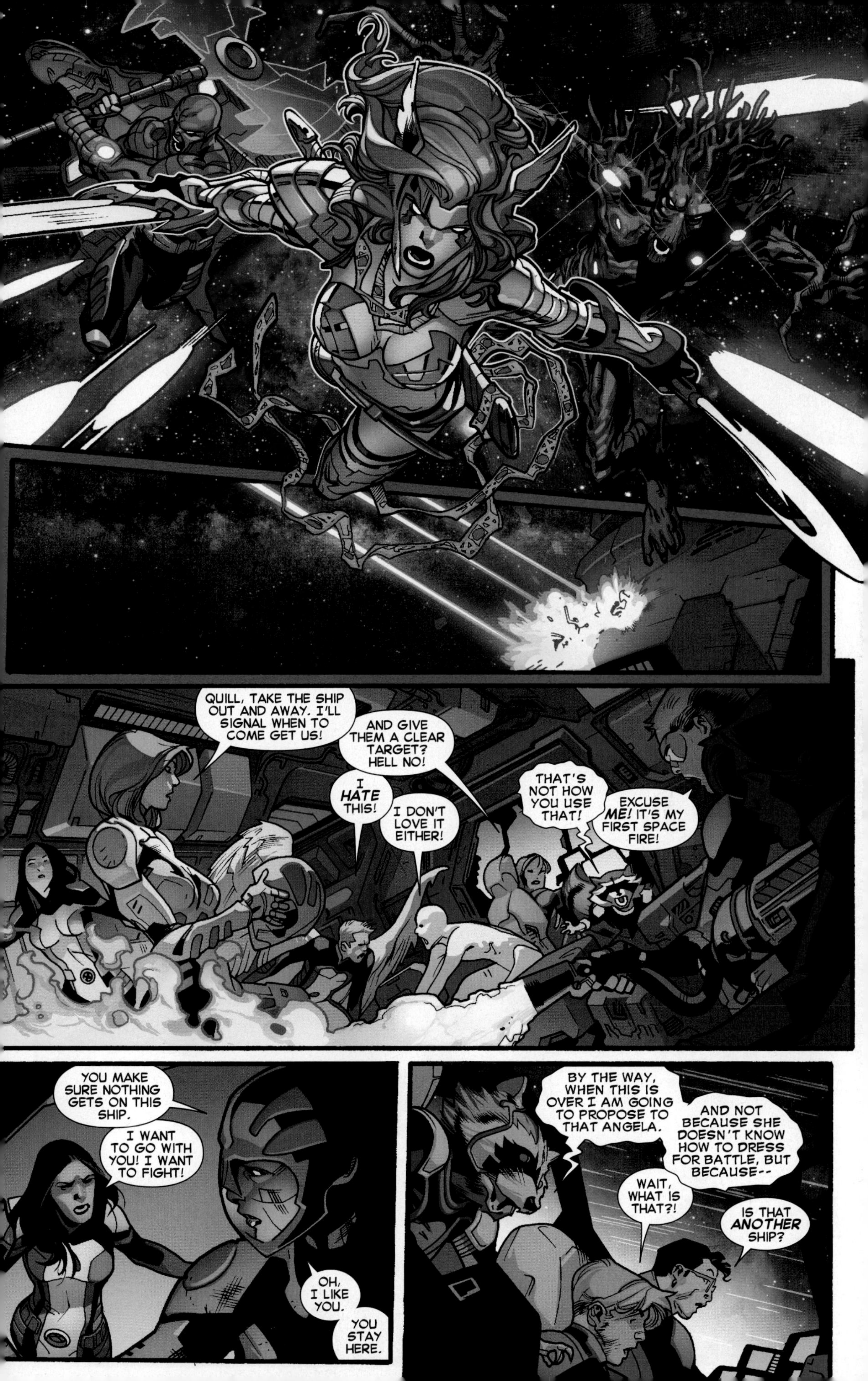
QUILL, TAKE THE SHIP OUT AND AWAY. I'LL SIGNAL WHEN TO COME GET US!
AND GIVE THEM A CLEAR TARGET? HELL NO!
I HATE THIS!
I DON'T LOVE IT EITHER!
THAT'S NOT HOW YOU USE THAT!
EXCUSE ME! IT'S MY FIRST SPACE FIRE!
YOU MAKE SURE NOTHING GETS ON THIS SHIP.
I WANT TO GO WITH YOU! I WANT TO FIGHT!
OH, I LIKE YOU.
YOU STAY HERE.
BY THE WAY, WHEN THIS IS OVER I AM GOING TO PROPOSE TO THAT ANGELA.
AND NOT BECAUSE SHE DOESN'T KNOW HOW TO DRESS FOR BATTLE, BUT BECAUSE--
WAIT, WHAT IS THAT?!
IS THAT ANOTHER SHIP?

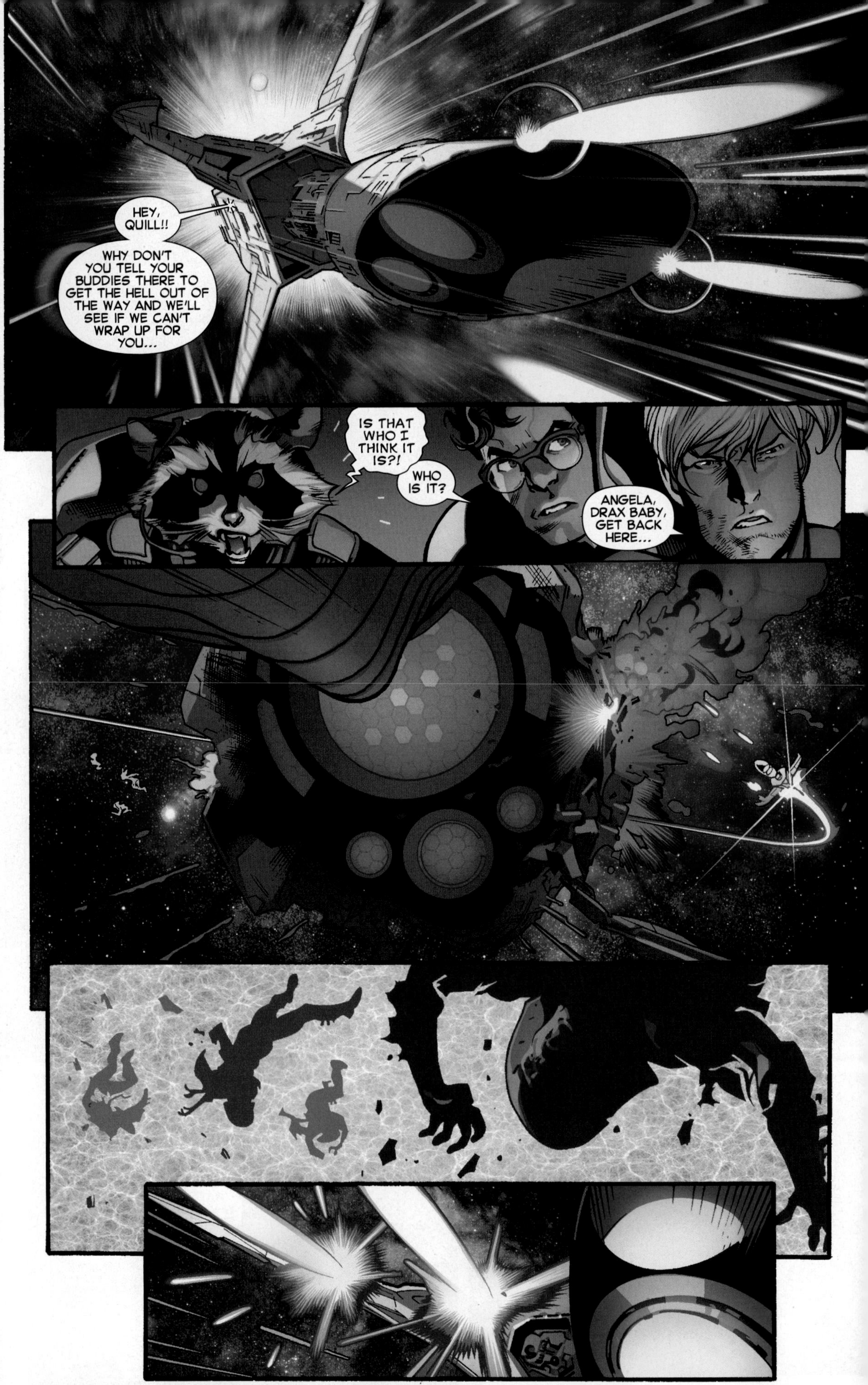
HEY, QUILL!!
WHY DON'T YOU TELL YOUR BUDDIES THERE TO GET THE HELL OUT OF THE WAY AND WE'LL SEE IF WE CAN'T WRAP UP FOR YOU...
IS THAT WHO I THINK IT IS?!
WHO IS IT?
ANGELA, DRAX BABY, GET BACK HERE...

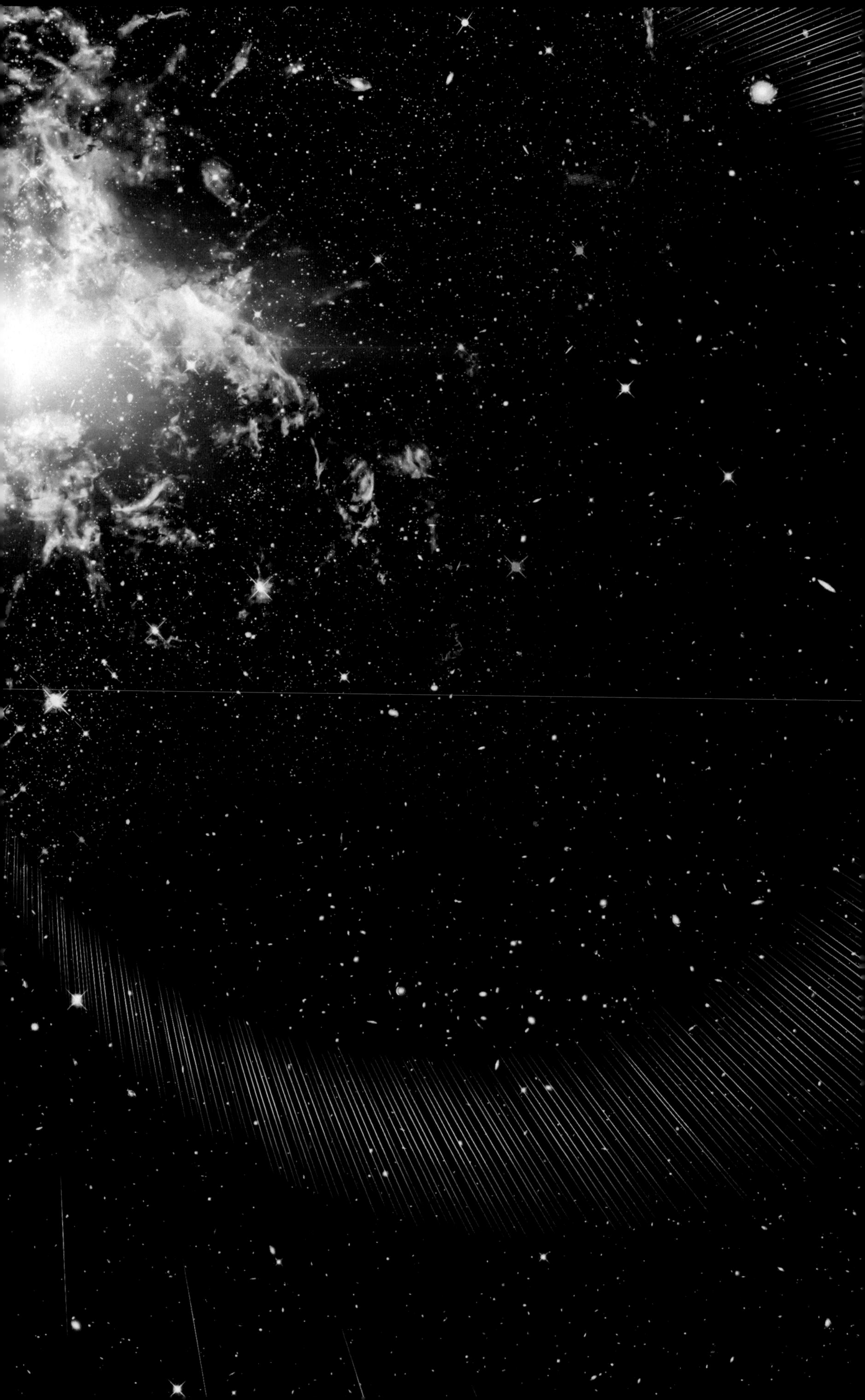

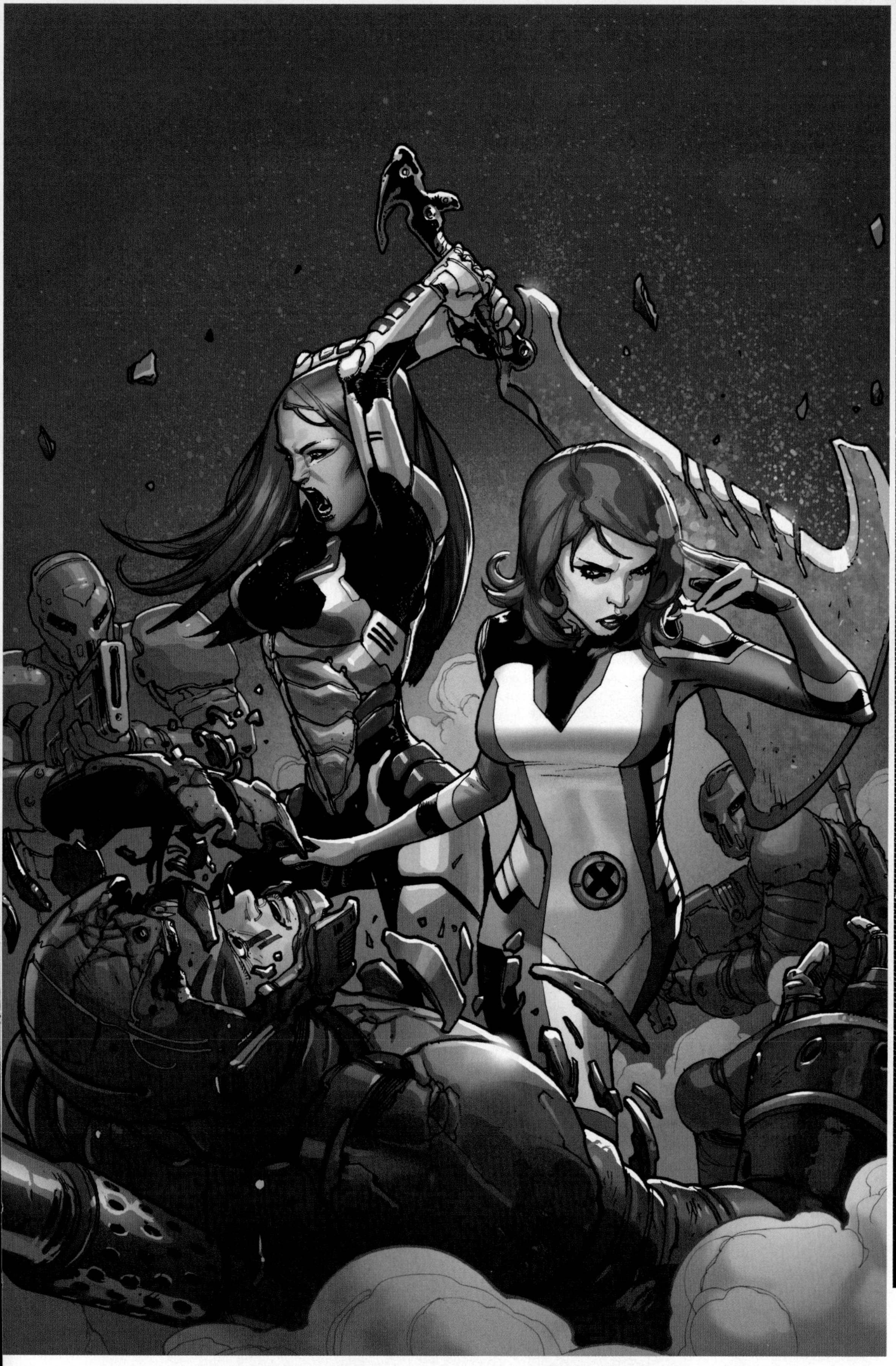

GUARDIANS OF THE GALAXY 12

ALASKA, YEARS AGO.

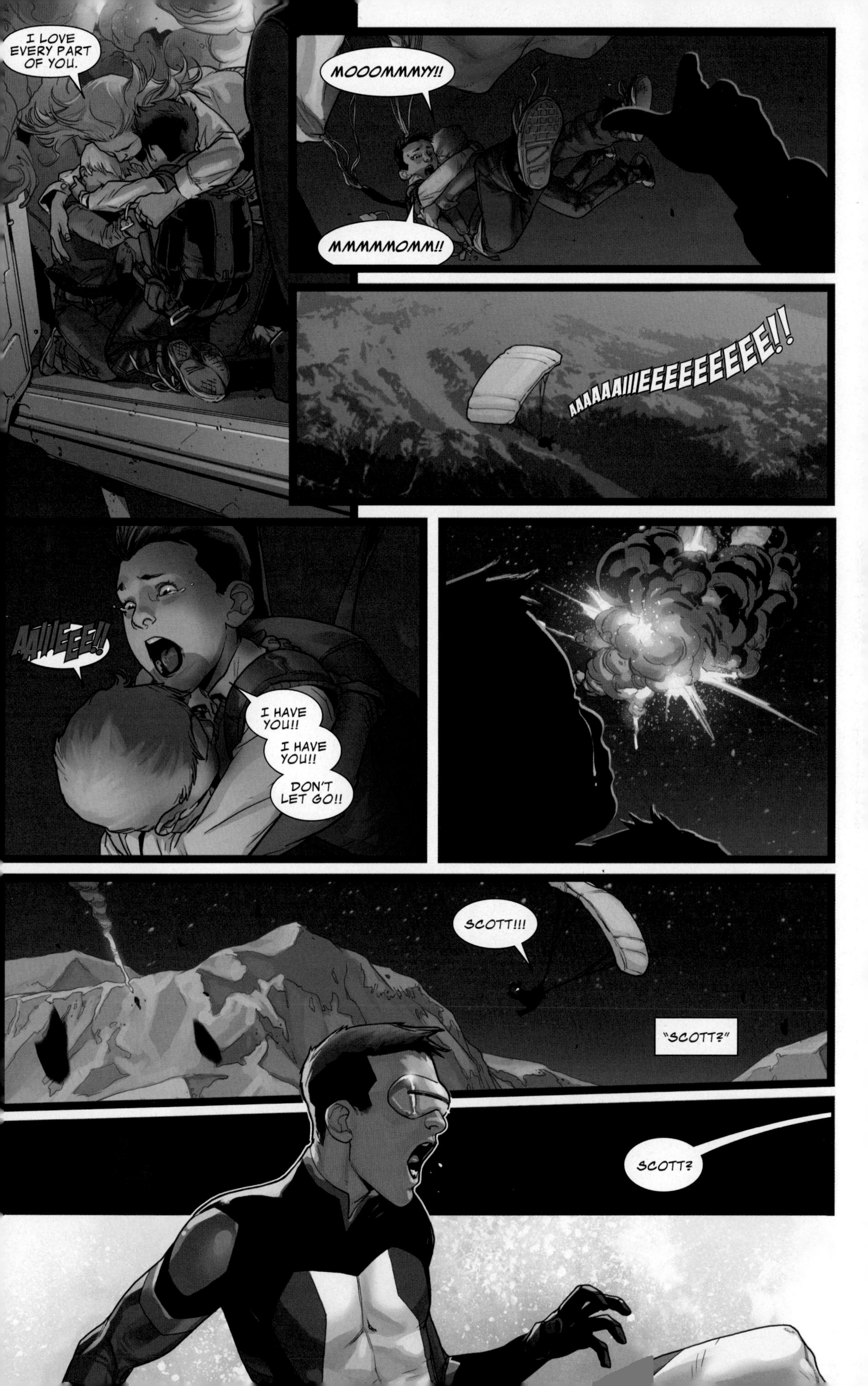

I LOVE EVERY PART OF YOU.
MOOOMMMYY!!
MMMMMOMM!!
AAAAAIIIIEEEEEEEEE!!
AAIIIEEE!!
I HAVE YOU!!
I HAVE YOU!!
DON'T LET GO!!
SCOTT!!!
"SCOTT?"
SCOTT?

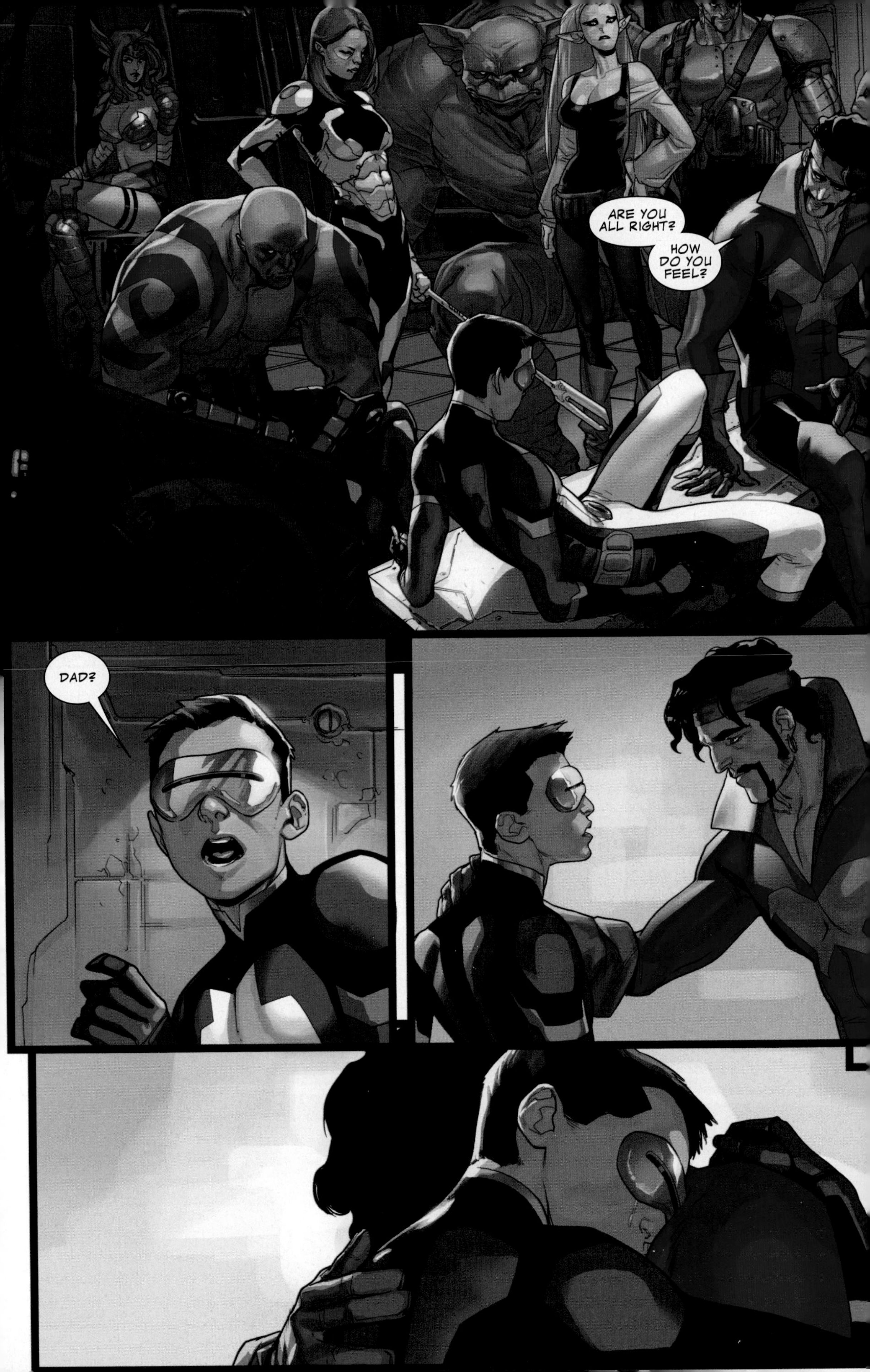
ARE YOU ALL RIGHT?
HOW DO YOU FEEL?
DAD?

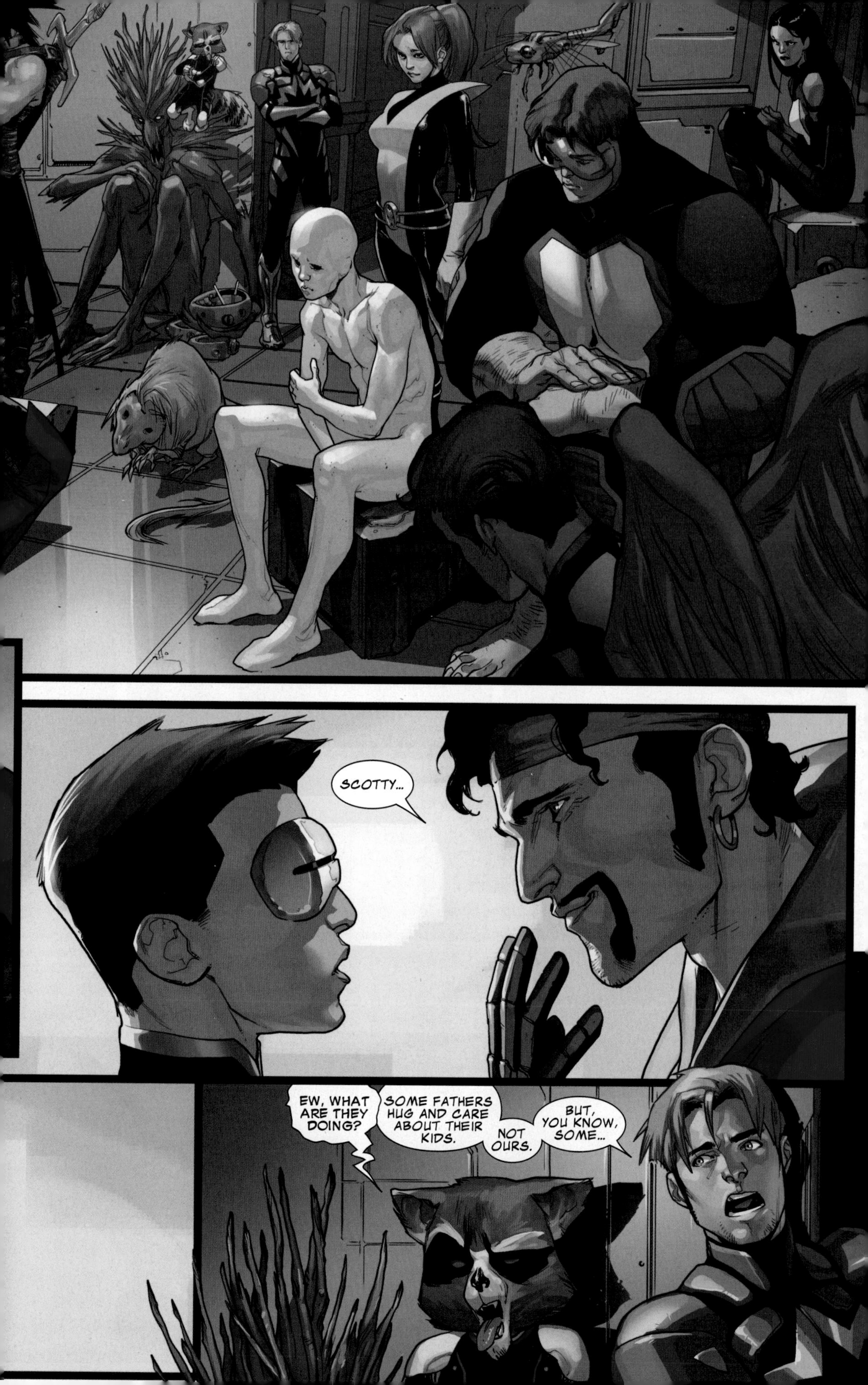
SCOTTY...
EW, WHAT ARE THEY DOING?
SOME FATHERS HUG AND CARE ABOUT THEIR KIDS.
NOT OURS.
BUT, YOU KNOW, SOME...

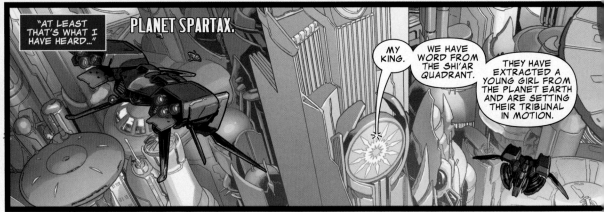

"AT LEAST THAT'S WHAT I HAVE HEARD..."

PLANET SPARTAX.

MY KING.

WE HAVE WORD FROM THE SHI'AR QUADRANT.

THEY HAVE EXTRACTED A YOUNG GIRL FROM THE PLANET EARTH AND ARE SETTING THEIR TRIBUNAL IN MOTION.

WHO AS YOU MAY KNOW WAS, AT ONE TIME OR ANOTHER, POSSESSED BY THE PHOENIX FORCE.

OUR INTEL CLEARLY SHOWS THAT JEAN GREY IS DEAD AND HAS BEEN FOR SOME TIME.

SO THIS NEW INTEL MUST BE FALSE.

DAMNED SHI'AR AND THEIR RELIGIOUS PRECISION.

I'M SORRY, SIR...DO YOU ALREADY KNOW OF THIS?

I DIDN'T THINK IT WAS GOING TO HAPPEN SO QUICKLY.

HAS THE EARTH RESPONDED?

WE DON'T BELIEVE THEY EVEN KNOW.

THE EXTRACTION HAPPENED COVERTLY.

WHY??

WHY DOES EVERYONE P[UT] ME IN THES[E] POSITIONS[?]

YOUR SON...

AND HIS GUARDIANS...

HOW DOES HE DO IT?

HOW DOES MY SON ALWAYS FIND A WAY TO PUT HIMSELF IN THE MIDDLE OF EVERYTHING??

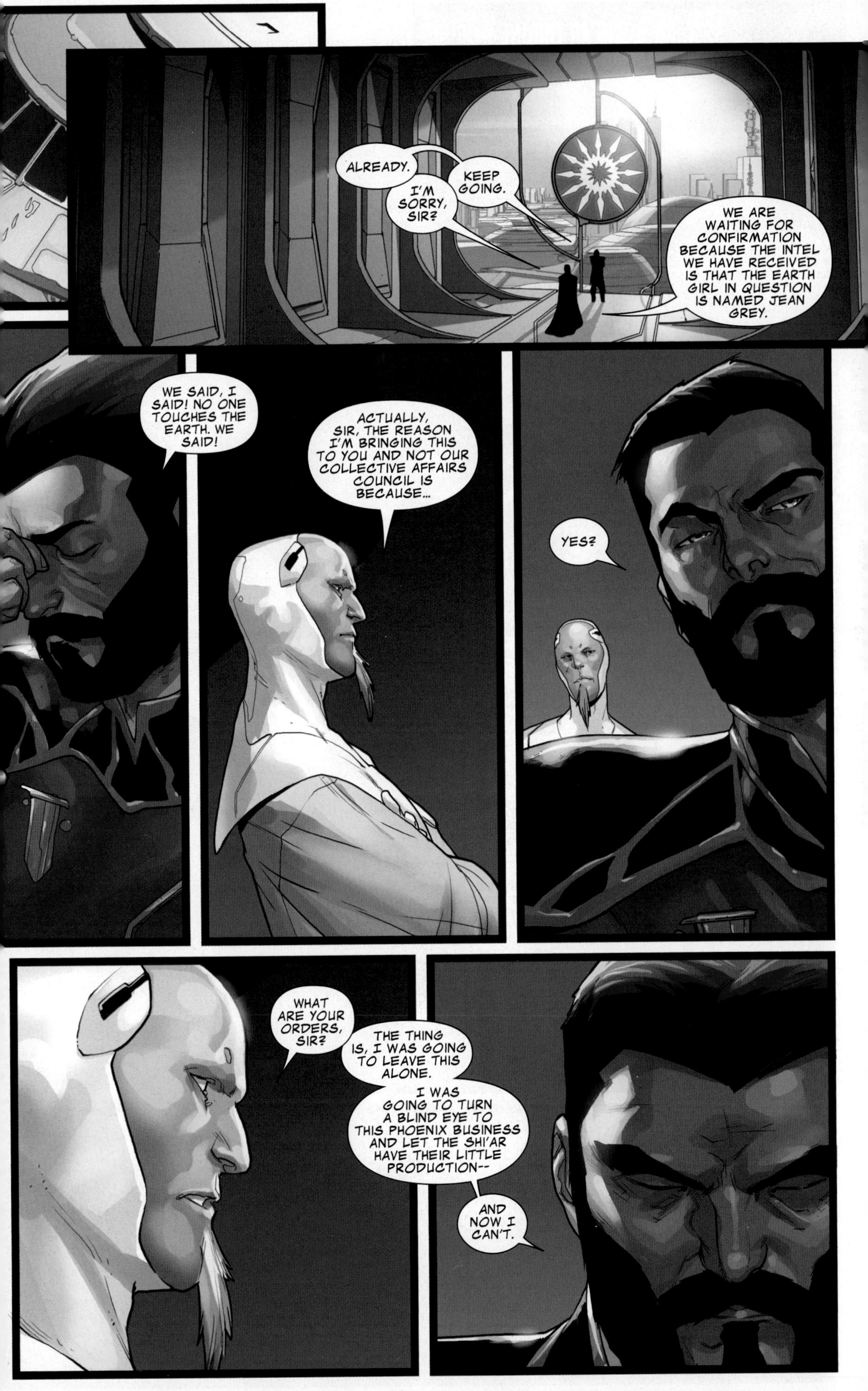
ALREADY.
KEEP GOING.
I'M SORRY, SIR?
WE ARE WAITING FOR CONFIRMATION BECAUSE THE INTEL WE HAVE RECEIVED IS THAT THE EARTH GIRL IN QUESTION IS NAMED JEAN GREY.
WE SAID, I SAID! NO ONE TOUCHES THE EARTH. WE SAID!
ACTUALLY, SIR, THE REASON I'M BRINGING THIS TO YOU AND NOT OUR COLLECTIVE AFFAIRS COUNCIL IS BECAUSE...
YES?
WHAT ARE YOUR ORDERS, SIR?
THE THING IS, I WAS GOING TO LEAVE THIS ALONE.
I WAS GOING TO TURN A BLIND EYE TO THIS PHOENIX BUSINESS AND LET THE SHI'AR HAVE THEIR LITTLE PRODUCTION--
AND NOW I CAN'T.

AND THE SHIP HAS NOT BEEN HEARD FROM SINCE?

NO.

WHAT DID YOU THINK WAS GOING TO HAPPEN, GLADIATOR?

PUT YOURSELF IN THEIR POSITION...

IF SOMEONE FROM ANOTHER SYSTEM CAME HERE AND TOOK ONE OF US, ONE OF YOUR IMPERIAL GUARD, WOULD YOU NOT FOLLOW THAT TRAIL TO THE ENDS OF THE GALAXY?

MANTA, A SHIP GOES MISSING IN THE VASTNESS OF THE GALAXY...THAT DOES NOT MEAN IT HAS ANYTHING TO DO WITH THIS.

IT IS THE X-MEN...

EARTHERS DO NOT HAVE THE TECHNOLOGICAL CAPACITY TO TRAVEL THIS FAR, THIS FAST.

NONE OF THEM.

YOU DON'T KNOW WHAT THOSE BARBARIANS CAN DO.

YOU STOLE ONE OF THEM AND THEY'RE COMING TO GET HER.

I DO NOT BELIEVE THEY HAVE THE POWER OR WHEREWITHAL TO REACH US IN TIME TO STOP WHAT IS ABOUT TO HAPPEN.

THEY WON'T JOIN US AS GALACTIC TRAVELERS FOR MANY GENERATIONS TO COME.

BY THE TIME THEY DISCOVER WHAT HAS HAPPENE AND BY WHOSE HAN IT WILL STILL TAKE THEM--

THEY ARE A FIERY AND PASSIONATE SPECIES AND YOU STOLE ONE OF THEM.

YOU STOLE ONE OF THE X-MEN.

YOU STOLE ONE OF THEIR FOUNDING MEMBERS.

YOU HAVE DECLARED WAR ON THE X-MEN.

WHICH MEANS YOU HAVE DECLARED WAR ON THE MUTANT POPULATION OF THE PLANET EARTH.

THEY WOULD COME FOR HER.

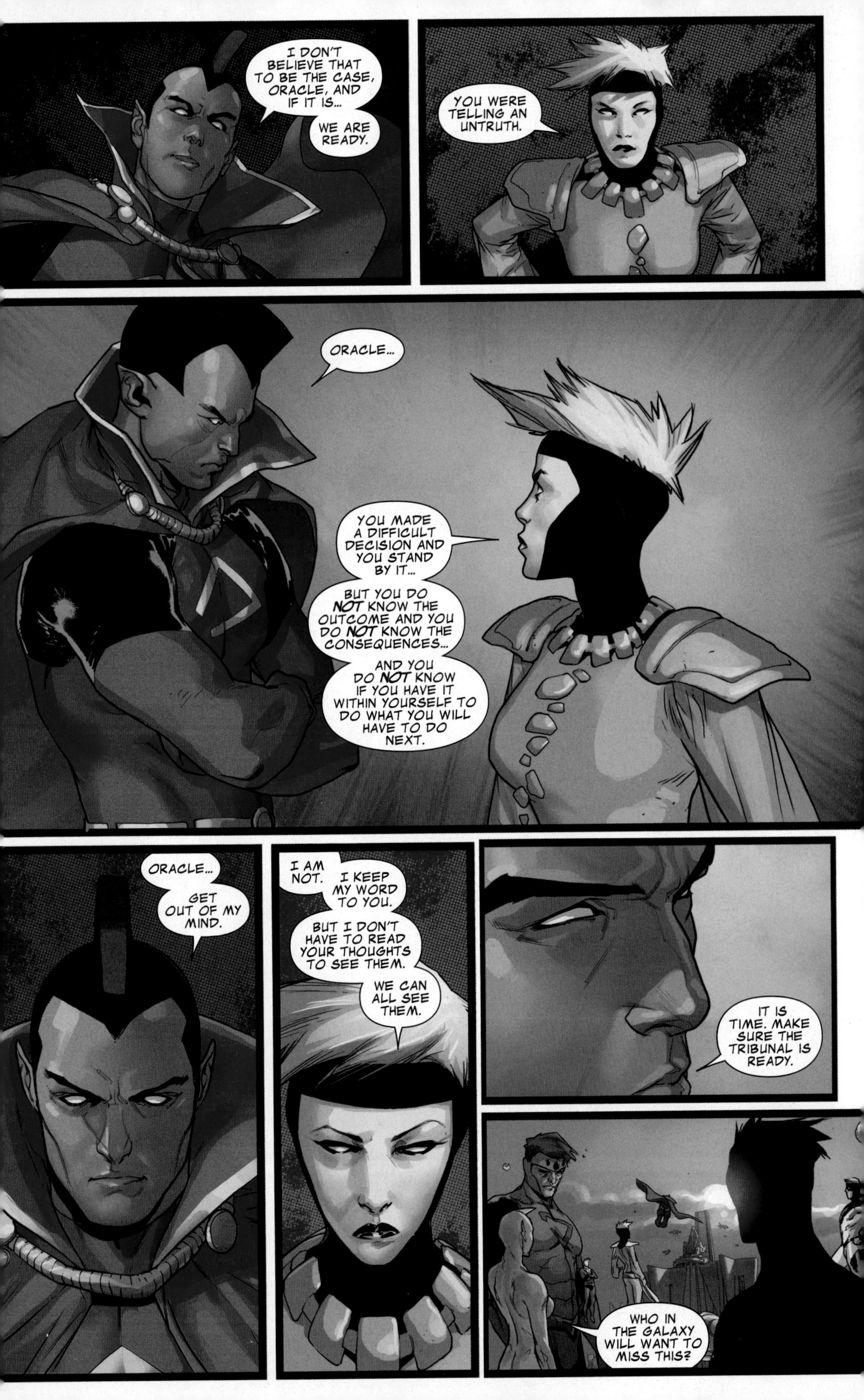
I DON'T BELIEVE THAT TO BE THE CASE, ORACLE, AND IF IT IS...
WE ARE READY.
YOU WERE TELLING AN UNTRUTH.
ORACLE...
YOU MADE A DIFFICULT DECISION AND YOU STAND BY IT...
BUT YOU DO NOT KNOW THE OUTCOME AND YOU DO NOT KNOW THE CONSEQUENCES...
AND YOU DO NOT KNOW IF YOU HAVE IT WITHIN YOURSELF TO DO WHAT YOU WILL HAVE TO DO NEXT.
ORACLE...
GET OUT OF MY MIND.
I AM NOT.
I KEEP MY WORD TO YOU.
BUT I DON'T HAVE TO READ YOUR THOUGHTS TO SEE THEM.
WE CAN ALL SEE THEM.
IT IS TIME. MAKE SURE THE TRIBUNAL IS READY.
WHO IN THE GALAXY WILL WANT TO MISS THIS?

OUTSKIRTS OF THE SHI'AR EMPIRE.
ARE YOU OKAY, SCOTTY?
I DON'T THINK THERE ARE WORDS TO DESCRIBE HOW I AM.
YOU'RE THE ONE WHO'S TRAVELED THROUGH TIME, KID.
COMPARATIVELY, I THINK MY STORY OF ALIEN ABDUCTIONS, PRISON BREAK, AND NOW SPACE PIRATES IS A LITTLE MORE CONVENTIONAL.
YOU'RE A SPACE PIRATE?
WE DON'T ACTUALLY CALL OURSELVES--WE CALL OURSELVES THE STARJAMMERS.
I THOUGHT YOU DIED.
YEAH, I KNOW, WE-- MMM! THIS IS SO ODD.
YOU KNOW, WE'VE, YOU AND I HAVE BEEN THROUGH THIS ALREADY.
WE'VE REUNITED. WE'VE MADE OUR PEACE WITH THE PAST.
ME AND, WELL, THE OLDER YOU.
YOU-- YOU AND I FOUND EACH OTHER?
YEARS AGO.
ARE WE-- ARE WE GOOD?
OF COURSE WE ARE. BOTH YOU AND YOUR BROTHER.
IN FACT, ALEX TRAVELED WITH ME FOR A--
AND MOM?

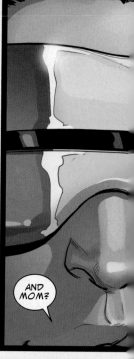

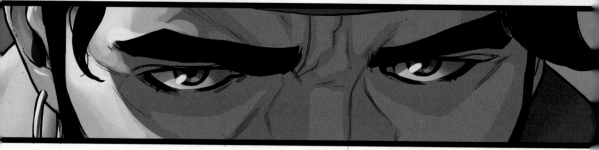

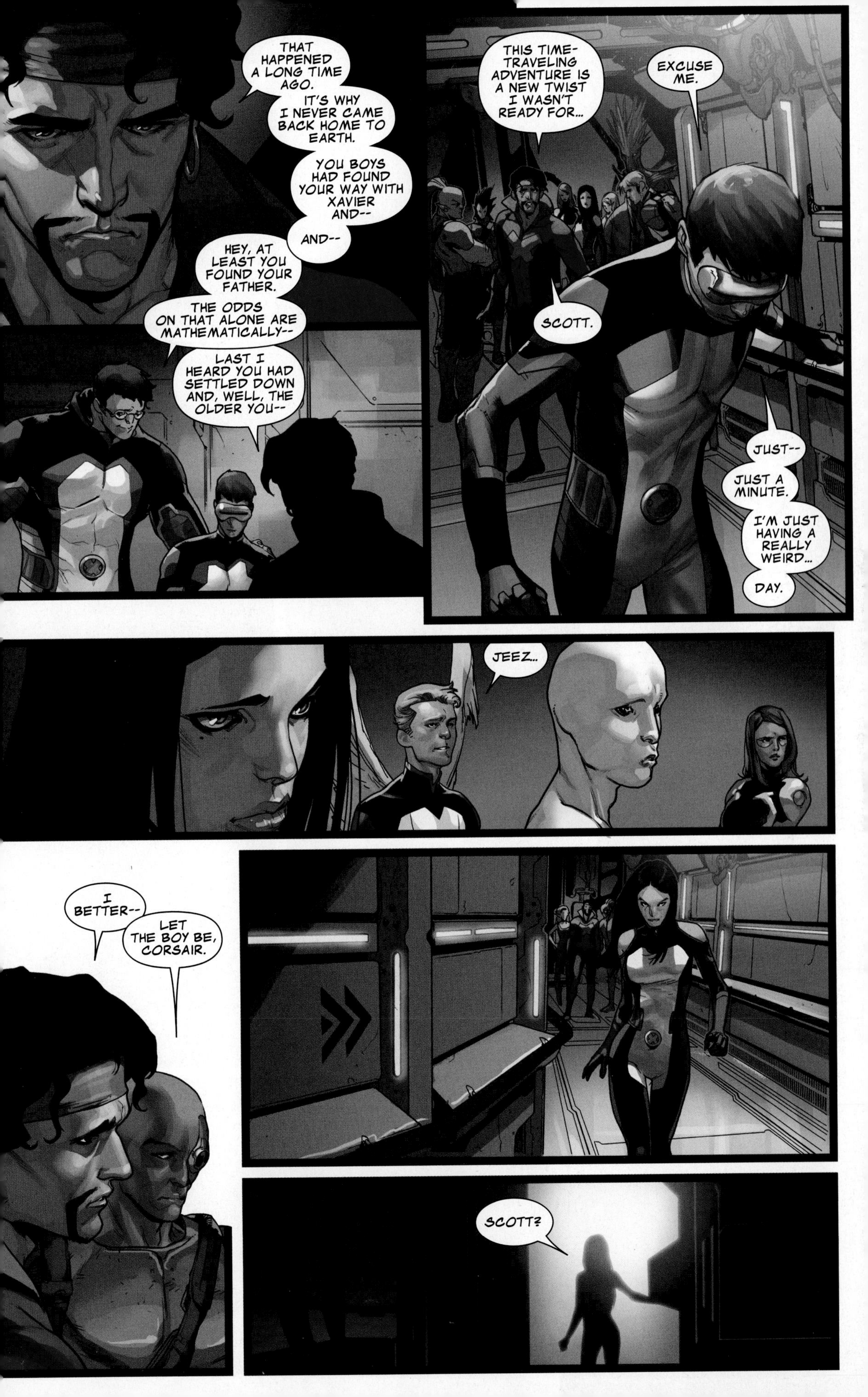

THAT HAPPENED A LONG TIME AGO.
IT'S WHY I NEVER CAME BACK HOME TO EARTH.
YOU BOYS HAD FOUND YOUR WAY WITH XAVIER AND--
AND--
HEY, AT LEAST YOU FOUND YOUR FATHER.
THE ODDS ON THAT ALONE ARE MATHEMATICALLY--
LAST I HEARD YOU HAD SETTLED DOWN AND, WELL, THE OLDER YOU--
THIS TIME-TRAVELING ADVENTURE IS A NEW TWIST I WASN'T READY FOR...
EXCUSE ME.
SCOTT.
JUST--
JUST A MINUTE.
I'M JUST HAVING A REALLY WEIRD...
DAY.
JEEZ...
I BETTER--
LET THE BOY BE, CORSAIR.
SCOTT?

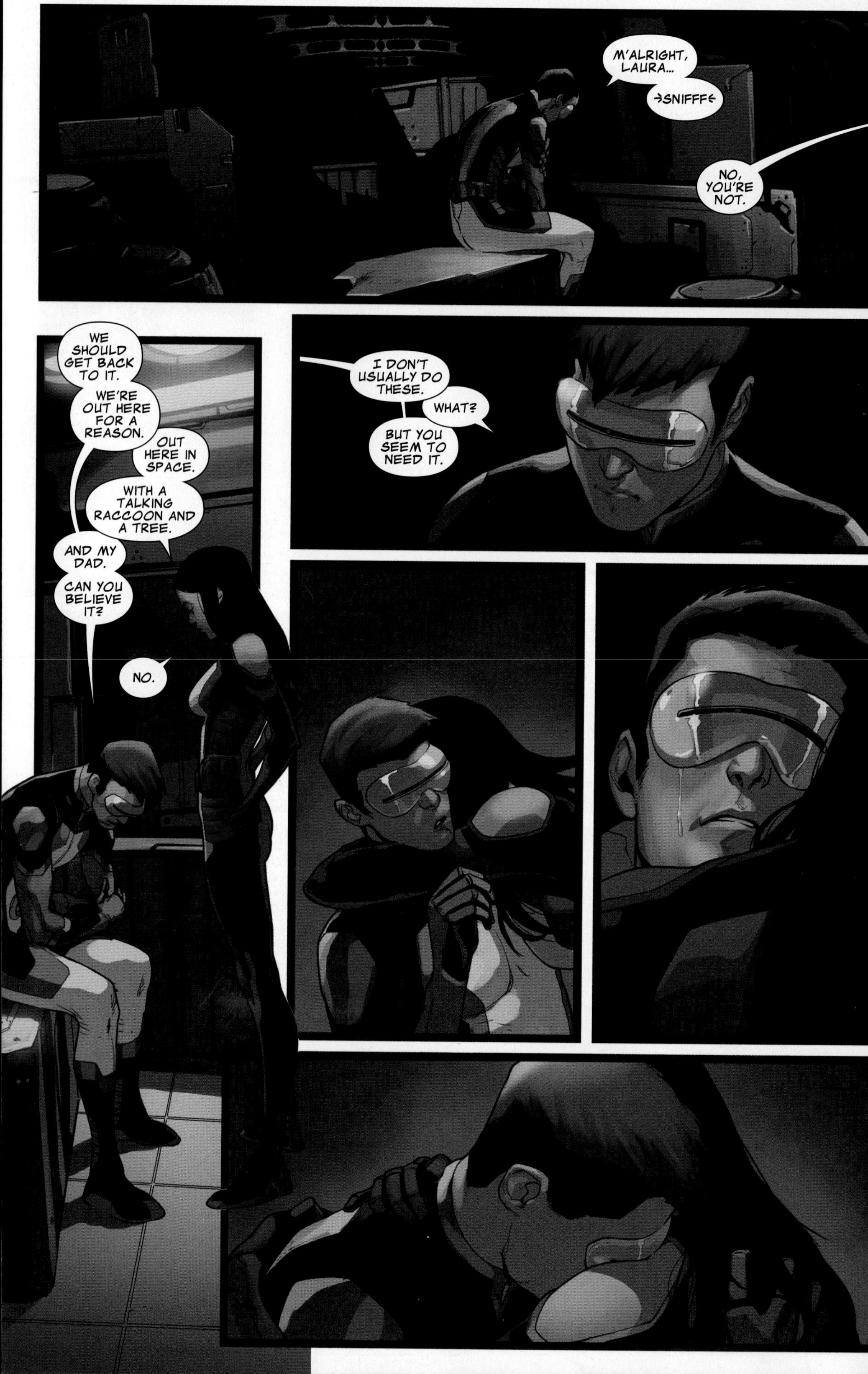
M'ALRIGHT, LAURA...
SNIFFF
NO, YOU'RE NOT.
WE SHOULD GET BACK TO IT.
WE'RE OUT HERE FOR A REASON.
OUT HERE IN SPACE.
WITH A TALKING RACCOON AND A TREE.
AND MY DAD.
CAN YOU BELIEVE IT?
NO.
I DON'T USUALLY DO THESE.
WHAT?
BUT YOU SEEM TO NEED IT.

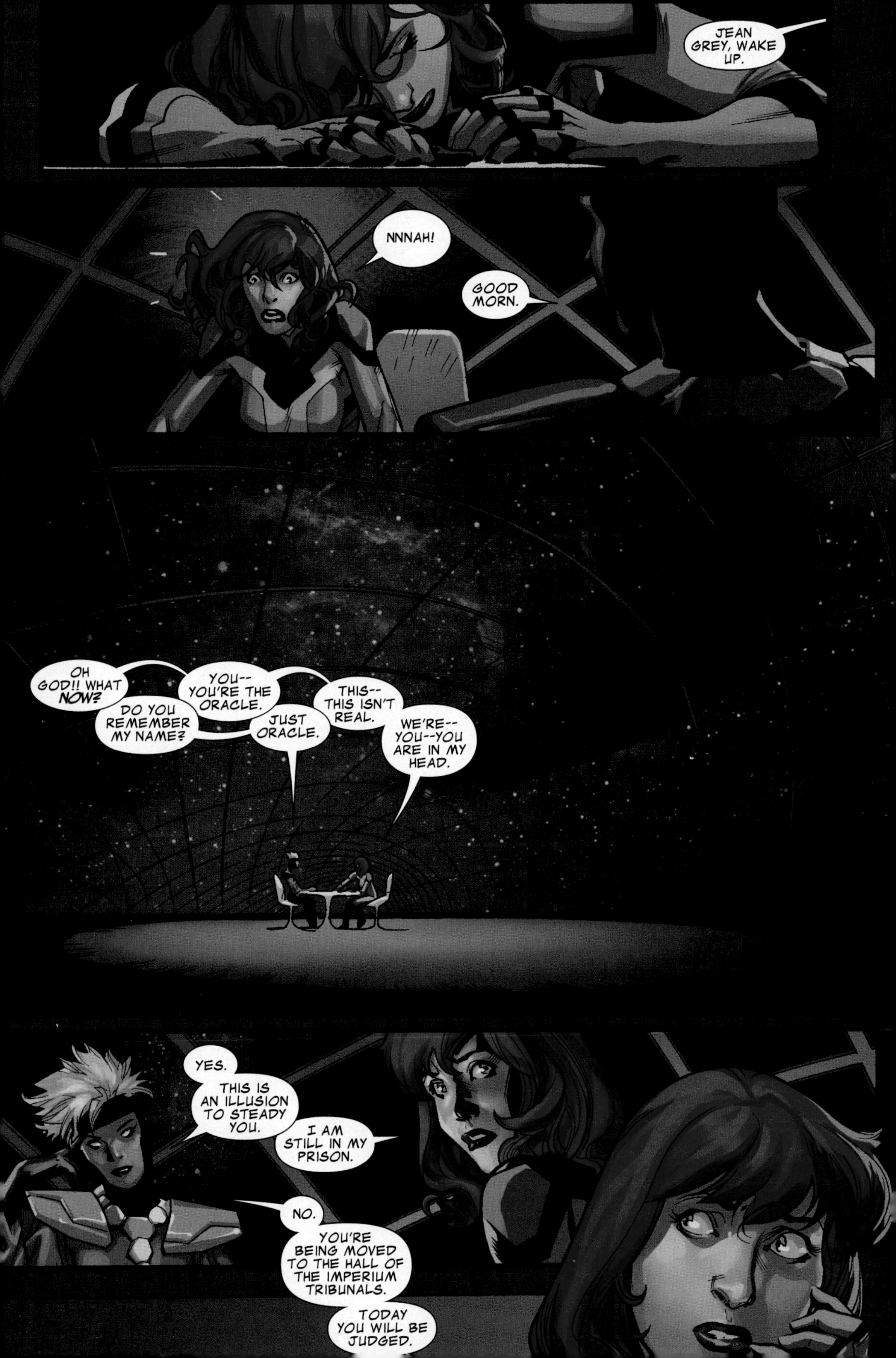
JEAN GREY, WAKE UP.
NNNAH!
GOOD MORN.
OH GOD!! WHAT NOW?
DO YOU REMEMBER MY NAME?
YOU-- YOU'RE THE ORACLE.
JUST ORACLE.
THIS-- THIS ISN'T REAL.
WE'RE-- YOU--YOU ARE IN MY HEAD.
YES.
THIS IS AN ILLUSION TO STEADY YOU.
I AM STILL IN MY PRISON.
NO.
YOU'RE BEING MOVED TO THE HALL OF THE IMPERIUM TRIBUNALS.
TODAY YOU WILL BE JUDGED.

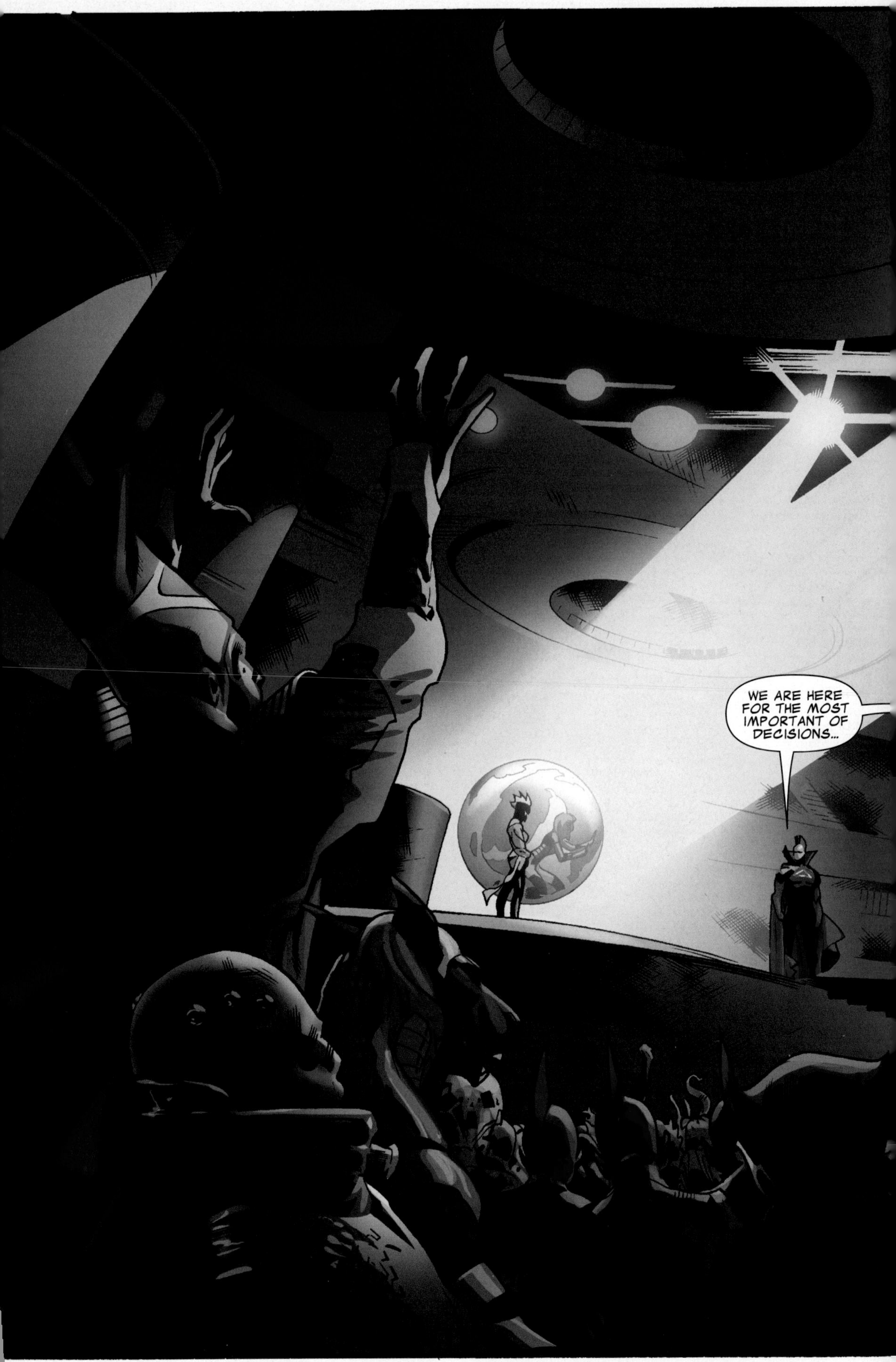
WE ARE HERE FOR THE MOST IMPORTANT OF DECISIONS...

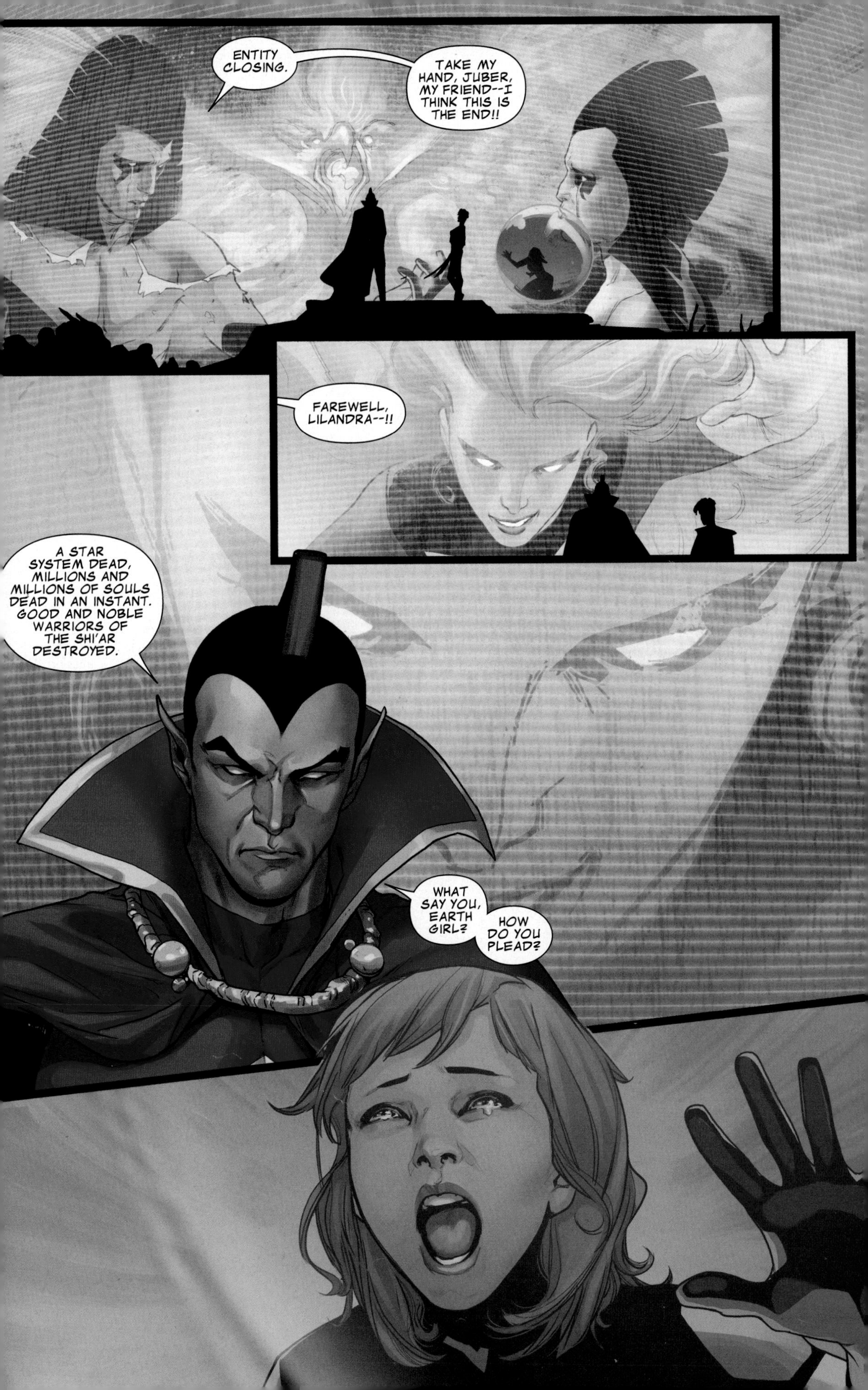
ENTITY CLOSING.
TAKE MY HAND, JUBER, MY FRIEND--I THINK THIS IS THE END!!
FAREWELL, LILANDRA--!!
A STAR SYSTEM DEAD, MILLIONS AND MILLIONS OF SOULS DEAD IN AN INSTANT. GOOD AND NOBLE WARRIORS OF THE SHI'AR DESTROYED.
WHAT SAY YOU, EARTH GIRL?
HOW DO YOU PLEAD?

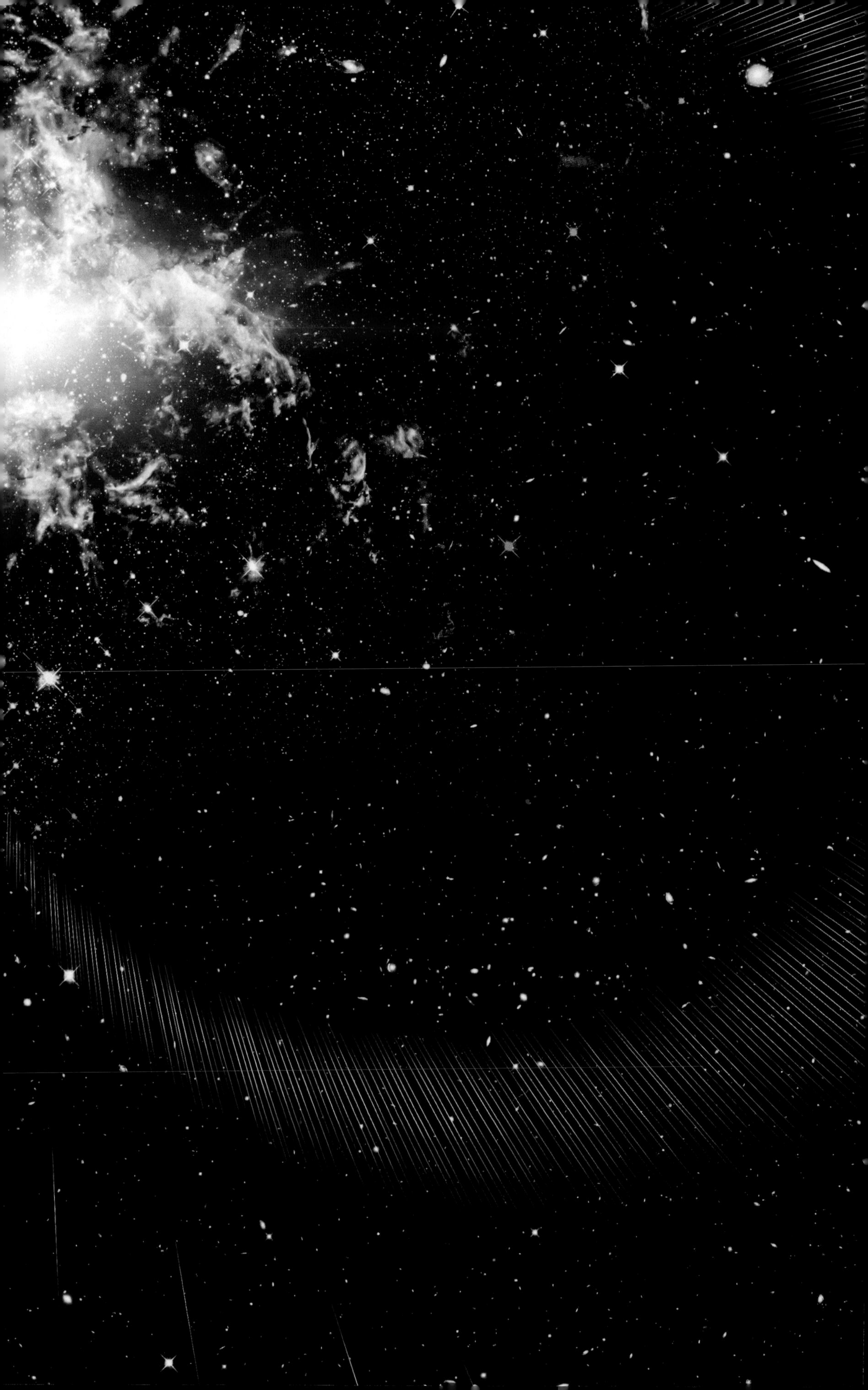

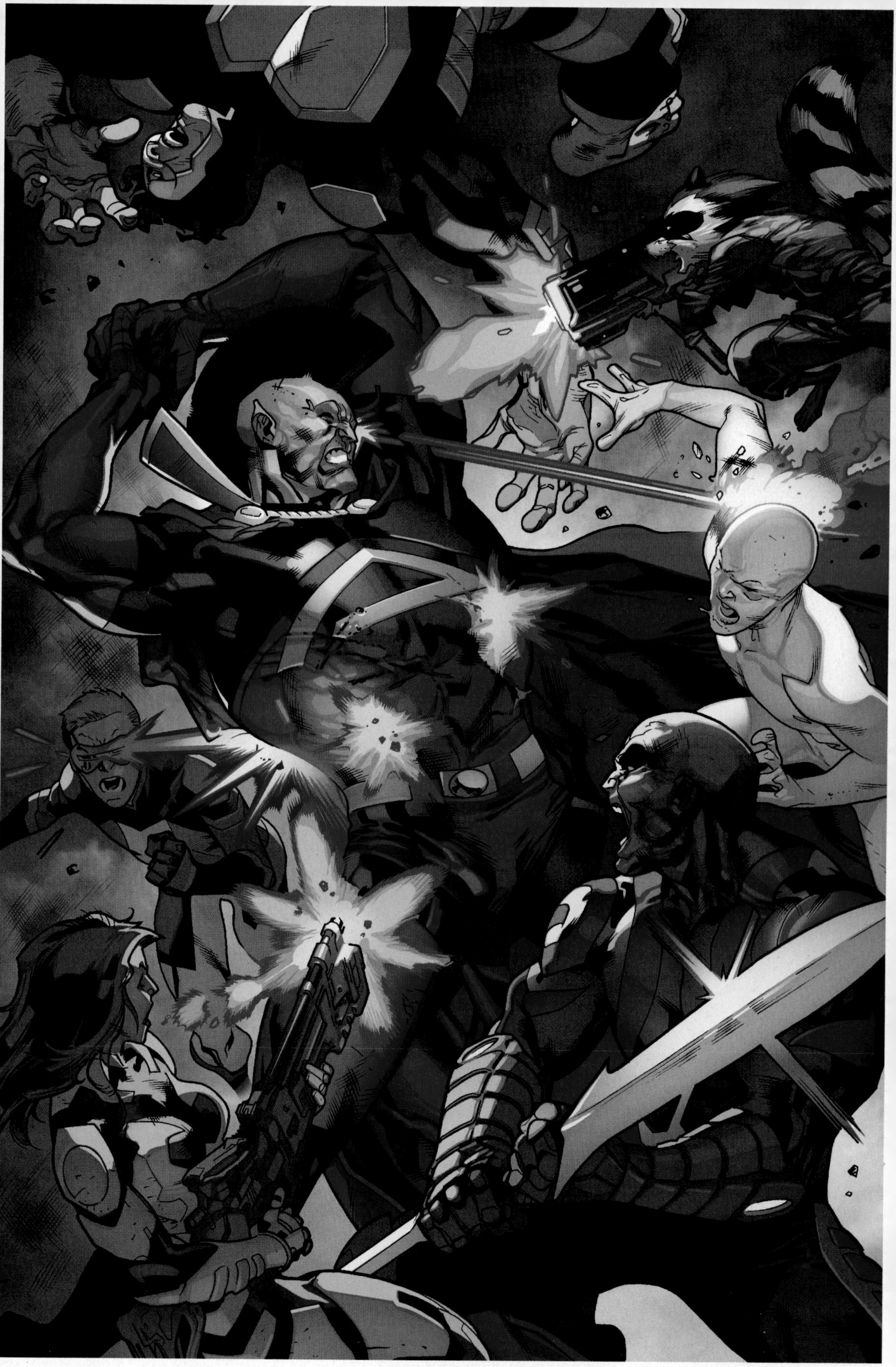

ALL-NEW X-MEN 24

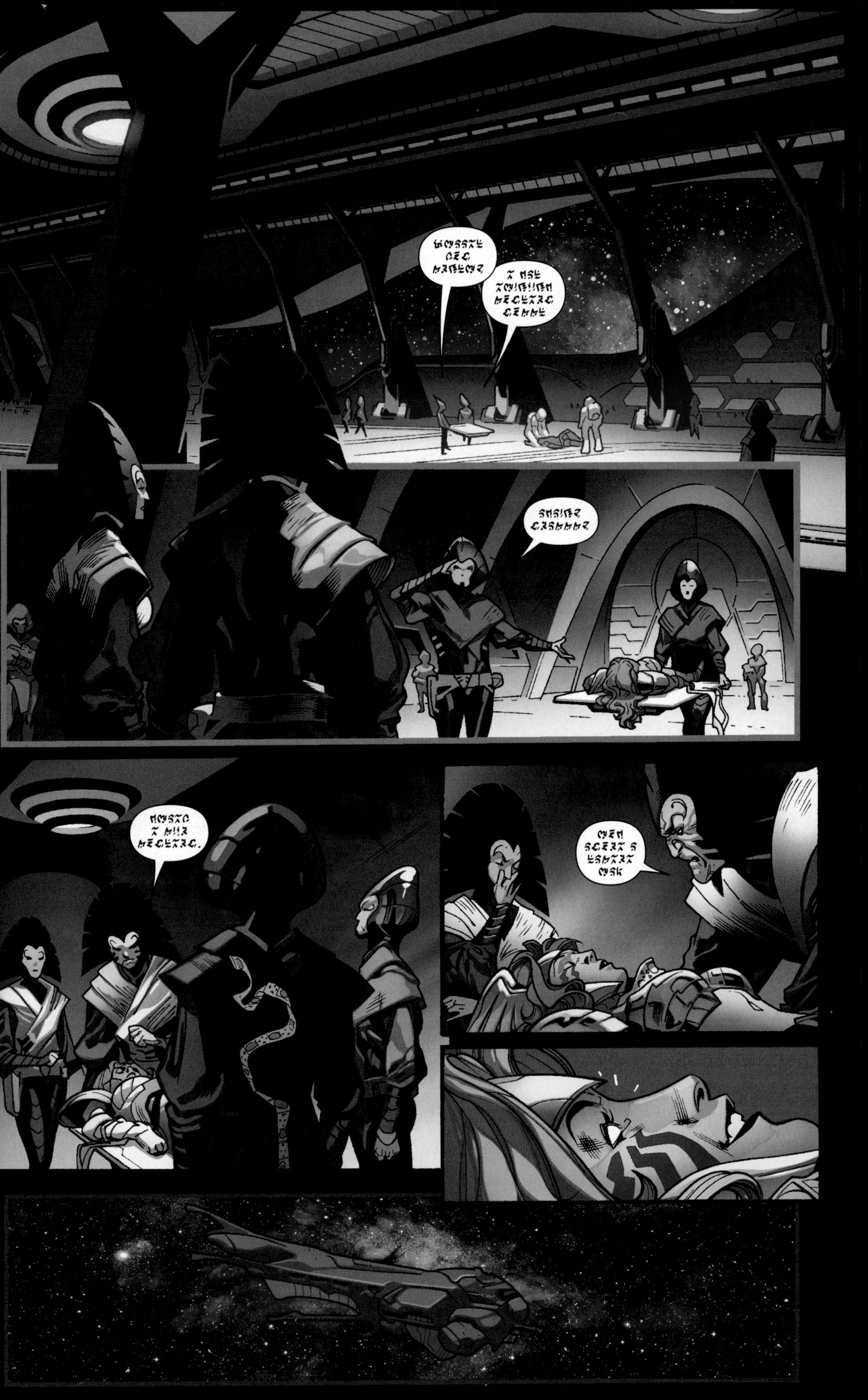

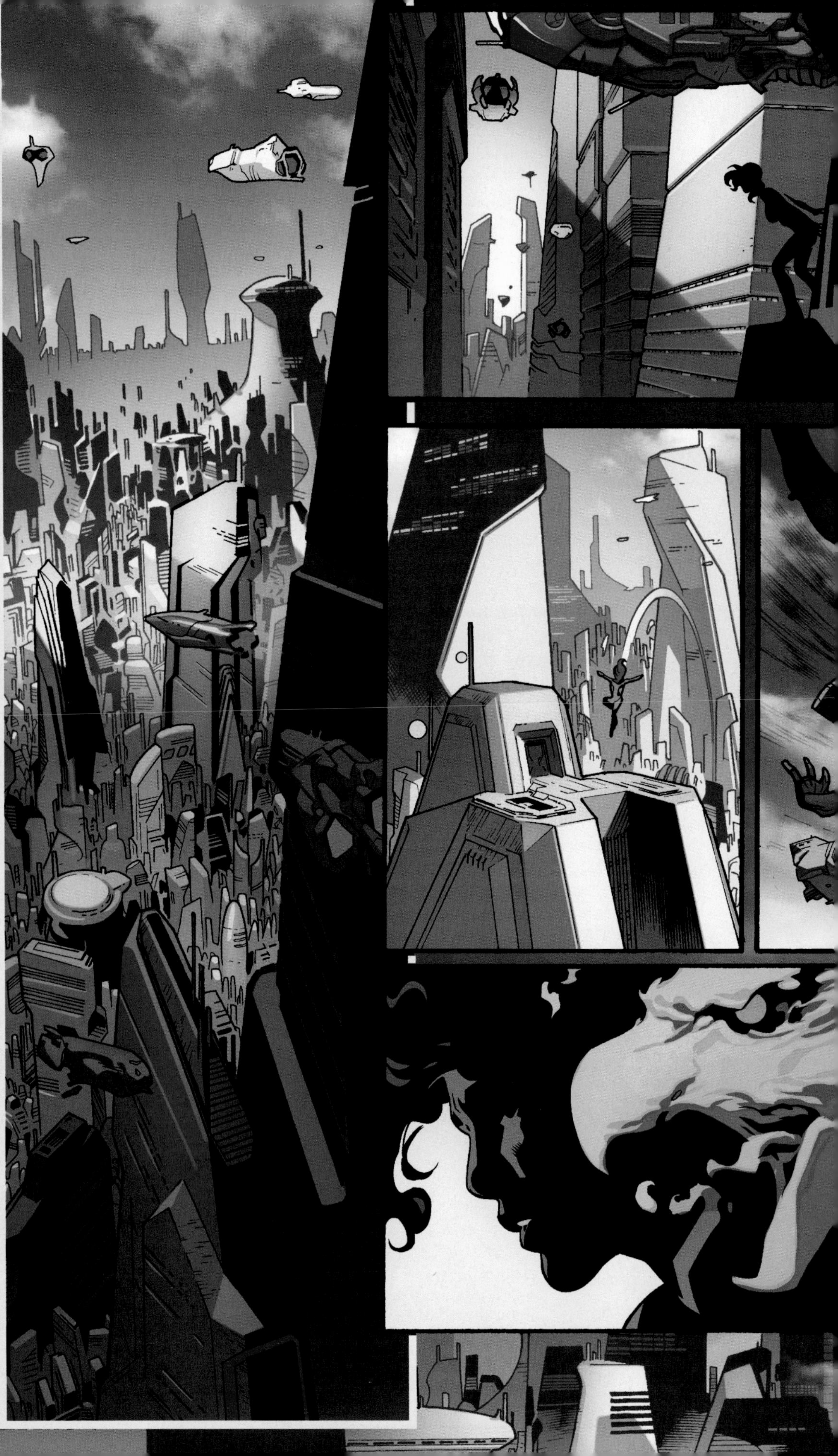

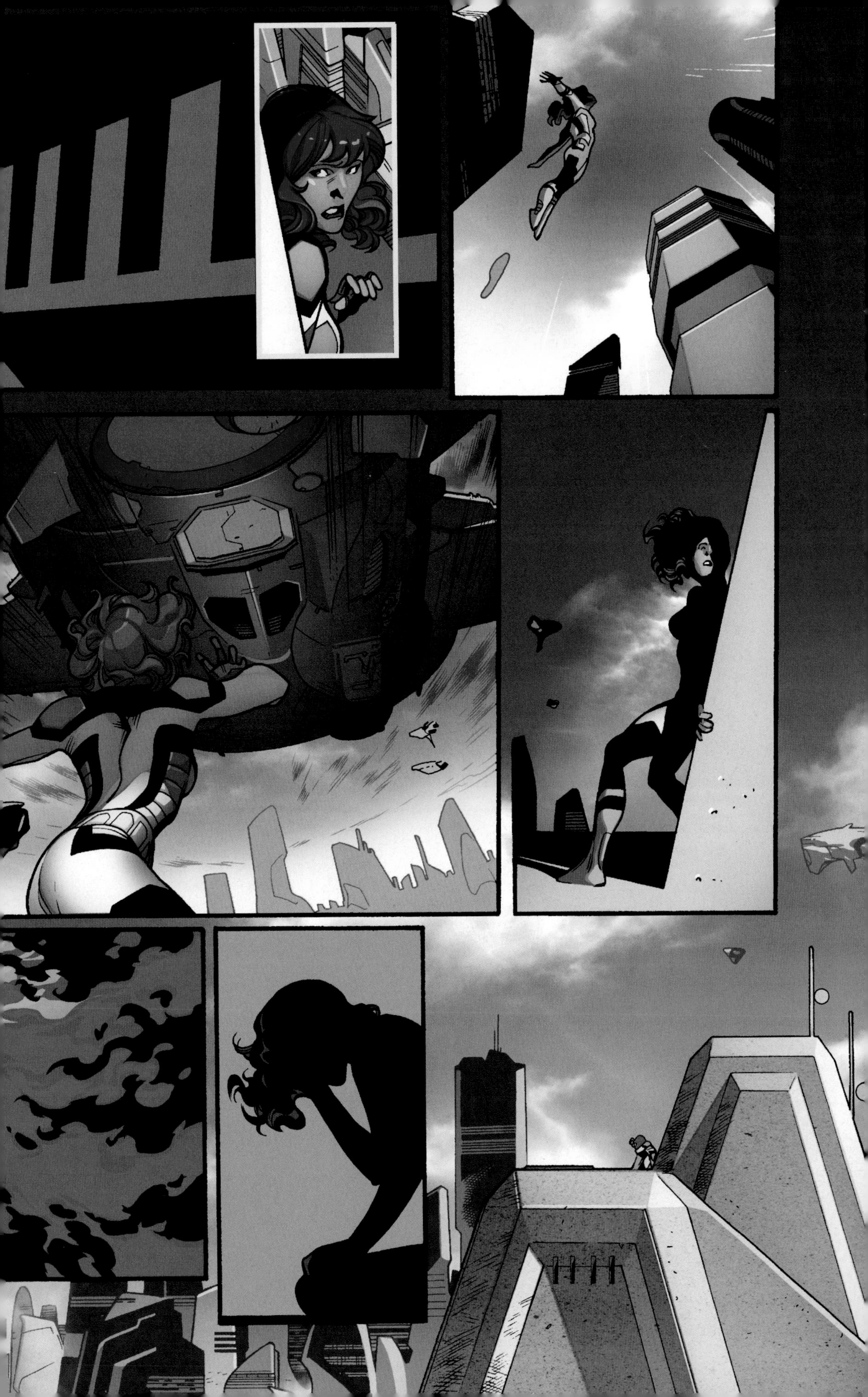

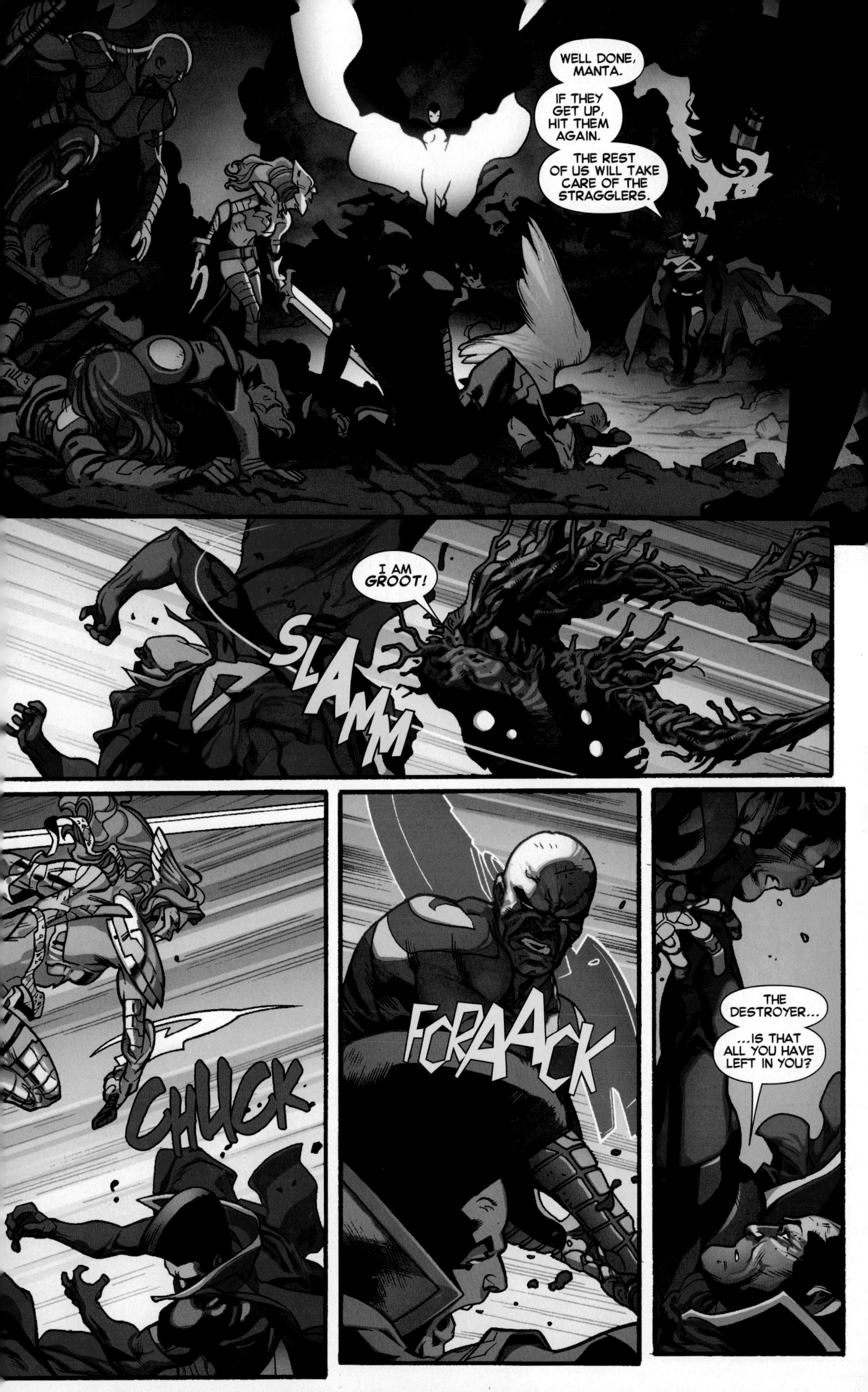
WELL DONE, MANTA.
IF THEY GET UP, HIT THEM AGAIN.
THE REST OF US WILL TAKE CARE OF THE STRAGGLERS.
I AM GROOT!
SLAMM
CHUCK
FCRAAACK
THE DESTROYER...
...IS THAT ALL YOU HAVE LEFT IN YOU?

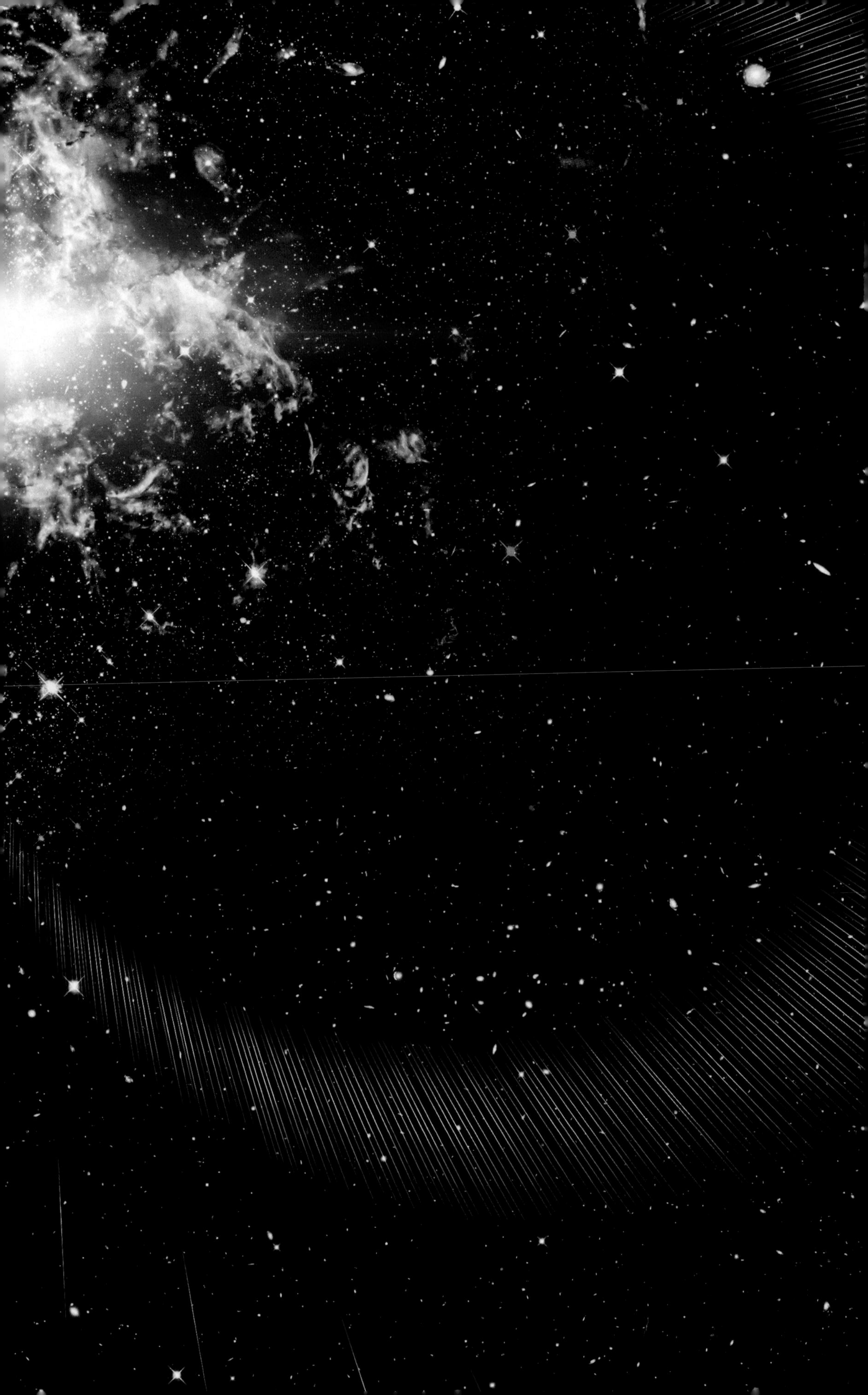

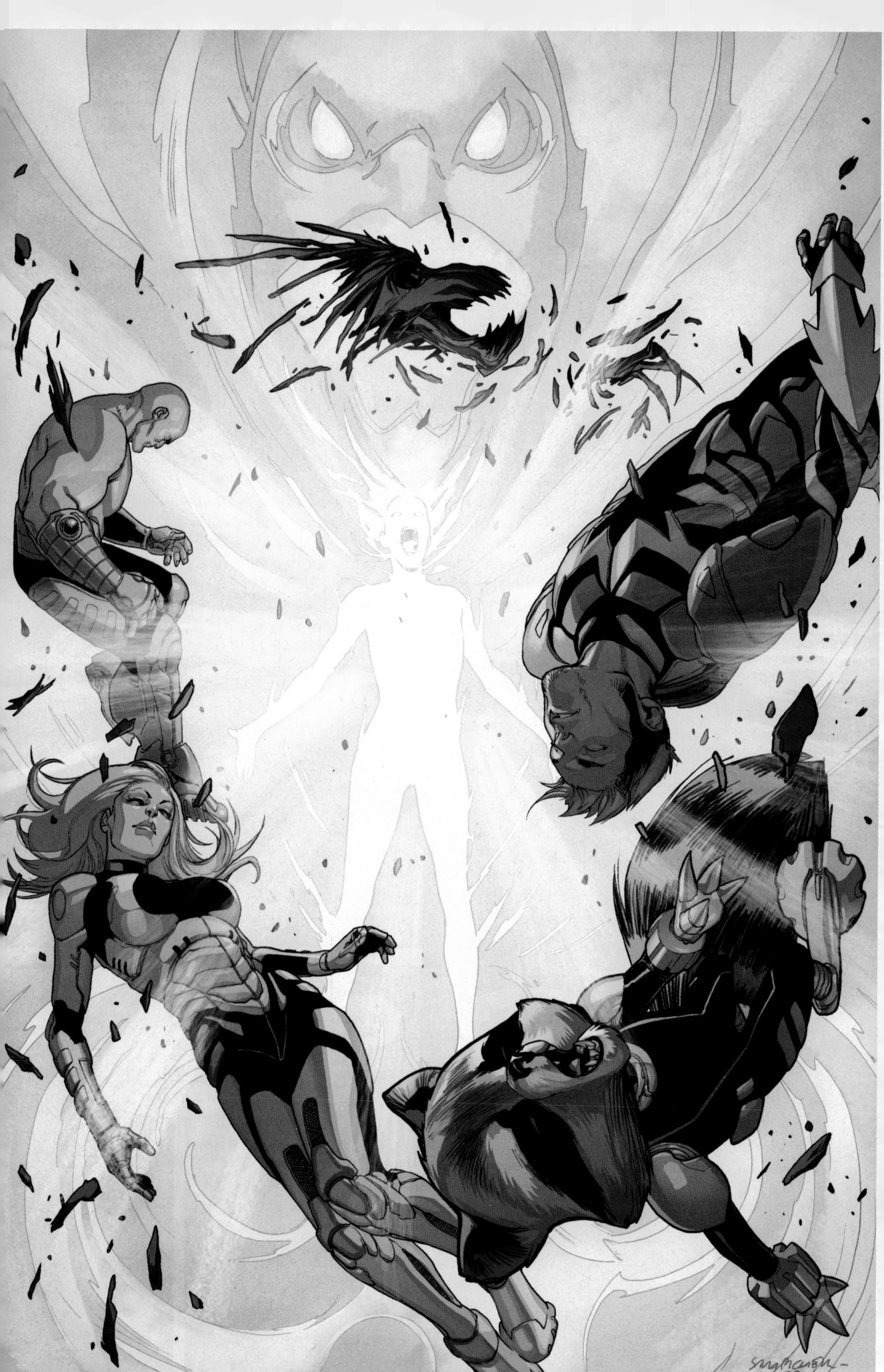

GUARDIANS OF THE GALAXY 13

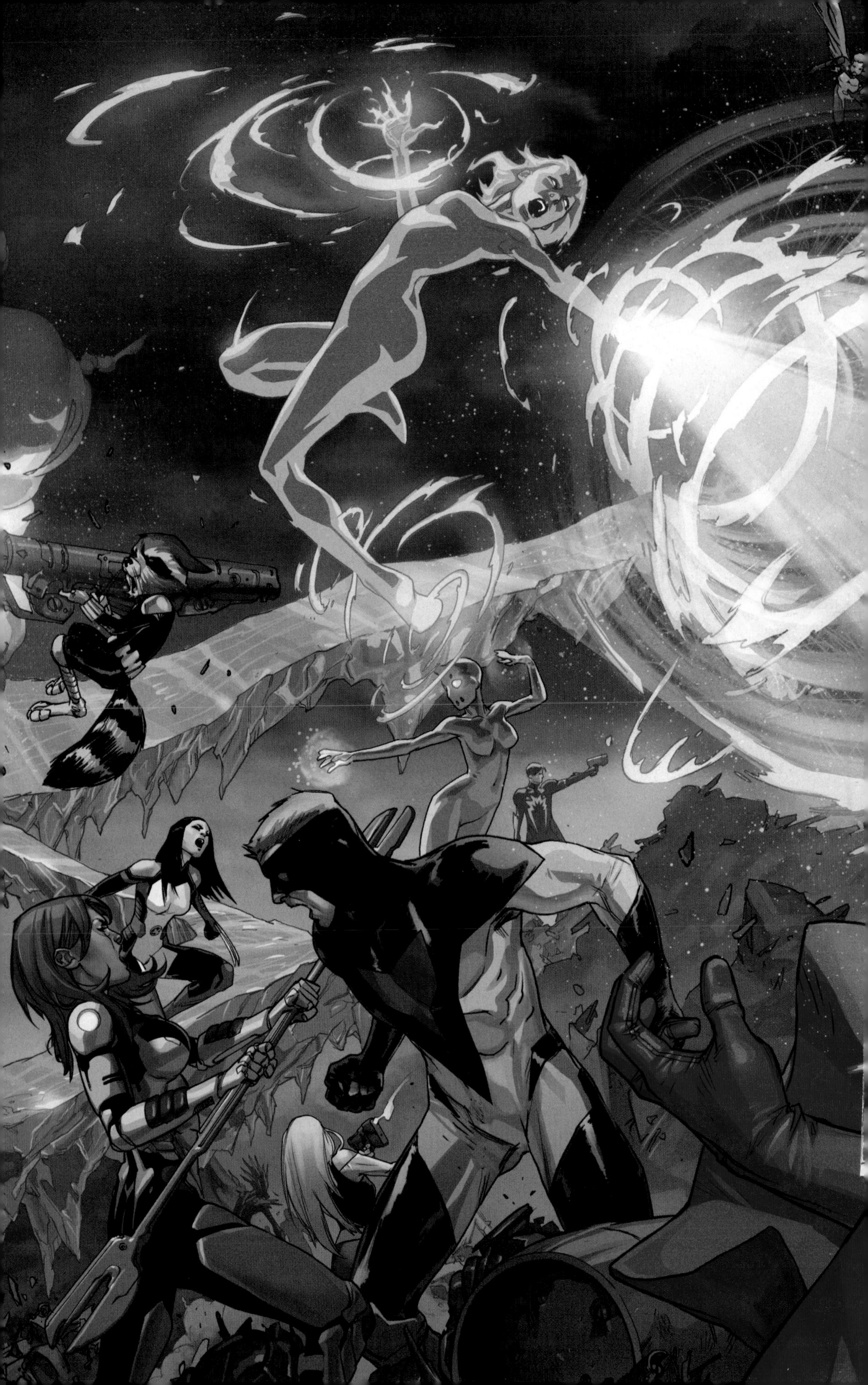

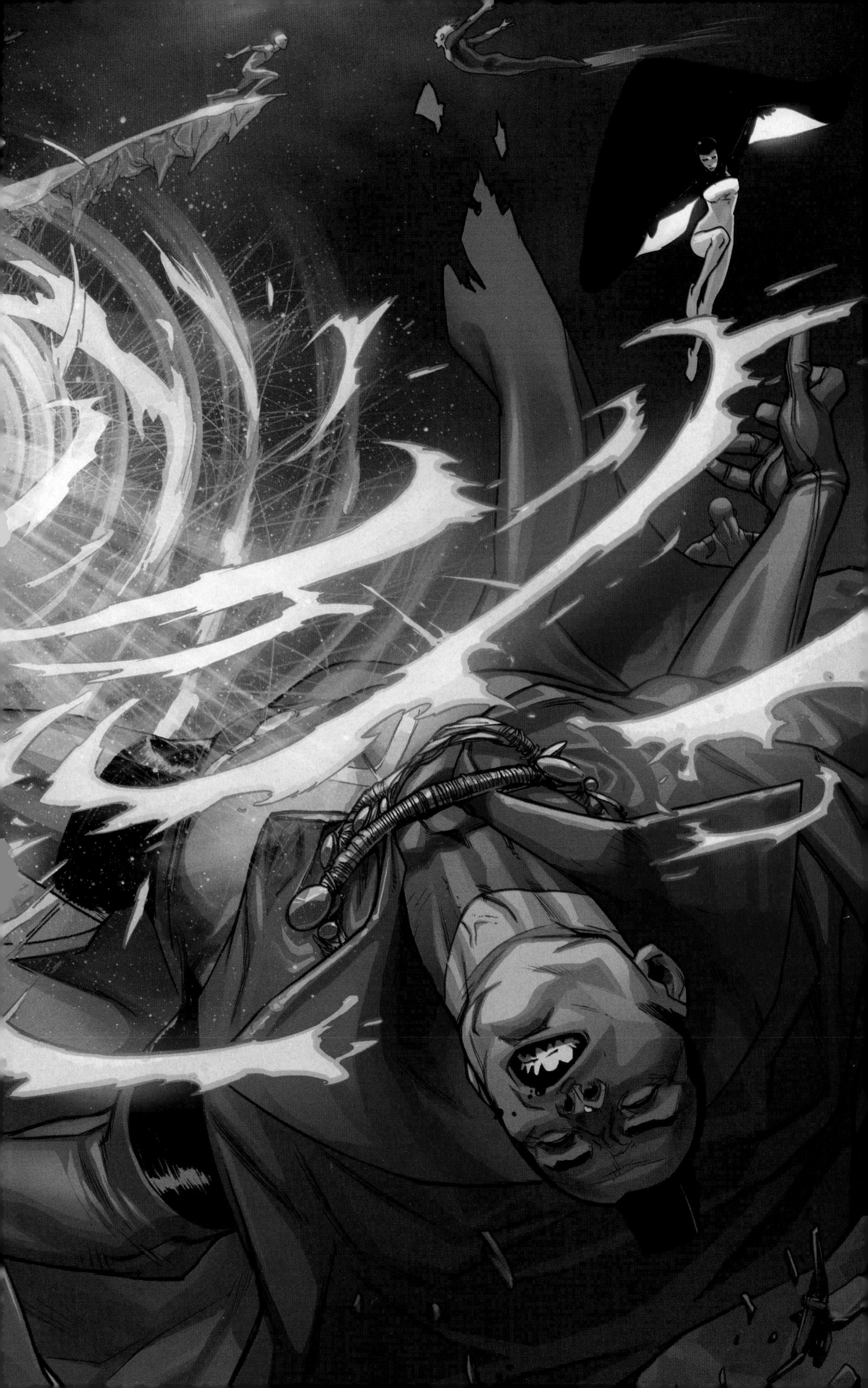

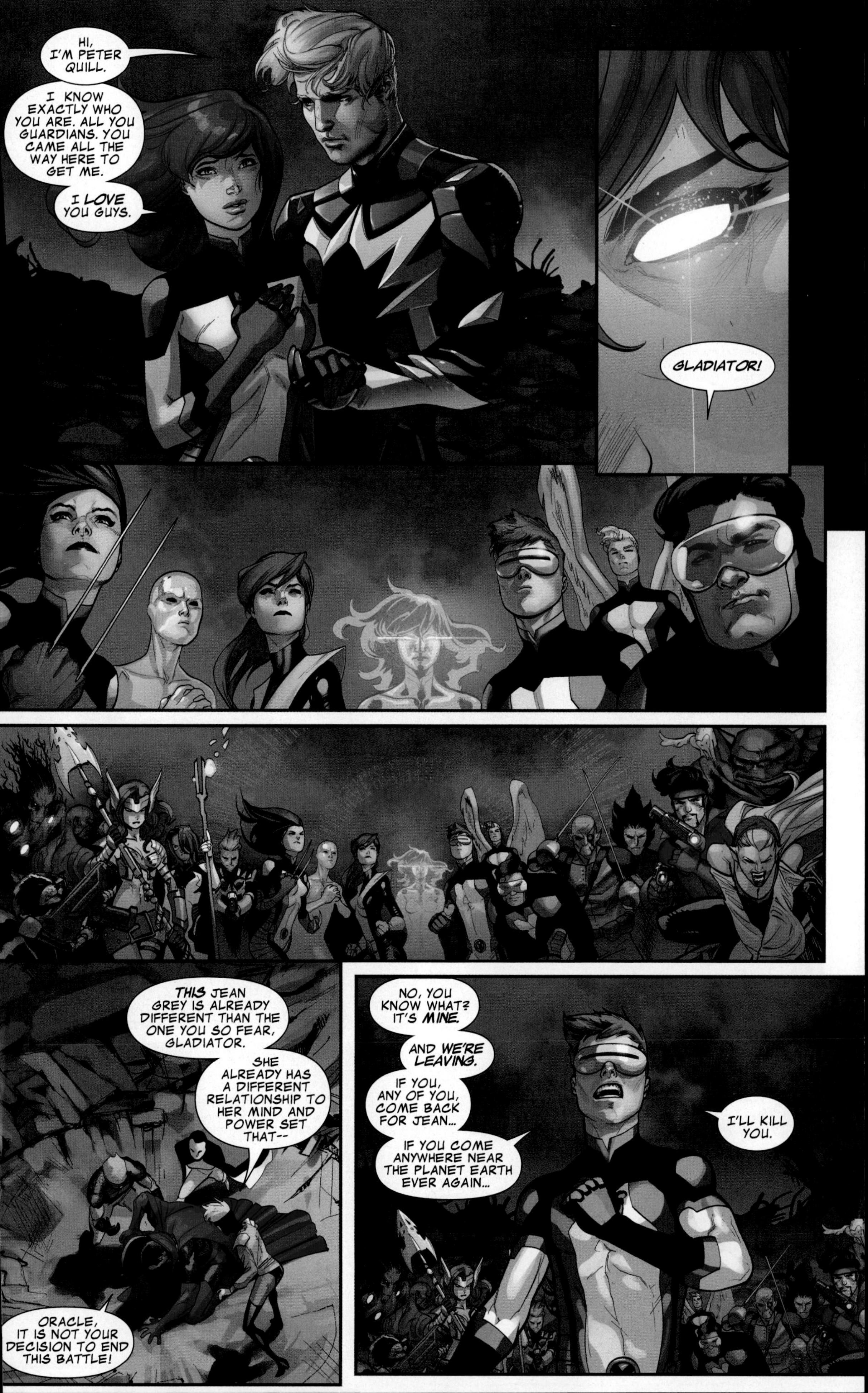
HI, I'M PETER QUILL.
I KNOW EXACTLY WHO YOU ARE. ALL YOU GUARDIANS. YOU CAME ALL THE WAY HERE TO GET ME.
I LOVE YOU GUYS.
GLADIATOR!
THIS JEAN GREY IS ALREADY DIFFERENT THAN THE ONE YOU SO FEAR, GLADIATOR.
SHE ALREADY HAS A DIFFERENT RELATIONSHIP TO HER MIND AND POWER SET THAT--
ORACLE, IT IS NOT YOUR DECISION TO END THIS BATTLE!
NO, YOU KNOW WHAT? IT'S MINE.
AND WE'RE LEAVING.
IF YOU, ANY OF YOU, COME BACK FOR JEAN...
IF YOU COME ANYWHERE NEAR THE PLANET EARTH EVER AGAIN...
I'LL KILL YOU.

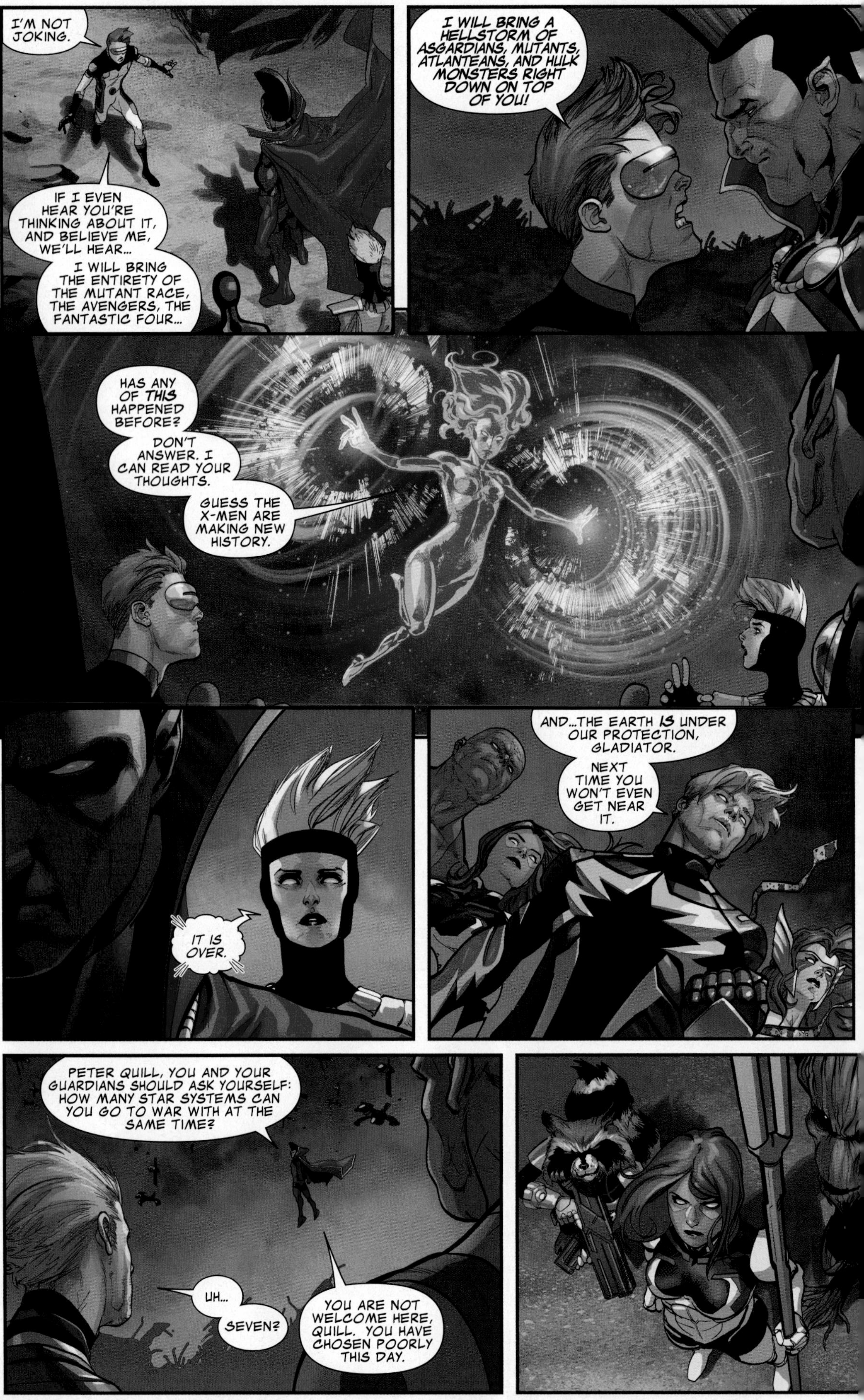
I'M NOT JOKING.
I WILL BRING A HELLSTORM OF ASGARDIANS, MUTANTS, ATLANTEANS, AND HULK MONSTERS RIGHT DOWN ON TOP OF YOU!
IF I EVEN HEAR YOU'RE THINKING ABOUT IT, AND BELIEVE ME, WE'LL HEAR...
I WILL BRING THE ENTIRETY OF THE MUTANT RACE, THE AVENGERS, THE FANTASTIC FOUR...
HAS ANY OF THIS HAPPENED BEFORE?
DON'T ANSWER. I CAN READ YOUR THOUGHTS.
GUESS THE X-MEN ARE MAKING NEW HISTORY.
IT IS OVER.
AND...THE EARTH IS UNDER OUR PROTECTION, GLADIATOR.
NEXT TIME YOU WON'T EVEN GET NEAR IT.
PETER QUILL, YOU AND YOUR GUARDIANS SHOULD ASK YOURSELF: HOW MANY STAR SYSTEMS CAN YOU GO TO WAR WITH AT THE SAME TIME?
UH...
SEVEN?
YOU ARE NOT WELCOME HERE, QUILL. YOU HAVE CHOSEN POORLY THIS DAY.

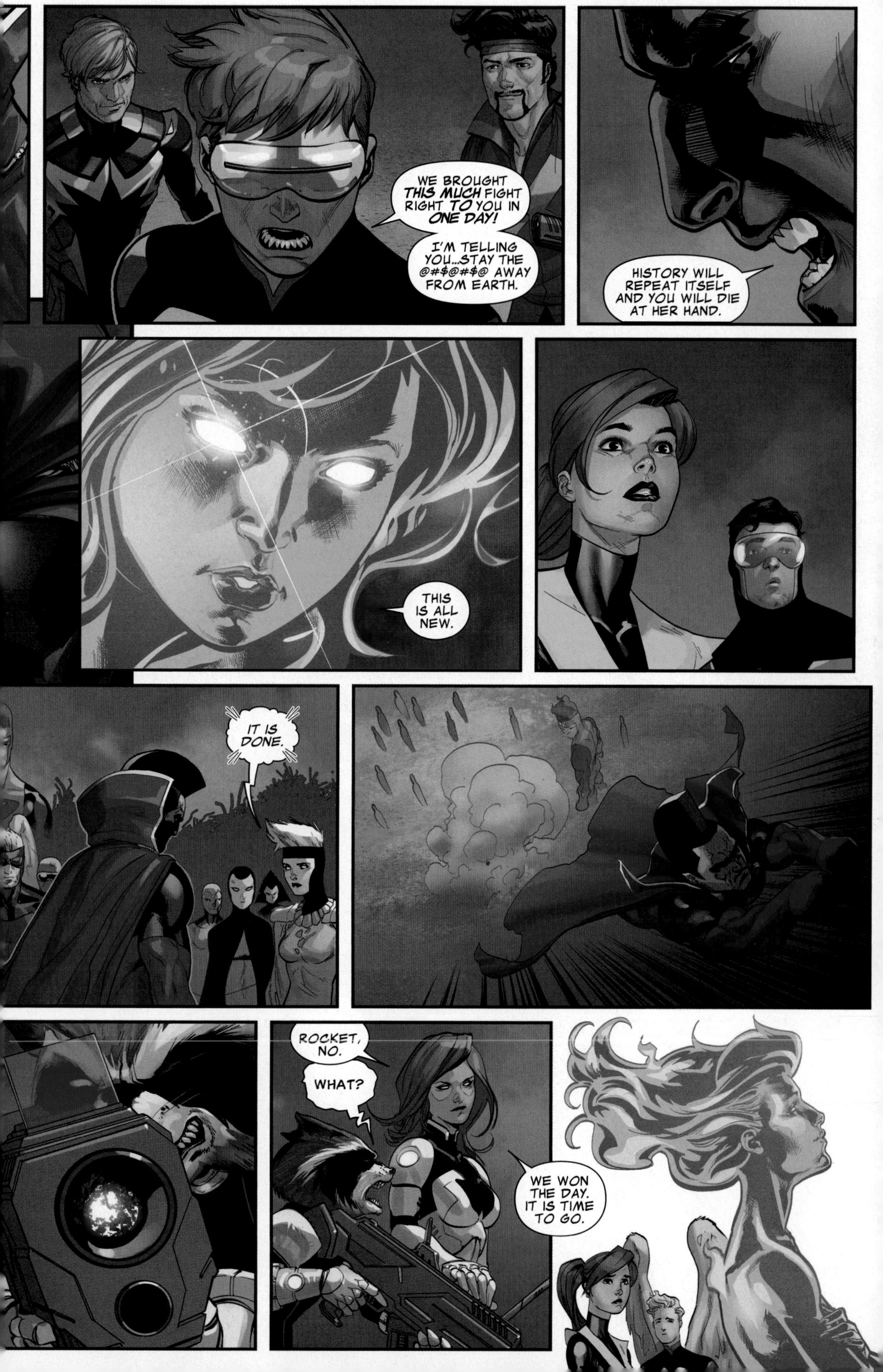
WE BROUGHT THIS MUCH FIGHT RIGHT TO YOU IN ONE DAY!
I'M TELLING YOU...STAY THE @#$@#$@ AWAY FROM EARTH.
HISTORY WILL REPEAT ITSELF AND YOU WILL DIE AT HER HAND.
THIS IS ALL NEW.
IT IS DONE.
ROCKET, NO.
WHAT?
WE WON THE DAY. IT IS TIME TO GO.

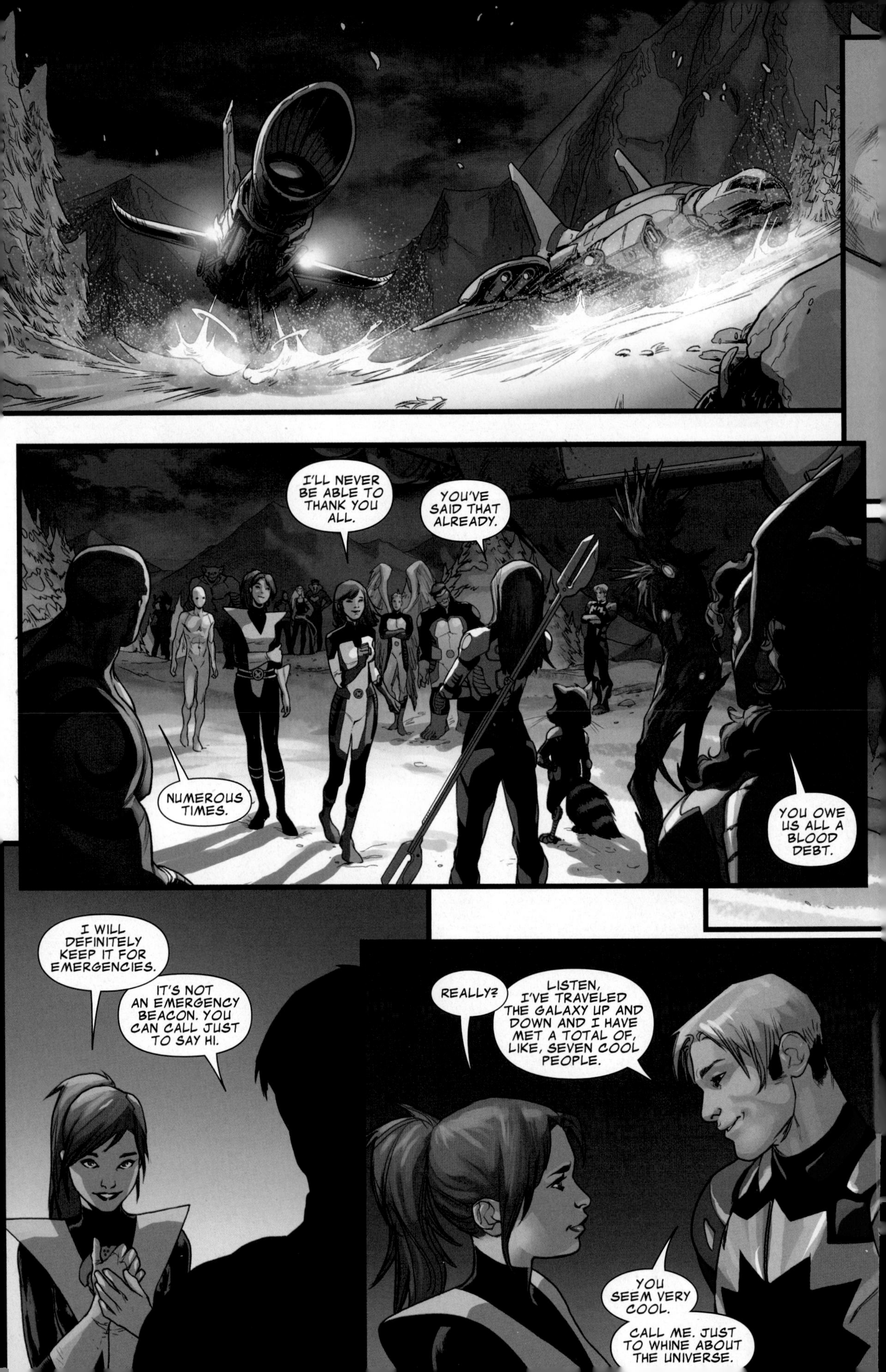
I'LL NEVER BE ABLE TO THANK YOU ALL.
YOU'VE SAID THAT ALREADY.
NUMEROUS TIMES.
YOU OWE US ALL A BLOOD DEBT.
I WILL DEFINITELY KEEP IT FOR EMERGENCIES.
IT'S NOT AN EMERGENCY BEACON. YOU CAN CALL JUST TO SAY HI.
REALLY?
LISTEN, I'VE TRAVELED THE GALAXY UP AND DOWN AND I HAVE MET A TOTAL OF, LIKE, SEVEN COOL PEOPLE.
YOU SEEM VERY COOL.
CALL ME. JUST TO WHINE ABOUT THE UNIVERSE.

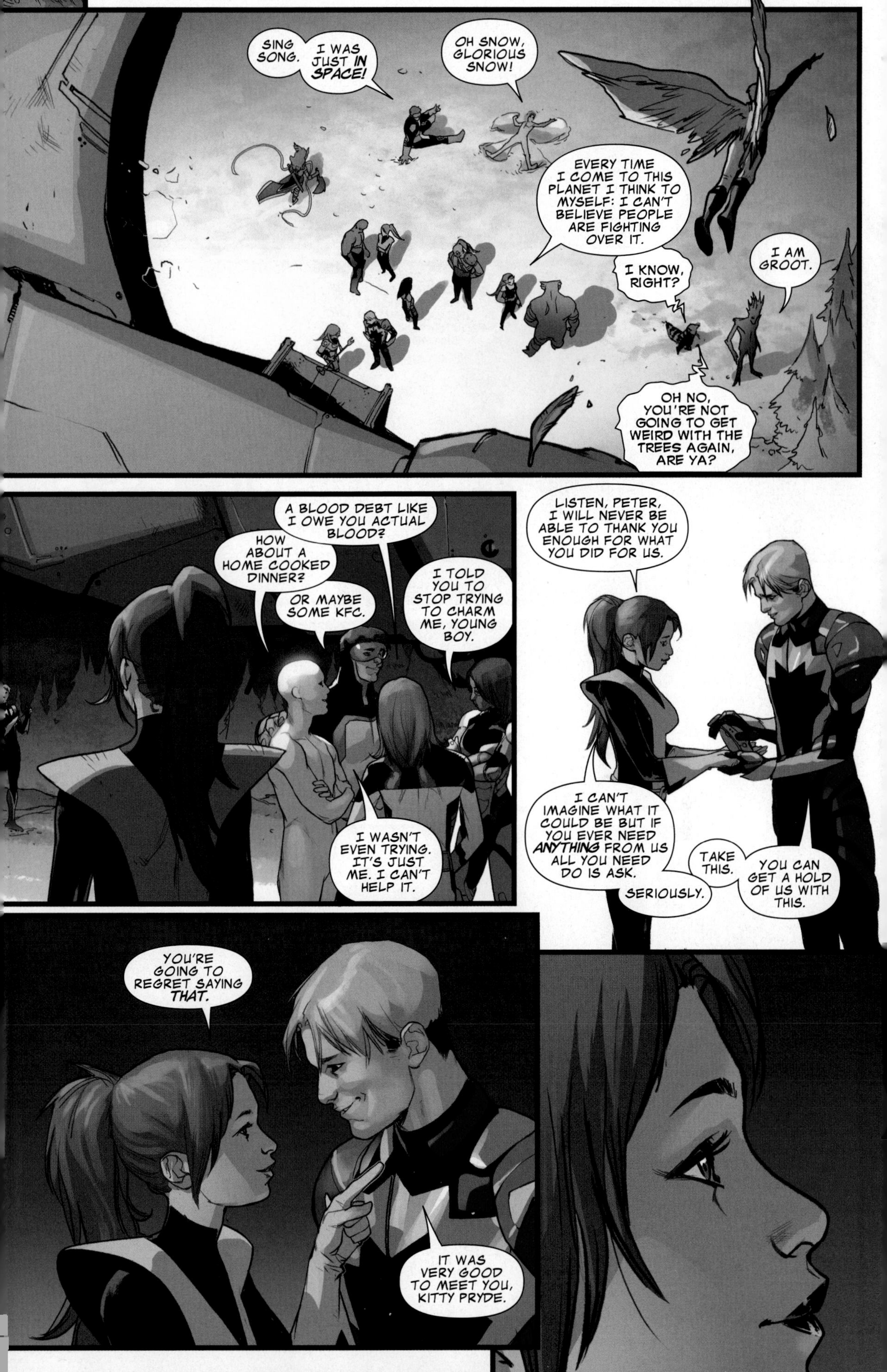
SING SONG.
I WAS JUST IN SPACE!
OH SNOW, GLORIOUS SNOW!
EVERY TIME I COME TO THIS PLANET I THINK TO MYSELF: I CAN'T BELIEVE PEOPLE ARE FIGHTING OVER IT.
I KNOW, RIGHT?
I AM GROOT.
OH NO, YOU'RE NOT GOING TO GET WEIRD WITH THE TREES AGAIN, ARE YA?
A BLOOD DEBT LIKE I OWE YOU ACTUAL BLOOD?
HOW ABOUT A HOME COOKED DINNER?
OR MAYBE SOME KFC.
I TOLD YOU TO STOP TRYING TO CHARM ME, YOUNG BOY.
I WASN'T EVEN TRYING. IT'S JUST ME. I CAN'T HELP IT.
LISTEN, PETER, I WILL NEVER BE ABLE TO THANK YOU ENOUGH FOR WHAT YOU DID FOR US.
I CAN'T IMAGINE WHAT IT COULD BE BUT IF YOU EVER NEED ANYTHING FROM US ALL YOU NEED DO IS ASK.
SERIOUSLY.
TAKE THIS.
YOU CAN GET A HOLD OF US WITH THIS.
YOU'RE GOING TO REGRET SAYING THAT.
IT WAS VERY GOOD TO MEET YOU, KITTY PRYDE.

YOU SURE WE CAN'T FEED YOU BEFORE YOU TAKE OFF?

YOU'RE MORE THAN WELCOME TO SPEND THE NIGHT IN OUR CONVERTED MUTANT TORTURE CHAMBER.

I AM GROOT.

WE TALKED ABOUT THIS, GROOT.

WE'RE GOING TO LEAVE NOW.

YOU'RE MAKING IT WEIRD.

I AM GROOT.

PUT ON SOME KRUTACKING PANTS.

HEY, UH, GUYS...

THIS IS A LITTLE HARD TO SAY SO I GUESS I'LL JUST COME OUT AND SAY IT...

YOU ALL KNOW THAT TWO DAYS AGO I THOUGHT MY DAD WAS DEAD.

I THOUGHT I WAS AN ORPHAN.

AND, WELL, I LOVE YOU GUYS AND IT'S BEEN CRAZY, ALL OF THIS, BUT...

I'M GOING TO GO WITH MY DAD.

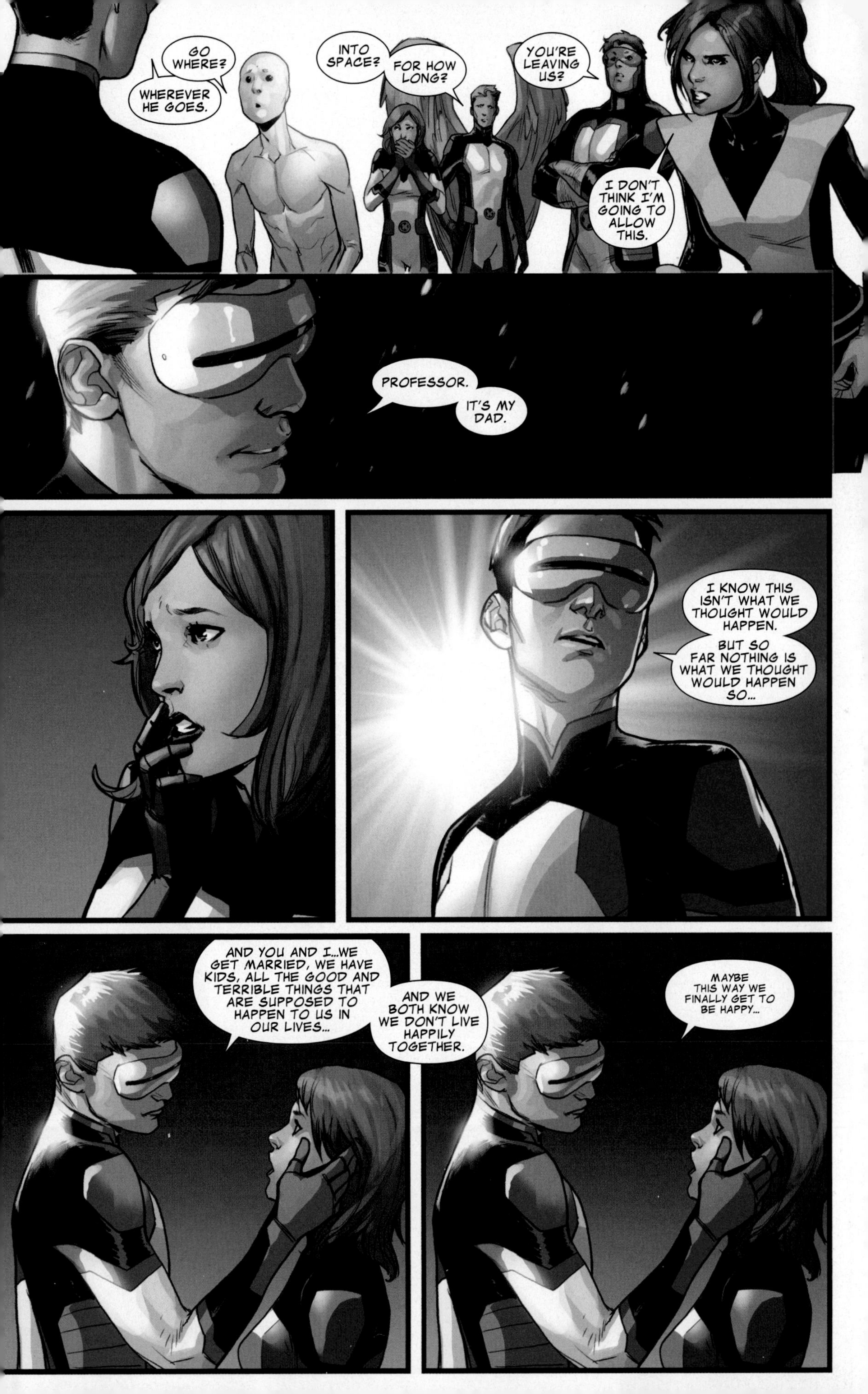
GO WHERE?
WHEREVER HE GOES.
INTO SPACE?
FOR HOW LONG?
YOU'RE LEAVING US?
I DON'T THINK I'M GOING TO ALLOW THIS.
PROFESSOR.
IT'S MY DAD.
I KNOW THIS ISN'T WHAT WE THOUGHT WOULD HAPPEN.
BUT SO FAR NOTHING IS WHAT WE THOUGHT WOULD HAPPEN SO...
AND YOU AND I...WE GET MARRIED, WE HAVE KIDS, ALL THE GOOD AND TERRIBLE THINGS THAT ARE SUPPOSED TO HAPPEN TO US IN OUR LIVES...
AND WE BOTH KNOW WE DON'T LIVE HAPPILY TOGETHER.
MAYBE THIS WAY WE FINALLY GET TO BE HAPPY...

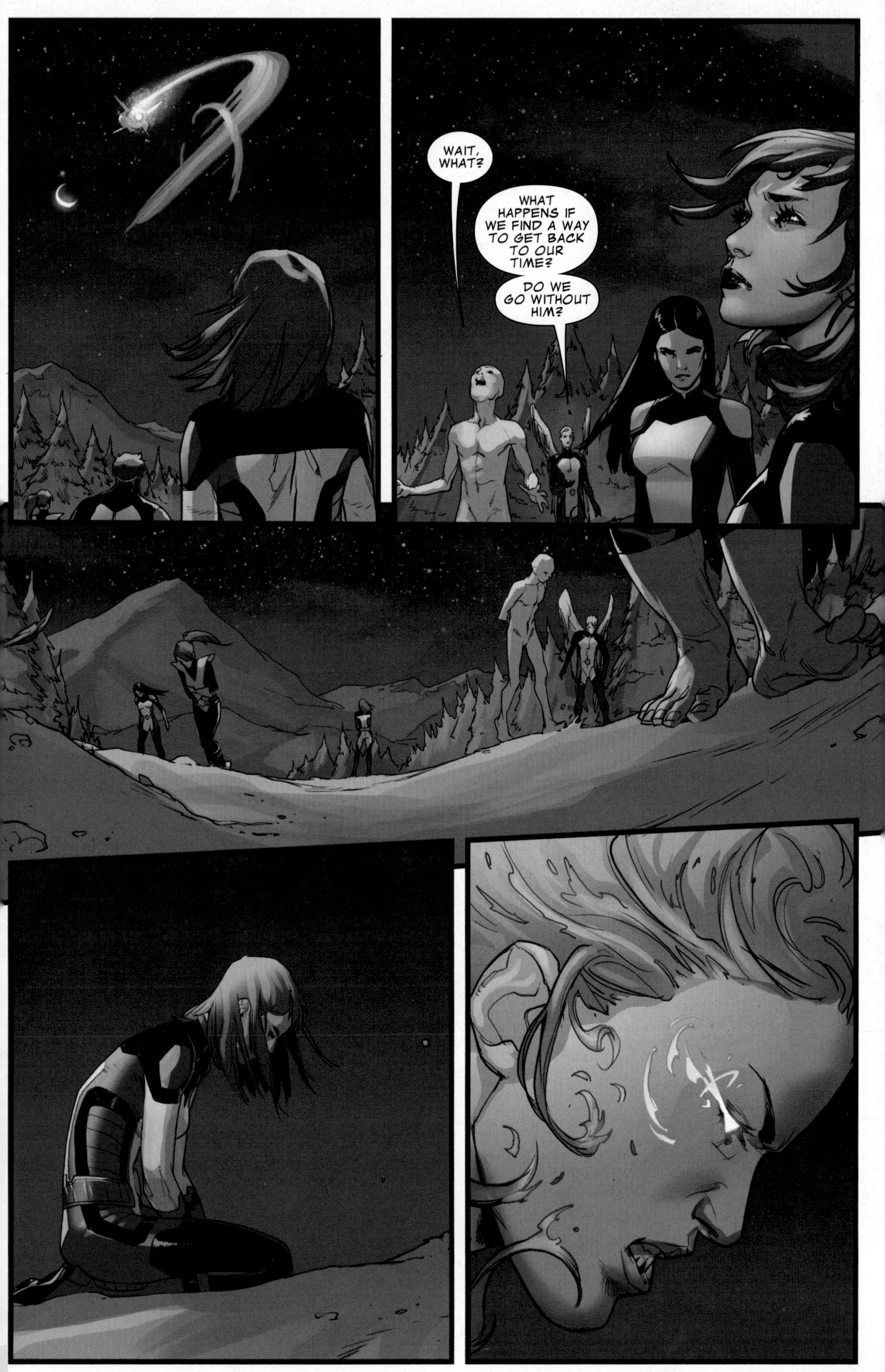
WAIT, WHAT?
WHAT HAPPENS IF WE FIND A WAY TO GET BACK TO OUR TIME?
DO WE GO WITHOUT HIM?

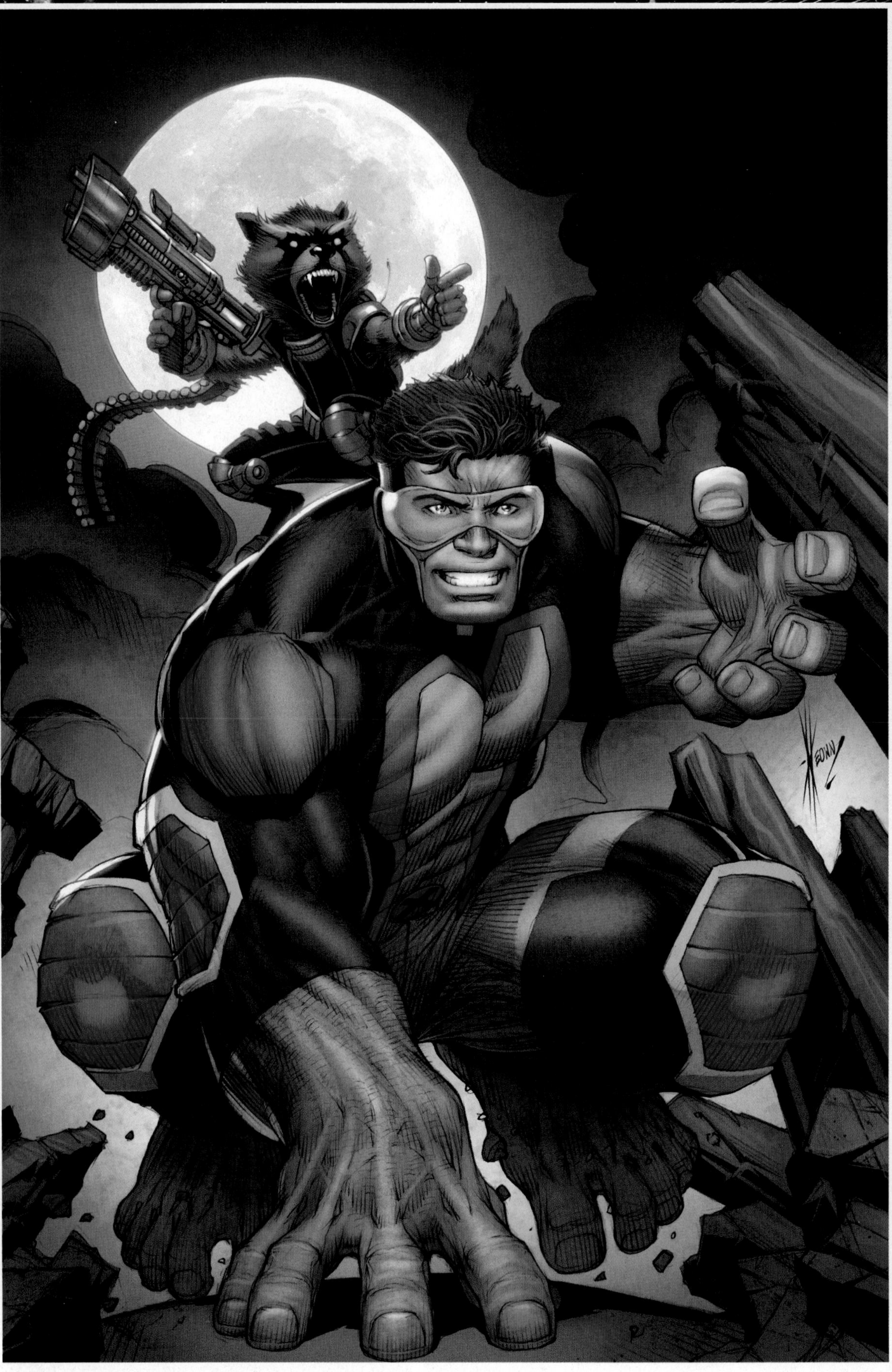

GUARDIANS OF THE GALAXY *#11* VARIANT
BY DALE KEOWN & JASON KEITH

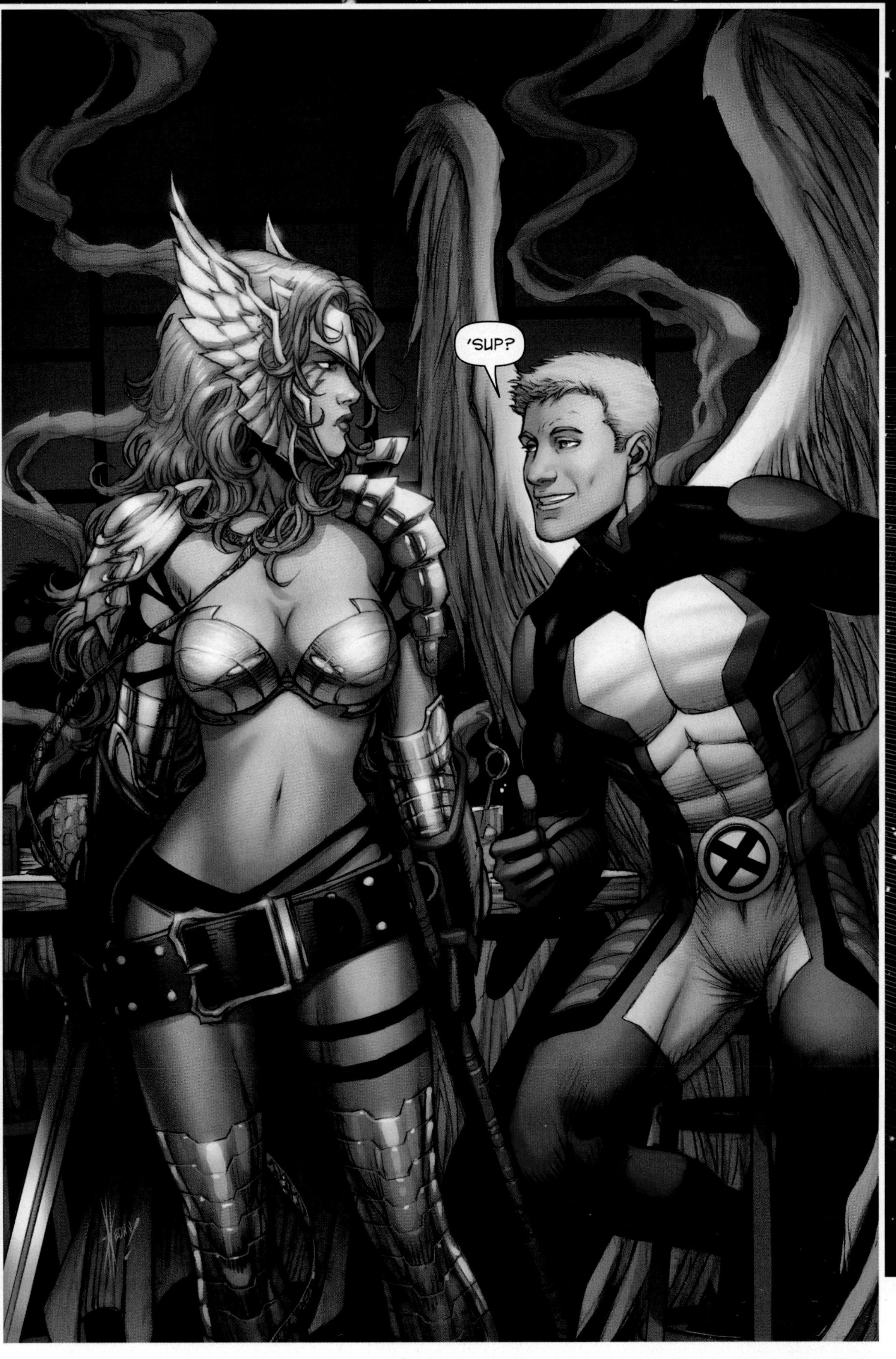
'SUP?

GUARDIANS OF THE GALAXY *#12* VARIANT
BY DALE KEOWN & JASON KEITH

GUARDIANS OF THE GALAXY _#13_ VARIANT
BY DALE KEOWN & JASON KEITH

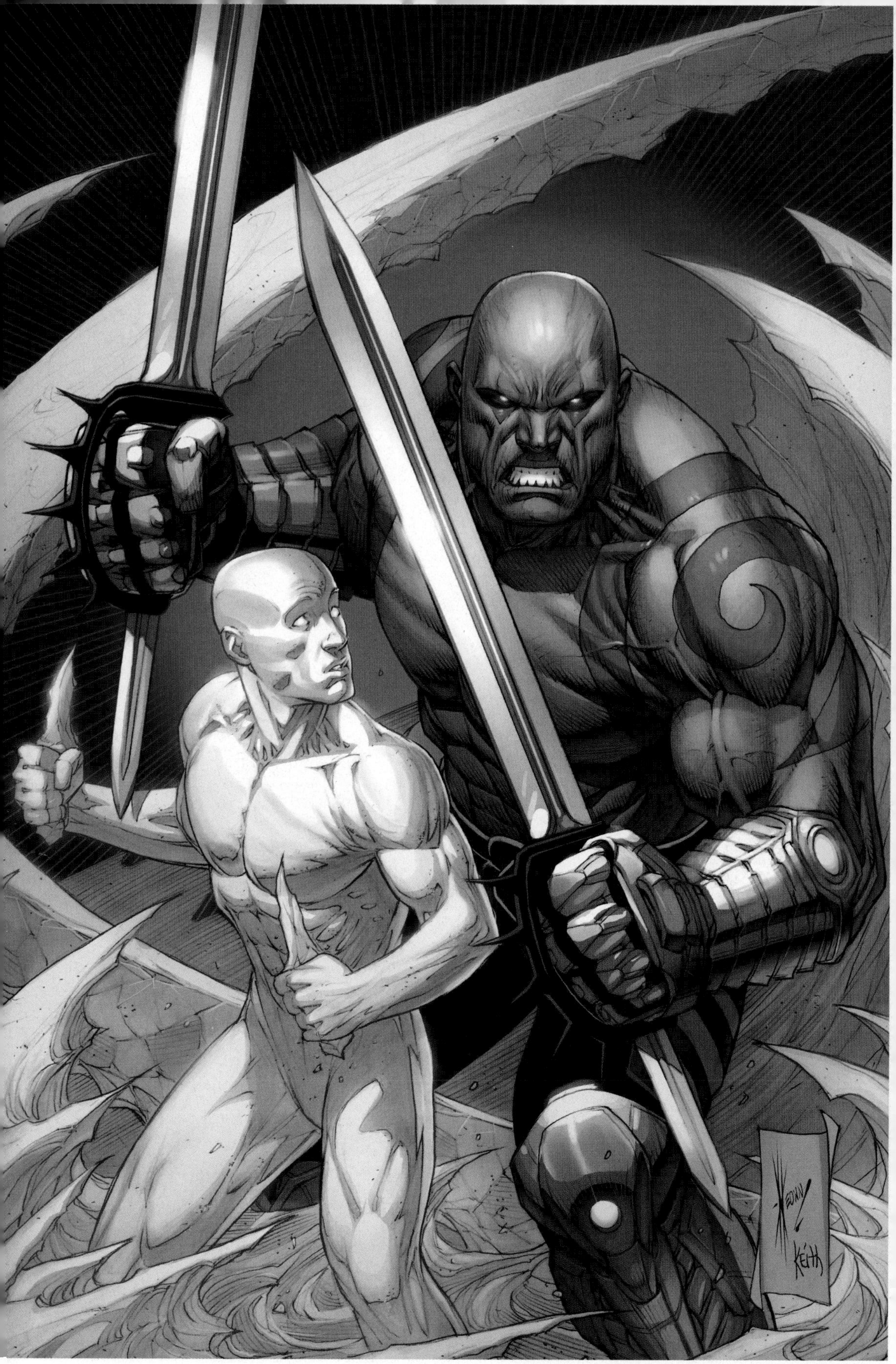

ALL-NEW X-MEN *#22* VARIANT
BY DALE KEOWN & JASON KEITH

ALL NEW X-MEN #23 VARIANT
BY DALE KEOWN & JASON KEITH

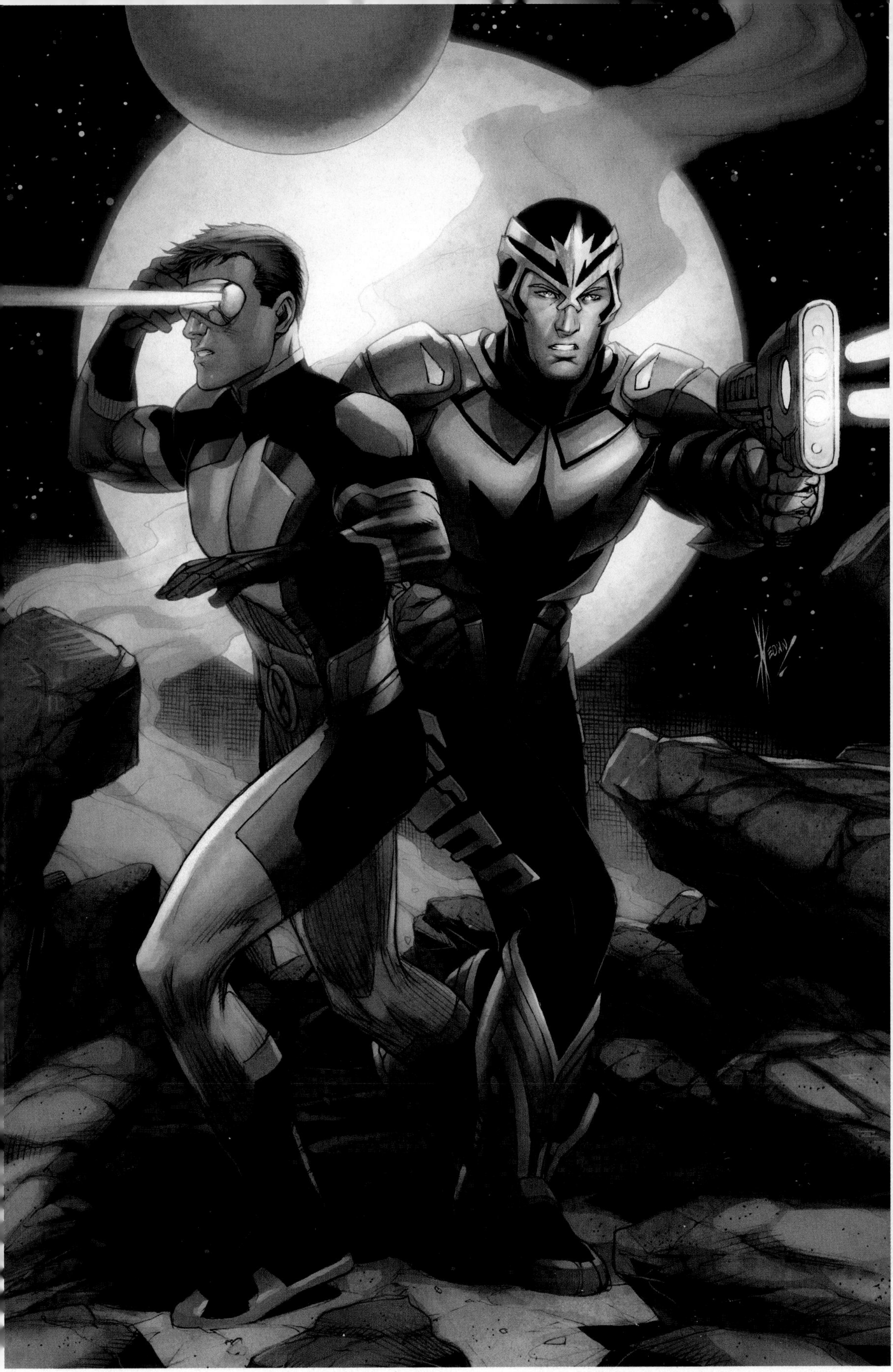

ALL-NEW X-MEN *#24* VARIANT
BY DALE KEOWN & JASON KEITH

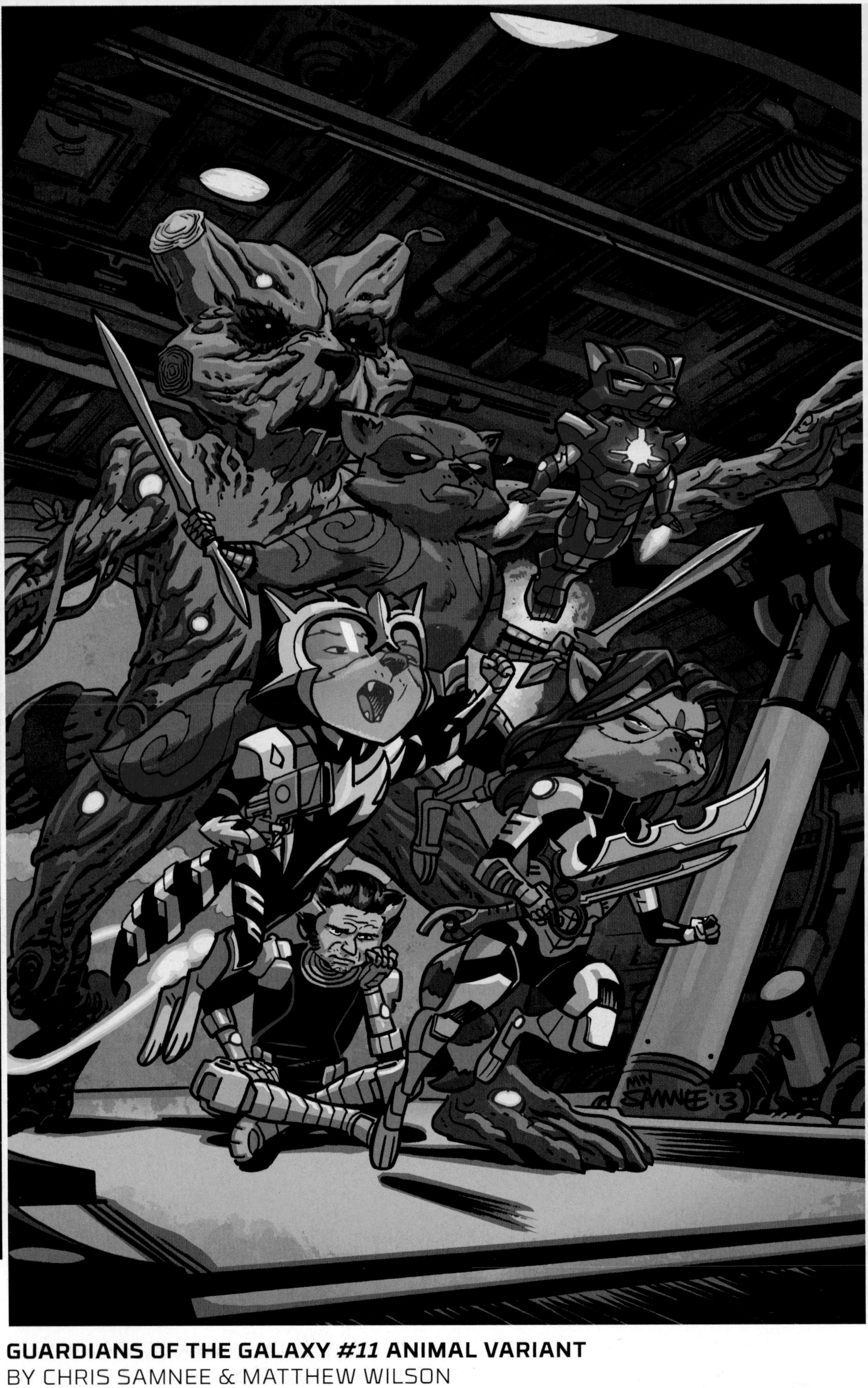
SAMNEE '13

GUARDIANS OF THE GALAXY *#11* ANIMAL VARIANT
BY CHRIS SAMNEE & MATTHEW WILSON

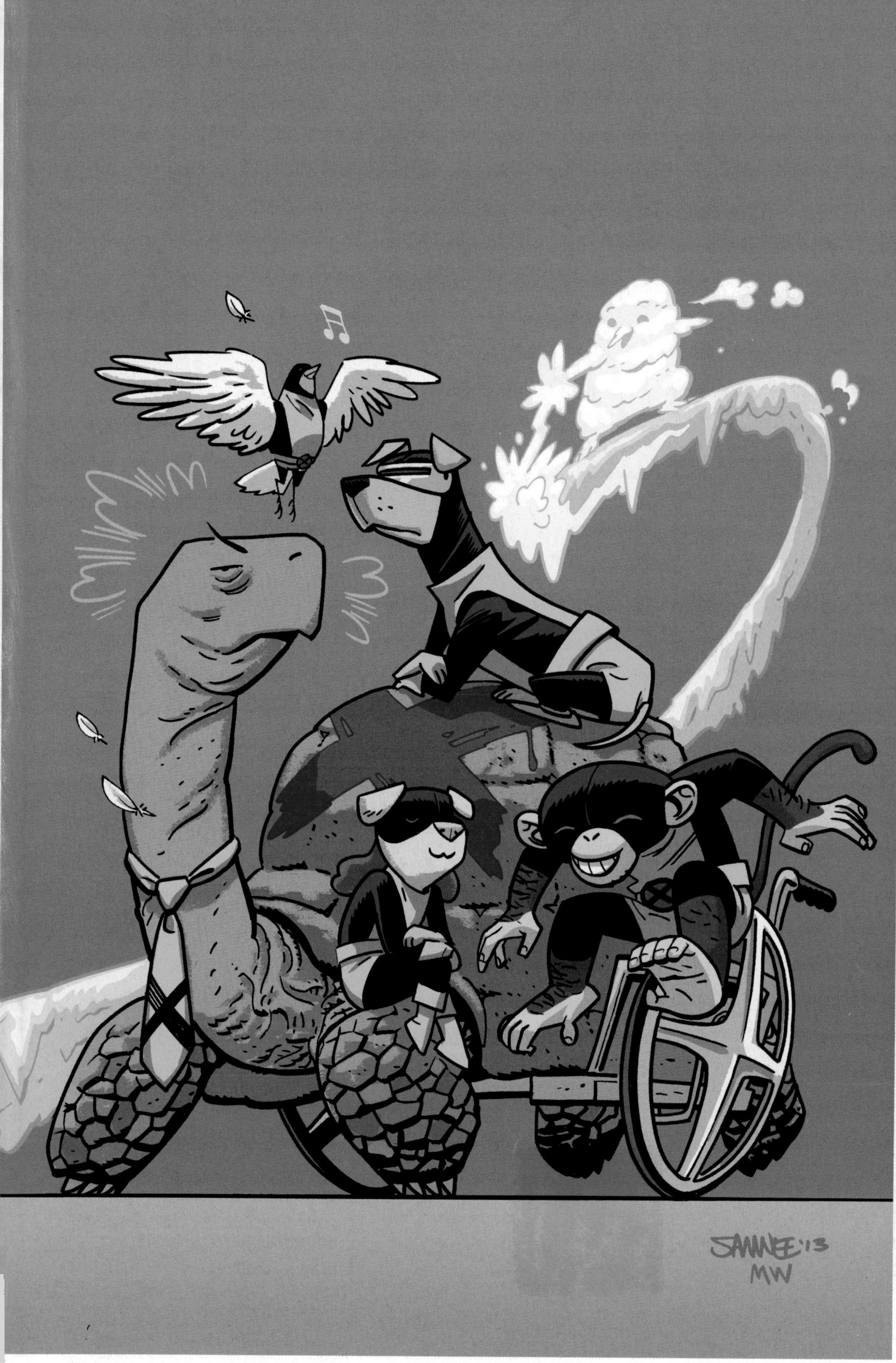
SAMNEE '13
MW

ALL-NEW X-MEN *#22* ANIMAL VARIANT
BY CHRIS SAMNEE & MATTHEW WILSON

MARVEL AUGMENTED REALITY (AR) ENHANCES AND CHANGES THE WAY YOU EXPERIENCE COMICS!

TO ACCESS THE FREE MARVEL AR CONTENT IN THIS BOOK*:

1. Locate the **AR** logo within the comic.
2. Go to Marvel.com/AR in your web browser.
3. Search by series title to find the corresponding AR.
4. Enjoy Marvel AR!

*All AR content that appears in this book has been archived and will be available only at Marvel.com/AR — no longer in the Marvel AR App. Content subject to change and availability.

MARVEL FREE DIGITAL COPY OFFER
PEEL HERE TO REVEAL CODE ▶

TO REDEEM YOUR CODE FOR A FREE DIGITAL COPY:

1. GO TO MARVEL.COM/REDEEM. OFFER EXPIRES ON 5/28/16.
2. FOLLOW THE ON-SCREEN INSTRUCTIONS TO REDEEM YOUR DIGITAL COPY.
3. LAUNCH THE MARVEL COMICS APP TO READ YOUR COMIC NOW!
4. YOUR DIGITAL COPY WILL BE FOUND UNDER THE *MY COMICS* TAB.
5. READ & ENJOY!

YOUR FREE DIGITAL COPY WILL BE AVAILABLE O

| MARVEL COMICS APP FOR APPLE® iOS DEVICES | MARVEL COMICS APP FOR ANDROID™ DEVICES |